"Where was this book when I needed it as a [...] forty-five years ago? Jay Moon truly brings i[...] volume chock-full of keen insights, case stu[...] from fields as far ranging as cultural anthropology, mission research, orality, symbolism and ritual studies, and ethnodoxology. This book is where you should start if you are a mission thinker or practitioner wanting to deepen your understanding of and effectiveness in intercultural Christian discipling. I could have and *would* have made good use of it a long time ago!"

—**James R. Krabill**, senior mission advocate, Mennonite Mission Network; general editor of *Worship and Mission for the Global Church: An Ethnodoxology Handbook*

"The cry for better discipleship methods is heard around the globe but most methods take a fill-in-the-blank approach, focused on acquiring more *information*, not the deep penetrating *formation* of disciples of Jesus that promotes personal and community transformation. Now Jay Moon in *Intercultural Discipleship* has charted a comprehensive and creative way forward like no other book in the field. Missiologically informed, cross-culturally relevant, and biblically faithful, this book draws on genres such as proverbs, drama, music, dance, rituals and ceremonies, and oral arts, together with riveting case studies to open the right side of our brains for disciple-makers around the world. I believe *Intercultural Discipleship* will soon become a classic text in the discipleship literature."

—**Darrell Whiteman**, publisher, American Society of Missiology

"Drawing on his extensive experience living cross-culturally, Jay Moon has produced a very readable and resourceful guide to making disciples. Enhanced by a global perspective, *Intercultural Discipleship* not only provides a valuable primer on understanding the relationship between faith and culture but also offers practical ways to utilize this knowledge for the sake of growing faithful and discerning disciples."

—**Bonnie Sue Lewis**, professor of mission and world Christianity, University of Dubuque Theological Seminary

"What could discipleship look, feel, smell, and sound like in this era of global cultural complexity? Immensely helpful in its integration of theory and practical know-how, *Intercultural Discipleship* is a resourceful pathway for deep learning and transformative growth for all teachers and students of culture, change agents, and hermeneutical communities interested in creative discipleship approaches that foster radical inclusion and participation in mission."

—**Uday Mark Balasundaram**, founder, Estuary Cultures and Order of Bezalel

"If this book gets the reading it deserves, we are at the dawning of a great new day for making disciples, and not just overseas. Skillfully drawing on several works that were ahead of their time (e.g., *Symbol and Ceremony* by A. H. Mathias Zahniser), Moon tells fascinating, instructive stories of those who practice what they preach. I had to keep putting the book down to add ideas to my to-do list."

—**Stan Nussbaum**, developer, SYNC Discipleship Program

A. Scott Moreau, *series editor*

ALSO IN THE SERIES:

INTERCULTURAL DISCIPLESHIP

Learning from Global Approaches to Spiritual Formation

W. JAY MOON

Baker Academic
a division of Baker Publishing Group
Grand Rapids, Michigan

© 2017 by W. Jay Moon

Published by Baker Academic
a division of Baker Publishing Group
P.O. Box 6287, Grand Rapids, MI 49516-6287
www.bakeracademic.com

Printed and bound by CPI Group (UK) Ltd, Croydon, CR0 4YY

Library of Congress Cataloging-in-Publication Data
Names: Moon, W. Jay, author.
Title: Intercultural discipleship : learning from global approaches to spiritual formation / W. Jay Moon.
Description: Grand Rapids : Baker Academic, 2017. | Series: Encountering mission | Includes bibliographical references and index.
Identifiers: LCCN 2017023409 | ISBN 9780801098499 (pbk. : alk. paper)
Subjects: LCSH: Spiritual formation. | Christianity and culture.
Classification: LCC BV4511 .M65 2017 | DDC 253—dc23
LC record available at https://lccn.loc.gov/2017023409

Scripture quotations are from the Holy Bible, New International Version®. NIV®. Copyright © 1973, 1978, 1984, 2011 by Biblica, Inc.™ Used by permission of Zondervan. All rights reserved worldwide. www.zondervan.com

17 18 19 20 21 22 23   7 6 5 4 3 2 1

This book is dedicated to my lovely wife
and the four blessings that God has given us:

Jeremy, Emily, Joshua, and Bethany;
as well our expanding family of Emily and Madison;
and the little bundle of joy, Audrey

Contents

Acknowledgments

Juum kan basi bu nyonowa zasimwa. (A fish always smells like its parents.)
—Builsa proverb

Notice Something "Fishy"?

Pastor Monday, seated with the other African pastors, arises from the wooden bench. With the smell of groundnut soup and goat meat still hanging in the air, we sit around finished plates, talking as only good friends can. I can't think of a better way to wrap up my parents' two-week visit to Ghana.

A smile flashes across Monday's face as he focuses his eyes on my parents and quips, "Juum kan basi bu nyonowa zasimwa" (A fish always smells like its parents).

The pastors erupt in laughter, shortly followed by applause of approval. A high compliment, the proverb is near the English equivalent of "like father, like son." Monday is thanking my parents for their role and influence to send me to Ghana.

My heart swells with pride and deep love as I look at my parents. I cannot express it any better. My parents supported and encouraged Pam and me at every turn, and I will never be able to fully express my gratitude for their continued support.

In the years since that day in Ghana, my parents have continued to be a great source of encouragement and inspiration. My mom has since passed away, but her influence is still felt every day.

God has also blessed me with an amazing woman to walk hand in hand on this faith journey. My wife, Pam, has lived out the pages of this book through her steady and consistent faithfulness to God. Her willingness to experience other cultures and take steps of faith is a testament to God's goodness and faithfulness. I have been privileged to walk alongside her for thirty years. Our children—Jeremy, Emily, Josh, Bethany—and our newest family members, Emily Julia, Madison, and Audrey, have also taught me how to learn from another generation. They are a constant source of joy to Pam and me. I can't think of a more fun group to share this journey of life with.

Along my journey, other key figures have shaped and molded this book. One of those friends is Darrell Whiteman, whose influence pervades this book. At times, I am not sure where his teaching leaves off and my own thoughts pick up. He has been a steady mentor and encourager since the day I first met him. His substantial comments and encouragement for this book provided helpful direction and guidance.

The idea for this book first came from Mathias Zahniser. Like a fish caught by a hook, I was reeled in by a course he taught, Cross-Cultural Discipling, at Asbury Theological Seminary. Matt opened my eyes to the role of symbols and ceremonies in the discipleship process. After I took the course as a doctoral student, Matt asked me to be a teaching assistant the following year. The third year, he asked me to help teach a portion of the course. The fourth year, Matt, exercising true discipleship, asked me to teach the entire course while he sat in the class as a student! Following each class period, he reviewed the entire class session with frank critique and encouragement.

Matt released this fish from his hands, and, humbled yet empowered, I have taught this course for the past ten years at both Sioux Falls Seminary and Asbury Theological Seminary. To trace the original smell of this book, read Matt's groundbreaking book *Symbols and Ceremonies* (1997). My hope is that this book in your hands will influence you in the same way that it has me.

Students from this class took these ideas and developed them in ways that I could not have imagined. While only a small portion of these examples appear in this book, I have learned much from my students' experiments. This experience has confirmed for me that alternate discipleship patterns are practical for many contexts.

I first observed the principles of intercultural discipleship through the actions of African church leaders with the Bible Church of Africa in Ghana. They demonstrated how oral learning patterns often result in different discipleship approaches. I have such admiration for the church leaders' patient and consistent witness of Christ amid difficult circumstances. Ministering alongside them was a privilege.

The Serving in Mission (SIM) missionaries in Ghana also taught me much about the role that cultural influences play in discipleship. These wonderful families and individuals patiently guided me to discover learning patterns that were culturally relevant to the local people.

I am also thankful for the many Native Americans whom I have met along the journey of faith. Both in seminary and on the Rosebud Lakota-Sioux reservation, they have demonstrated potent discipleship patterns from Native perspectives. One of the most important lessons I learned from them is the need to respect the past in order to make sense of the present.

I also want to acknowledge the gracious permission granted by the publishers of previous articles and books from which I drew excerpts. In particular, chapter 8 provides new material while also drawing heavily from my dissertation research in the book *African Proverbs Reveal Christianity in Culture: A Narrative Portrayal of Builsa Proverbs Contextualizing Christianity in Ghana* (2009). The excerpts are used by permission of Wipf and Stock Publishers (http://www.wipfandstock.com).

While I take credit for all the mistakes that you may find in this book, I hope you are left with a pleasant "smell" from the book in your hands. If so, I am indebted to all of those mentioned above.

Preface

This book is written for people who are stuck in spiritual ruts—and they do not know how to get out. Too often, either Christians are conformed to the local culture, or they separate their spiritual life from the surrounding culture. Aren't Christians supposed to be transformed and then change their culture? Without knowing it, we have fallen into ruts that the apostle Paul warned his disciples about many years ago (Rom. 12:1–2).

We have forgotten some of the early methods of discipleship that the church long ago depended on to transform people and cultures. This book remedies our amnesia by recovering methods from the early church during a time of significant growth and culture change.

We have also overlooked options that are available for discipleship by limiting ourselves to approaches from our own culture alone. By probing other cultures around the world, we will discover potent discipleship methods to apply to our own culture. In addition, we will also become aware of how our own tunnel vision prevents us from seeing the creative genres already in a culture that can be appropriated for discipleship.

The bottom line is this: God has given us a wealth of cultural tools to promote spiritual growth, but we often overlook them and settle for just one! I have seen the transformation that can happen when disciples put into practice the entire toolbox. Instead of limiting ourselves to one approach, consider how individuals, families, and whole cultures could be transformed if we recovered discipleship methods from previous times and various cultures. In this book we will explore multiple cultures across the globe and many generations across time in our search for intercultural discipleship practices that produce spiritual growth.

I am writing, first and foremost, for the practitioner. The disciplers of today are not failing simply due to a lack of information. Rather, instead of mere information, they need transformation. This transformation should reach to the very core of our worldview. To this end, I will provide some theory to undergird our approach, but I will not remain at the top of the abstraction ladder indefinitely. Rather, I will climb down this ladder and apply theory on the ground—where we live. I will also deliver a generous dose of personal narratives and hope that you find glimpses of yourself in the stories so that you begin thinking about and then experimenting with new possibilities for spiritual growth.

Each chapter begins with a cultural proverb and personal story of mine to give you clues about where the chapter is headed. Throughout the chapter, I have also dropped some gold coins for you to gather. These coins come in the form of short narratives, proverbs, figures/tables, memorable characters, and personal experiences. While names have occasionally been changed out of respect for the privacy and sensitivity of the people involved, these stories faithfully portray the truth as I perceived it at the time.

At the end of each chapter you will find suggestions and activities to perform with a small group of disciples. Instead of providing another curriculum of topics to discuss, these suggestions guide the discipler in how to apply intercultural discipling.

In appendix B you will find suggestions and exercises for instructors, drawn from my ten years' experience in teaching the Cross-Cultural Discipling course to seminary students. The exercises can be applied in homes, church small groups, retreats, or classrooms. I hope these suggestions assist you in teaching others about this topic and also encourage you to conduct your own experiments.

This generation is experiencing a growth spurt in Christian expansion worldwide that is unprecedented since the beginning of the church. However, some have described the church as a mile wide but an inch deep. I am dreaming that this generation will have a qualitative discipleship growth spurt that matches the numerical growth. This requires a journey in discipleship that few have been willing to take. Will you ride with me?

Roadmap for the Journey

The roadmap for the journey is straightforward. In the first chapter I discuss how we got stuck. This overview alerts us to the worldview assumptions that limit our perspectives on discipleship. In chapter 2 we discuss two ruts in the road that have jarred many travelers (buckle your seat belt!), namely, syncretism and split-level Christianity, along with the recommended middle approach of critical contextualization. Chapter 3 defines and describes intercultural discipleship. Like a headlight shining on the road ahead, a case study exposes the path that the rest of the book will follow.

The succeeding chapters each focus on different cultural genres that are useful for discipleship. Symbols are examined in chapter 4, new rituals are discussed in chapter 5, and the contextualization of existing rituals is demonstrated in chapter 6. The process of critical contextualization for discipleship is introduced through the real stories of friends we meet along the road in these initial chapters.

Chapter 7 turns to a favorite genre of many disciples: stories. Chapter 8 then addresses proverbs, a personal favorite of mine. In chapter 9 the atmosphere is energized as we explore dance, music, and drama for discipleship. Chapter 10 then gets us out of the car and into the streets for holistic discipleship, where words and deeds are integrated.

To leave the reader stranded far from home, though, seems a bit inconsiderate of my passengers. In order to find our way home, chapter 11 summarizes and applies each of the previous chapters to discipleship for a specific context: postmodern culture. Finally, the conclusion offers some tips for escaping the tire ruts that often bog down disciplers.

I hope you enjoy this lifelong journey of discipleship. It will likely contain more surprises than you can ever anticipate.

1

How Did We Get in This Spiritual Rut?

Gandiok yeng kan kaw banga. (One giant alone cannot catch a lizard.)
—Builsa proverb

Stuck in the Mud

The truck slows to a grinding halt. It finally dawns on me that the thirsty African soil has soaked up the heavy rains during the church service. The tan dirt road has turned into a deep brown mud pit. Gradually, the truck stops as the tires form two deep ruts in the mud.

"No problem. I have four-wheel drive," I say out loud, perhaps to reassure myself. I have since learned that a truck's four wheels are no match for muddy roads seeking a victim.

"Whiiiiiiiiiiir," whine the tires as they spin in place. Trying to back out now, the tires, desperate for any type of traction, grasp only mud that is slung out the back.

Stuck.

No way forward. No way backward.

Everyone jumps out of the truck, including the half-dozen people in the back. Now they are pushing and pulling the truck as I try to rock the tires back and forth. This only seems to make matters worse, as the tires become wedged even deeper into the mud, which is not going to give up its prey so easily. In the tug-of-war between the tires and the mud, the mud is clearly the victor.

Eventually, some men arrive with arms full of logs and sticks.

"When you rock forward, we will put the logs into the tire ruts. That way, the tires will have something to grab on to when you rock back. This will work—we have done it before," they explain. Like a patient in the emergency room, I am more desperate for help than a prolonged explanation. I will try anything.

With a surge on the gas pedal and the straining of human muscle against the metal truck body, the truck tires crunch over the logs as they are released from the clutches of the reluctant mud. Free at last . . . with the help of others.

Breathing a sigh of relief, everyone hops back in the truck.

We try a different way home.

From Decisions to Baptisms to Church Commitment

Several church leaders have openly decried the lack of discipleship in the church to transform individuals and communities. While many "decisions for Christ" are made, few of these decisions result in further discipleship. For example, Waylon Moore notes, "In the United States, pastors have indicated that up to fifty percent of those making decisions in their churches are not baptized afterward" (1981, 42). Charles Crabtree fears that the numbers are even worse than that. He admits, "We cannot say with integrity that the Assemblies of God [in the US] retained more than 10 percent of those who made a decision for Christ as Savior. . . . The lack of retention of new converts in the Assemblies of God is a spiritual tragedy" (2008).

This discipleship concern is not limited to the West alone. As Moore notes, "In South America some pastors have said that eight out of ten of those who make a decision for Christ in an evangelistic meeting never come back to the church. The same thing is happening in Africa and Asia" (1981, 42). Allen Swanson's research in Taiwan indicates that it took a staggering fifty to sixty evangelistic decisions to result in one lasting convert who remained in the church (1989, 54)! The International Consultation on Discipleship meeting in Eastbourne, England, reports, "Our zeal to go wider has not been matched by a commitment to go deeper" (Weber 2003, 182).

Reflection and Discussion

1. Consider your experience with people making decisions for Christ at evangelistic rallies or events. What percentage do you estimate continue for baptism and church involvement?
2. For those who do get baptized and continue in the church, what do you think made the difference?
3. Why do you think that this lack of discipleship is so widespread?

Coming Home

Like me and my companions in this story, disciplers are looking for a way home. Well-intended Christians are getting stuck in their spiritual growth. Instead of moving on to Christian maturity and transformation, they are stagnating and cannot seem to move forward, like tires spinning in place, forming deeper ruts. Disciplers are searching for discipleship patterns that will free them from the tight grip of the surrounding culture that conforms them. They are also trying to find ways for faith to interact with the local culture in order to be relevant at work, at home, and among friends. By practicing the same methods, over and again, disciplers seem to be wedged even deeper in the mud. Stuck.

This is not simply a problem for one particular culture. Leaders from around the world have expressed concerns about the lack of discipleship in the church. Western and majority world churches are facing a similar dilemma.

While people may respond to Christ for salvation, they are not deepening their faith and maturing as disciples of Jesus.

Since Jesus's Great Commission (Matt. 28:16–20) contains the central command to make disciples of all the nations, churches largely agree that

---

The American church is dying, not from lack of effective evangelism, nor from lack of resources, but from lack of effective discipleship.

Michael Ramsden (in "Decade of Discipleship" 2017)

---

discipleship should be a priority for the mission of the church. Unfortunately, they would also usually agree on another point: their track record for discipleship is not so good. They have fallen into the two ruts of being conformed to the local culture, on one hand, or separating their faith from large areas of life, on the other. Surely the church could do a better job of finding logs to dislodge the spinning tires. Can churches from other cultures and other time periods provide some needed guidance in this important process of discipleship?

Removing the Straitjacket

There is great value in stepping out of your own culture for a period of time in order to gain a fresh perspective, as anyone who has lived deeply in another culture can attest. In order to get a wider perspective on the process of discipleship, I take an intercultural approach in this book. Viewing how discipleship is done in other cultures, we gain fresh perspectives that can be helpful in our own cultural contexts. Culture has been described as a "comfortable straitjacket," since every culture highlights certain options for how things should be done correctly and filters out others. An intercultural perspective makes us aware of some of the options for discipleship that other cultures have filtered out and disregarded. As we will see, many of these options have been around since the beginning of the church (during another time of rapid church growth), but they have been overlooked in recent years. An intercultural approach combines the strengths of various cultures over various time periods in order to overcome the limitations of individual cultures and generations.

Intercultural discipleship is similar to the combination of gasoline and a match. When lessons from various cultures are combined, powerful results emerge! When isolated from one another, they are powerless. Monocultural discipleship approaches likewise miss the potential power in discipleship, since it isolates cultures from one another. An intercultural approach, however, learns from other cultures, resulting in powerful transformation.

The Builsa proverb advises us, "Gandiok yeng kan kaw banga" (One giant alone cannot catch a lizard). No matter how powerful an individual person is, he or she is unable to single-handedly catch this small animal—a task that two children can easily accomplish. Likewise, churches in individual cultures need the help of other cultural perspectives in order to fulfill the Great Commission and make disciples of all nations. Instead of trying to be a more powerful giant (and not accomplishing the task), we need to look for discipleship practices from other cultures.

Widening the Community

This intercultural approach will show how discipleship is a communal process that addresses intimate issues involving the whole individual and the community. I will also highlight the value of oral literature (particularly symbols, rituals, proverbs, stories, music, dance, and drama). While these genres are often overlooked in cultures that prefer print learning, intercultural disciplers recognize that they have been tested over centuries and are laden with discipleship potential. Like logs grown from local trees, these genres can assist disciplers in dislodging us from spiritual ruts.

A multigenerational perspective reveals how previous generations have successfully approached discipleship. Snapshots from earlier stages of church

> **When a person makes a confession of faith and is never taken through a formal discipleship process, there is little hope of seeing genuine spiritual transformation.**
>
> Howard Hendricks (in "Decade of Discipleship" 2017)

growth demonstrate practical applications of cultural genres for discipleship. History agrees with the men who shoved logs under the spinning tires: "This will work—we have done it before."

Along with using an intercultural and multigenerational approach, I compare and contrast other religions in this book. This process reveals how religions around the world use sacred myths, symbols, and rituals to form worldviews and transform disciples, and it can be appropriated for Christian discipleship. To guard against the two ruts of syncretism (culture is not sufficiently critiqued by Scripture, thereby blending two faith systems) and isolation (culture is rejected or ignored, thereby separating faith from large sectors of life), the process of contextual discipleship should promote biblically faithful and culturally appropriate discipleship.

Instead of limiting us to one culture in one time period, discipleship approaches from various cultures and time periods present new options to transform the worldviews of maturing followers of Jesus. This brings hope for disciples of the future.

How Did We Get Here?

While I am hopeful that the intercultural discipleship approaches I describe will transform the disciples of the future, we first need to look to the past in order to understand how we arrived at this point today. We will see that our monocultural approaches slip a comfortable straitjacket on young disciples without their knowing it.

Table 1.1 summarizes some of the assumptions that individual cultures highlight for discipleship. Monocultural discipleship approaches emphasize one side to the neglect of the other. Without knowing it, the worldview assumptions of individual cultures limit how discipleship is usually carried out.

TABLE 1.1

Comparison of Cultural Assumptions That Affect Discipleship

Western Culture	Majority World Culture
Print learning preference	Oral learning preference
Individual identity	Collective identity
Justice (guilt) orientation	Honor (shame) orientation
Cognitive focus	Emotive focus
Material/scientific reality	Spirit-power reality
Redemption theology	Creation theology
Assembly-line production	Handcrafted production

While the cultural assumptions listed in table 1.1 are helpful during times of cultural stability, they serve as straitjackets that prevent us from trying out other options. This is particularly important during times of rapid cultural change, when other options are needed to cope with the new questions and issues being faced. The intercultural discipleship approach I advocate in this book recognizes and then integrates both sides of table 1.1. As evidenced by the pleas of churches, this is sorely needed amid the rapid and pervasive changes that globalization presents. Let's consider each of the cultural assumptions in table 1.1 in more detail.

Print versus Oral Learning Preference

More than any other single invention, writing has changed the way people think (Ong 1982, 78). Disciplers in print-based cultures tend to approach the discipleship process with a strong preference for print materials. During my early discipleship days in college, I met with a mentor who gave me a book to read that discussed important biblical topics. I diligently read the book and wrote my answers to the questions posed in the spaces provided in the book. We then met to discuss the book. After weeks of diligent work, I finally completed the book. As a result, I then graduated to . . . another book! I never questioned this approach, since I assumed that it was the best and logical one for discipleship in the surrounding print culture.

This preference for print learning shaped how I started the discipleship of new believers in Africa. As a young missionary, I was eager to meet with new believers to read and discuss written Bible studies that focused on important biblical topics. As I began teaching these lessons to prepare new believers for baptism, I quickly noticed how the topical studies were hard for people to grasp and did not easily engage these eager disciples. Instead, I noticed how the pastor used oral learning approaches that were memorable and engaging, employing local proverbs, songs, dance, and stories to connect with the disciples' thinking and memory patterns. As I witnessed his approach, it became clear that disciples were being transformed. I was changed as well (see sidebar 1.2).

I realized that the monocultural discipleship approach was not enough. Art forms such as proverbs, stories, dance, and music (discussed in chaps. 7–9) were helpful discipleship tools. A print-based approach was not wrong—it was just not enough. While chapter 3 discusses oral discipleship further, the point here is that a monocultural approach focusing on print learning assumptions alone will miss the value of oral learning assumptions (and vice versa). A combination of oral and print learning preferences together is needed. This is becoming more and more relevant in Western as well as majority world cultures in the postmodern era, when learners increasingly prefer oral approaches (discussed further in chap. 11). Monocultural discipleship approaches are simply not sufficient.

Individual versus Collective Identity

Another cultural assumption that affects the process of discipleship is the degree of individual versus collective identity (see, e.g., Moreau, Campbell, and Greener 2014, 154–64). In the Western world, people generally find their identity in their personal accomplishments. When two individuals meet for the first time, they will often inquire about the other's occupation. From an early age, children are taught to be independent and do their own work in

Print Assumptions in an Oral Culture

I walk toward the lone lantern, excited to meet this group of new believers. The only light for miles, the weak kerosene flame wobbles in the cool night air, flickering shadows against the mud hut that serves as a church.

Stepping through the church door, I am greeted by a large gathering anticipating my arrival. I approach the front of the room, armed with prepared lessons on sin, salvation, and how to walk in this newfound faith. It is the method I learned when I first accepted Christ. I am eager to teach, and they are excited to hear.

Well, at first they are.

It isn't long before their eyes start shifting, their eyelids start to droop, and this energetic room that I walked into is now—and I cringe to say it—completely bored.

"How is this possible?" I think. I consider pushing forward, like forcing children to eat the vegetables on their plate—they may not like it, but it's for their own good! Seeing the downward spiral that I am falling into, a young pastor steps forward and begins with a proverb,

"Fi mabiik dan bo cham zuk, fi kan de teng chainya." (If your relative is at the top of the sheanut fruit tree, you do not have to eat the sheanut fruit that lies on the ground.)

He continues, "What the white man is trying to explain is that Jesus sits in the top of the tree right next to God. You can call on him in prayer and be assured that he will hear you. The idols in our homes are like sheanut fruit that have fallen to the ground. Why would you want these bruised fruits when Jesus provides the good fruit at the top of the tree?"

Smiles and laughter burst forth, and the audience is once again energized. Even more important, they are learning and growing in a way that connects deeply within them.

The pastor continues with a local story and ends with a locally composed song. The drums burst forth, and people dance in a circle as they belt out statements such as, "Jesus is a lorry. Enter in and he will take you to heaven."

To conclude, the pastor asks them to recall what they have learned. I am amazed at how the group recounts the biblical lesson in sharp clarity, drawing from local proverbs, stories, and songs.

Adapted from Moon (2015, 166–67)

Reflection and Discussion

1. Why didn't Jesus write a book for his disciples? Wouldn't it have been a lot easier to use a book to instruct his disciples?
2. Instead of print approaches to discipleship, what oral genres did Jesus use (e.g., see Mark 4:33–34)?
3. How might print versus oral learning preference differences affect discipleship practices in various cultures worldwide?

school. This highly individualized culture leads to everything from personal license plates for cars to personal evangelism and personal discipleship! While it is important to focus on a personal relationship with Jesus Christ that is vibrant and nurturing, this monocultural approach overlooks the value of discipleship that is rooted in collective identity.

Collectivist cultures generally find their identity in their clan. When two individuals meet for the first time, they will often inquire about their relational networks to people that they may commonly know. From an early age, they are taught to place the needs of the group above their individual concerns. This collective identity also shapes how spirituality is experienced and nurtured. Communal cultures revel in shared spiritual experiences. For example, the Sicangu Lakota Sioux gather together for the sun dance ceremony. While only a few brave souls will be tethered to the tree of life by rope skewered to their skin, family, friends, and well-wishers circle around them to experience the spiritual ceremony together for several days. A monocultural approach to discipleship misses the critical role that rituals play in the discipleship process. Chapter 5 focuses on rituals to illuminate the role of the community and the individual in discipleship.

Justice (Guilt) versus Honor (Shame) Orientation

Related to the individual versus collective identity discussed above is the difference between justice-oriented versus honor-oriented societies (see also Moreau, Campbell, and Greener 2014, 195–209). While the terms "guilt" and "shame" are often used to describe these differences, Ruth Lienhard points out that "honor is a basic cultural value. Shame is a mechanism for punishment and keeping individuals in line" (2001, 133). Scott Moreau, Evvy Campbell, and Susan Greener add, "In similar fashion, justice should be understood as a basic cultural value, with guilt as the corresponding mechanism for social conformity" (2014, 196).

The Western world has largely been characterized as justice oriented. Justice-oriented cultures use a set of rules to uniformly bind their society together such that all people are treated equally and fairly regardless of their role or position in society. When a rule or law is broken, the guilty person should acknowledge his or her guilt, confess it to others, and then pay the penalty. Once this is accomplished, the individual is then forgiven for what he or she has done and restored. In Christian discipleship, individuals are expected to confess their sins to Jesus so that they receive forgiveness based on Jesus paying the penalty of sin, resulting in the restoration of the sinner.

Honor-oriented cultures, however, are bound together by a set of relationships whereby people are expected to act according to the expectations of their own in-group or patron. Individuals are expected to favor their own in-group members. If someone breaks these expectations, then shame is brought on him and his entire group. Moreau, Campbell, and Greener note, "When a person brings dishonor (shame) to the in-group, the only way to restore purity or expunge shame is through some type of ritual that will erase the impurity and restore the relationship" (2014, 197). For Christian discipleship in honor-oriented societies, rituals play a prominent role in deeply embedding values and maintaining relationships.

Misunderstanding and problems occur when people from justice-oriented cultures engage those from honor-oriented cultures, and vice versa. Moreau, Campbell, and Greener note that cross-cultural workers from justice-oriented cultures "are likely to ignore or suppress important indigenous rituals that may be adaptable to church life, such as rituals for conflict resolution, life transitions, and socialization—in other words, rituals important for discipleship" (2014, 275).

For example, after I had lived in Africa for several years, a misunderstanding arose between a church leader and me. I tried to address the problem by going directly to the person and discussing the issue. I was hoping for a confession of guilt such that restoration would occur. After a period of time, the African invited me and another missionary friend to join him and two other African church leaders for dinner together. We had a wonderful meal that was cooked and served by the wives of the church leaders. During the meal, the misunderstanding was mentioned, but it was not overtly discussed. Jokes and smiles were exchanged such that we all departed with laughter and in high spirits.

On the way home from the dinner, the missionary friend said to me, "Our African friends sure knew how to delicately solve that misunderstanding and restore relational harmony, didn't they?"

I was dumbfounded and responded, "We really did not discuss the misunderstanding very much at all. How can you say this was solved?"

Growing up as a missionary kid in an honor-oriented culture, my friend quickly saw what I had overlooked. He explained, "The church leaders gathered together and even asked their wives to prepare a delicious meal for us. This meal and gathering communicated very loudly that they understood and acknowledged the misunderstanding. The meal together was a way to restore the relational harmony."

Stunned, I sat in silence as I started to realize how blind I was to the use of this "ritual meal" to restore the relationships that are so important in honor-oriented cultures. I gradually observed the importance of gift giving along with rituals for discipleship. Intercultural disciplers learn how to apply the lessons from both justice-oriented and honor-oriented cultures for discipleship in various cultural contexts. The use of gift giving and rituals will be discussed further in chapters 5 and 6.

Cognitive versus Emotive Focus

The emphasis of cognitive understanding versus emotive experience is another cultural assumption that affects the discipleship process. For cognitive-based cultures, discipleship focuses on understanding the correct content. It is important to know very clearly what is fact and what is error. Truth will be learned and upheld, while errors will be guarded against. The main focus is to maintain a correct ideology that clearly articulates the correct beliefs, norms, and values. Zahniser (1997) calls these the "ultimate issues." This cognitive focus helps determine who is "with us" and who is holding on to heresy, as disciplers understand the ultimate God correctly.

Other cultures value the emotive experience very highly. It is not enough just to know the correct answers; people in these cultures want to experience the truth. They want to feel the presence of God and experience this presence in their lives. God should be concerned about the daily concerns of life, such as my marriage, if and when to start a new business, infertility, and so on. Zahniser (1997) calls these the "intimate issues." This emotive focus will help disciplers to experience the intimacy of God in their daily lives.

While a monocultural approach focuses on either side of the equation, intercultural discipleship combines both the cognitive understanding and the emotive experience of God such that the ultimate God becomes intimate. Victor Turner (1967) has observed how symbols play an important role in connecting the two. Using slightly different terms, he notes that the ideology (cognitive) and the sensory (emotive) are two very distinct aspects of our lives. They are polar opposites, and cultures tend to emphasize one pole more than the other. Table 1.2 describes these two polar opposites.

TABLE 1.2	
Contrasting Poles United by Symbols	
Ideological (Cognitive) Pole	Sensory (Emotive) Pole
Beliefs	Feelings
Norms	Needs
Values	Appetites and desires
Head	Heart
What you SHOULD do	What you WANT to do

While these two poles describe opposite aspects of our lives, symbols have a unique way of connecting these two poles. Turner calls this the polarization property of symbols. The symbol places the emotive (sensory) pole at the service of the cognitive (ideological) pole. The end result is that a symbol helps stir the desire (emotive experience) within a person to do what is right (cognitive understanding). Put more simply, well-utilized symbols help people *want* to do what they *should* do.

As we walked into a Native American ceremony one day, the Native American woman next to me breathed in deeply as the aroma of burning sage saturated the room. Smiling widely, she exclaimed, "That is the smell of forgiveness!" This important value of forgiveness was brought to her mind and heart by the sweet-smelling sage that suffused her senses. The smell of the burning sage was a powerful symbol that helped her to connect a cognitive understanding to an emotive experience, which was an important step in her discipleship process. The role of symbols is so important in understanding and applying intercultural discipleship that it is the focus of chapter 4.

Material/Scientific versus Spirit-Power Reality

Intercultural disciplers also need to recognize the fundamental assumptions that various cultures make concerning a material/scientific reality versus a spirit-power reality. Philip Jenkins notes, "If there is a single key area of faith and practice that divides Northern [Hemisphere] and Southern [Hemisphere] Christians, it is the matter of spiritual forces and their effects on the everyday human world" (2011, 123). Overlooking this key area often leads to inadequate discipleship.

In a culture with a material/scientific worldview assumption, the "scientific method" trumps all other truth. This method sets up experiments with tight controls to determine an exact outcome. If the same outcome occurs again and again, it is considered a valid scientific fact and strong evidence of underlying scientific laws or principles. Anything outside this process is considered skeptically at best or dismissed as invalid or not real. When discipleship occurs

---

Because metaphors communicate with emotive power as well as cognitive content, use of biblical metaphors in the communication process can be used by the Holy Spirit to stimulate such faith. They can speak to both the mind and the heart, and often appeal to the senses.

Craig Ott (2014, 358)

---

in this type of context, legal and historiographic approaches to the Bible are used to discover incontrovertible truths that can be systematized into categories such as the doctrines of God, humanity, and church. Textual studies that accurately detail the origin, author, dates, and so on of the biblical books become very important exegetical tools to parse the text itself and derive the meaning. The aim is to articulate biblical truth that can be defensible against attack, like a bomb-proof shelter.

The assumptions in a spirit-power-oriented culture are very different. Instead of basing truth on scientific claims, spiritual power is at the center of daily life. Humans inhabit a world full of spirit activity that needs to be carefully navigated despite human weakness and vulnerability. Kwame Bediako notes the difference that this makes for discipleship: "Primal religion deals with a source of power, while Western theology has centered on a system of ideas" (1995, 106). As an African friend mentioned to me, "Systematic theology is not wrong—it is just not enough to help me make it through the day. I need a theology to protect me from witchcraft, curses, or juju."

Marguerite Kraft (1995) portrays the two different worldview assumptions by comparing them to eyeglasses, as shown in figure 1.1. I will use an example to clarify the figure. A man comes to someone's house one day. The look on his face reveals that he is in obvious pain. After lowering himself into a chair, he barely has enough strength to describe the pain in his stomach. From the material/scientific worldview (left side of the figure), someone might advise him to go to a medical doctor so that the disease can be identified and the proper medicine be prescribed to treat it. However, in that same event from the spirit-power-oriented worldview (right side of the figure), someone might take a different approach. They might take him to a local healer to find out *who* had caused the sickness, not *what* had caused it. The healer would determine what relationship has been fractured or upset that resulted in this sickness. The healer would then prescribe the proper procedure to treat the person. Each of these monocultural approaches highlights one area but misses another important aspect of discipleship.

Figure 1.1
Worldview lens affects discipleship response

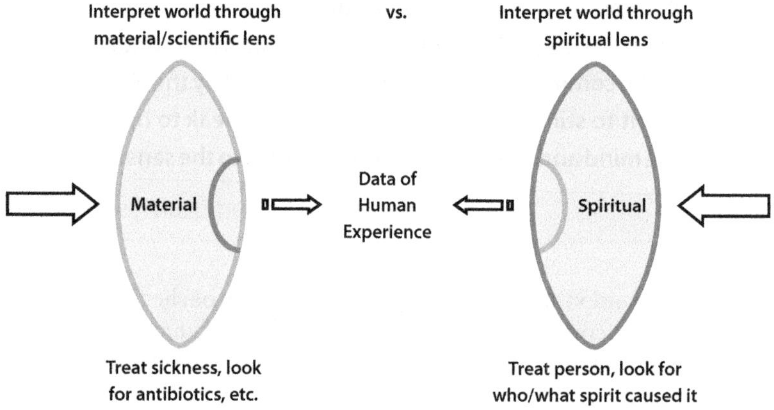

Interpret world through material/scientific lens   vs.   Interpret world through spiritual lens

Material   Data of Human Experience   Spiritual

Treat sickness, look for antibiotics, etc.   Treat person, look for who/what spirit caused it

By taking an intercultural discipleship approach, Kraft notes that there is value in *both* treating the disease and treating the person. She recommends a set of bifocals. Although they advise the person to go to the doctor, people from a materialistic/scientific worldview miss the opportunity to pray with him or her and ask about the relationships that may be fractured, thereby resulting in stomach pain. While counseling the patient about his relationships with others, those from a spirit-power-oriented culture miss the opportunity

Theology Affects Starting Points for Intercultural Discipleship

Jesus never presented a simple formula to describe salvation. New Testament theologian Brenda Colijn notes that there are various starting points to describe salvation in the New Testament:

> The New Testament does not develop a systematic doctrine of salvation. Instead, it presents us with a variety of pictures taken from different perspectives. . . . The variety of images attests to both the complexity of the human problem and its solution. No single picture is adequate to express the whole. . . . Each image is a picture of salvation from one perspective, posing and answering one set of questions. When seen together, they balance and qualify one another. We need all of them in order to gain a comprehensive understanding of salvation. (2010, 14–16)

The question becomes, then, where do disciplers start? Colijn develops twelve images of salvation from the New Testament that are possible starting points for discipleship. Without an intercultural discipleship approach, disciplers will likely start with the image of salvation that resonates most with their own culture. For example, someone with a justice-guilt worldview will probably connect with the penal substitution image of salvation, which will likely fall on deaf ears when he or she disciples people with an honor-shame or power-fear worldview (spirit-power reality).

Craig Ott notes that "one can begin with a biblical analogy that has the most common ground with the hearer's worldview, experience, and frame of reference" (2014, 359). Intercultural disciplers can identify the context in which they are ministering and then start with the image of salvation that connects to the plausibility structure of the disciple. Ott identifies four starting points for four different cultural contexts, as follows:

	Penal Substitution	Reconciliation	Power	Sacrifice
Cultural context	Justice-guilt	Honor-shame	Power-fear	Clean-polluted
God	Judge	Father	Source of blessing/life	Holy, pure
Humans	Subjects	Children	Subject to spirit forces	Worshipers
Sin	Breaking law	Rebellion	Unfaithfulness	Defilement
Sin's Result	Death/separation	Shame	Curse/bondage	Banishment
Solution	Payment	Propitiation	Deliverance	Cleansing
Christ	Substitute	Mediator	Deliverer	Sacrifice
Salvation	Justification	Restore harmony	Liberation, blessing	Purification
Image	Courtroom	Prodigal son	Redemption	Baptism

Adapted from Ott (2014, 363–70).

Reflection and Discussion

1. Consider which images of salvation utilize the plausibility structures of various cultures. How could this alter the starting point for discipleship in various cultural contexts?

2. How would the local cultural understanding need to be corrected in order to convey the biblical image accurately?

3. How would this change the starting point for discipleship in various cultures?

to find healing from the medicine God has provided through the wisdom passed on to the doctor. A monocultural approach misses the discipleship opportunities that intercultural discipleship affords.

Kraft's husband, Charles Kraft, laments,

> For what is probably the majority of the peoples of the world, the most important questions of life revolve around what to do about (or with) the supernatural powers that they believe surround them and constantly influence their lives. It is unfortunate that most of the Westerners . . . hold secularized Western assumptions rather than biblical assumptions concerning such powers. (1996, 201)

Aspects of material/scientific worldview assumptions can be contextualized with aspects of spirit-power worldview assumptions to promote holistic discipleship (discussed in chap. 10). If we neglect this step, monocultural discipleship approaches affect our theology to the point that our theology can be "culturally captive," thereby limiting the discipleship process in key areas of life.

Redemption versus Creation Theology

Underlying theological positions (shaped by worldview assumptions) affect the discipleship process in other important areas. Western Christians are usually very familiar with a redemption theology, based on the penal substitution image of salvation. Simplified by Bill Bright in the Four Spiritual Laws, it proceeds like this:

1. God offers a wonderful plan for your life (John 10:10).
2. All have sinned (Rom. 3:23).
3. The result of sin is death (separation from God) (Rom. 6:23).
4. Jesus is the substitute for our sins to bring us back to God (John 3:16).

The end result of this presentation is that someone is asked whether she is assured that she will go to heaven when she dies. If not, she will pray to receive Jesus Christ, assuring her of salvation. This penal substitution image of salvation is biblically sound and reminds us of reproducible methods for disciples to articulate their faith clearly and concisely.

One of the outcomes of using this approach alone, though, is that people then associate salvation almost exclusively with the future (i.e., salvation addresses what happens when they die and want to go to heaven). The matter of what happens while they are still alive is not as important. Salvation is strongly tied to the words that are heard and then spoken in prayer by the new believer.

While a redemption theology emphasizes the sin of humanity (starting in Gen. 3), other cultures emphasize a creation theology. Creation theology reaches back a bit further, to Genesis 1, and emphasizes that whatever God creates is good. God even dares to call the creation good. Even though God's creation is stained by sin, there is still value in creation because God made it and called it good. Folk cultures often emphasize a creation theology. Consider the words of Chief Luther Standing Bear of the Teton Sioux.

> It was good for the skin to touch the earth, and the old people liked to remove their moccasins and walk with bare feet on the sacred earth. Their tipis were built upon the earth and their altars were made of earth. The birds that flew in the air came to rest upon the earth, and it was the final abiding place of all things that lived and grew. The soil was soothing, strengthening, cleansing, and healing. This is why the old Indian still sits upon the earth instead of propping himself up and away from its life-giving forces. For him, to sit or lie upon the ground is to be able to think more deeply and to feel more keenly; he can see more clearly into the mysteries of life and come closer in kinship to other lives about him. (Nerburn 1999, 5–6)

One of the outcomes of a creation theology is that salvation includes the present—what happens while we are alive on earth is still important. It focuses on the prayer that Jesus taught his disciples (Matt. 6:9), echoed in churches around the world each week. This prayer asks for the kingdom of God to come on *earth* as it is in heaven. While the kingdom will be fully experienced in heaven, it is to be partly fulfilled on earth. Lester Ruth compares this to eating cookie dough before it goes into the oven (*The Feast* 2011). While we anticipate that the fully baked cookies will taste delicious in the near future, the cookie dough is a present foretaste of what is to come.

While salvation is through faith alone (Eph. 2:8–10), faith is displayed through the deeds done on earth, since faith without works is dead (James 2:17). A creation theology reminds us of the important place of deeds. It also reminds us that if we start to devalue one aspect of God's creation (e.g., the land), this eventually leads to devaluing other elements in God's creation (e.g., the unborn, the elderly, and the marginalized).

Instead of considering creation theology and redemption theology as two competing theologies, intercultural disciplers recognize them as two sides of the same coin. Holding them in creative tension with each other results in discipleship that integrates both words and deeds, future and present, and heaven and earth perspectives. This holds in tension Jesus's Great Commandment (Matt. 22:34–39) to "love the Lord your God" (who is in heaven) *and* "love your neighbor as yourself" (who is on earth). This topic of holistic discipleship is discussed in chapter 10.

Assembly-Line versus Handcrafted Production

The cultural view of production (shaped by worldview) also affects how discipleship is carried out. Whether the items produced are goods, services, or even disciples, cultures regard production differently.

In the Western world, Henry Ford developed the moving assembly line in 1913 to produce Model T automobiles. The goal of the assembly line is uniformity. The driving force behind the conveyor belt is efficiency. The assumption is "if it is efficient, then it is good." The end result is a large quantity of cars produced in a short time with minimal cost. What a powerful concept!

This concept is also applied beyond cars to include discipleship in the Western world. For example, in *No Man Left Behind*, Patrick Morley, David Delk, and Brett Clemmer advocate an assembly-line discipleship model, as they claim that "this model demonstrates how to build a 'people mover' or 'conveyor belt' to disciple men within your church. Just like a moving sidewalk at an airport or an assembly line at Henry Ford's factory, this process helps men get from where they are to where God wants them to be" (2006, 21).

The value of this assembly-line production approach is that large quantities of people can move through the discipleship process. This often results in discipleship programs using large seminars and curriculum that is mass-produced in an efficient manner. An obstacle to this approach, however, is that assembly lines are meant to result in a finished product. Once the line is finished, so is the product. Likewise, disciples may feel that once they have finished the particular discipleship program advocated, they are a "finished product." Instead of regarding discipleship as an ongoing process, they regard it as something from which they graduate. Bill Hull notes, "The most common mistake made by well-intentioned leaders, particularly acute in the Global North, is turning discipleship into a curriculum that a serious disciple completes and then graduates from" (2006, 36). Focusing on uniformity, efficiency, and finished products, the assembly-line production mentality has limitations.

Majority world societies, however, have a different focus for production. Instead of the high-technology assembly-line model, they advocate a hand-crafted model of production. The goal of handcrafted production is uniqueness. The driving force behind the handiwork is creativity. The assumption is "if it is creative, then it is good." The end result is that a small quantity of crafts is produced, with each one being an authentic and creative original. What a powerful concept!

The value of handcrafted production is that the unique qualities of the local culture and artist are expressed in each product. When applied to discipleship, the handcrafted approach recognizes that each disciple has a unique set of circumstances. Differences in gender, age, life-cycle stage, social power, personal temperament, learning style, culture, and family position are all considered in the discipleship process. As opposed to mass production in the assembly-line model, the handcrafted model creates a unique disciple based on the unique set of circumstances that the person finds himself or herself in, throughout the life cycle. Fortunately, there are predictable stages in the life cycle that humans usually encounter (e.g., birth, adolescence, marriage, death). These unique circumstances are incorporated in rituals during these stages in order to move people from one level of faith to another. Rituals are so important in the discipleship process that this is the focus of chapters 5 and 6. Once again, a combination of both processes can help intercultural disciplers produce many disciples who are each unique.

Worldview Formation

The assumptions discussed above help form a person's worldview. Paul Hiebert defines worldview as "the foundational cognitive, affective, and evaluative assumptions and frameworks a group of people makes about the nature of reality which they use to order their lives. It encompasses people's images or maps of the reality of all things that they use for living their lives" (2008, 25–26). In this definition, note that these underlying assumptions that comprise a worldview form the foundational beliefs, feelings, and values. Clifford Geertz affirms that the worldview then provides a model of reality and also a model for action (1973, 169). Charles Kraft further notes that these models are not complete; rather, they are based on perceptions of reality, in his definition of worldview as "the culturally structured assumptions, values, and commitments/allegiances underlying a people's *perception of reality* and their responses to those perceptions" (1996, 52; emphasis mine).

Worldviews, then, are not complete, since they limit what people perceive. As a result, monocultural disciplers are often oblivious to how their worldview assumptions are shaping their Christian faith . . . until there is an intercultural encounter. When this occurs, disciplers better understand their own worldview and are more open to transformation.

Worldview Transformation

Discipleship must recognize and transform the worldview if the discipleship process is to result in transformed lives. Hiebert (2008, 319–24) notes three ways we can change worldviews:

1. *Examine worldviews*: Bring the worldview assumptions to the surface and "make explicit what is implicit" (319).
2. *Be exposed to other worldviews*: "Step outside our culture and look at it from the outside, and . . . have outsiders tell us what they perceive as our worldview" (321).

3. *Create living rituals*: To help express our worldviews, living rituals "affirm our deepest beliefs, feelings, and morals, which lead to new lives in a new community and in the world" (324).

Discipleship must use all three methods to transform the worldviews of growing disciples. Intercultural discipleship examines the disciple's worldview assumptions (demonstrated above), exposes this to other worldviews (the focus of the remaining chapters), and creates living rituals (discussed in

> **Culture hides much more than it reveals, and strangely enough what it hides, it hides most effectively from its own participants.**
>
> Edward T. Hall (1959, 29–30)

chaps. 5 and 6). This approach can result in worldview transformation. When we ignore this process, worldviews are often left untouched. The result is all too common: disciples get stuck in spiritual ruts.

Stuck in Spiritual Ruts

The cultural assumptions discussed above explain how easy it is to get stuck in spiritual ruts. Monocultural disciplers are limited, since they emphasize one side of discipleship to the neglect of the other side. The result is insufficient discipleship. In monocultural discipleship, major cultural features are

> **If you make disciples, you always get the church. But if you make a church, you rarely get disciples.**
>
> Mike Breen and Steve Cockram
> (2011, Kindle location 81)

"hidden"; therefore, they are not addressed. One giant alone, no matter how big or fast, cannot catch this lizard!

Spiritual growth stagnates.

The spiritual ruts grow deeper.

To probe a bit further to find the depth of these ruts, in the next chapter we discuss some of the major issues that get us stuck in the discipleship process. Once these discipleship issues are identified, we can then describe an intercultural discipleship approach to move forward.

Summary

Churches around the world are searching for discipleship methods to transform Christ followers. Whereas monocultural methods limit the options for discipleship, combining methods from multiple cultures and worldviews overcomes the limitations of one culture and historical period alone. In this chapter we examined the following:

1. When discipleship is based on a Western perspective, the following factors are often assumed: print learning preference, individual identity, justice (guilt) orientations, cognitive focus, material/scientific reality, redemption theology, and assembly-line production.
2. When discipleship is based on a majority world perspective, the following factors are often assumed: oral learning preference, collective identity, honor (shame) orientation, emotive focus, spirit-power reality, creation theology, and handcrafted production.
3. Each of these assumptions has strengths and weaknesses. Combining aspects of both cultural perspectives can result in greater discipleship than limiting ourselves to the assumptions in one perspective alone.
4. These assumptions, among others, form the disciple's worldview. For a disciple to be transformed, his or her worldview must be transformed. This is often made possible by intercultural engagement.

Activity for Discipling

1. To really learn the practice of intercultural discipling, we must be apply it in the context of close relationships that balance both affirmation and challenge. Breen and Cockram have observed, "A gifted discipler is someone who invites people into a covenantal relationship with him or her, but challenges that person to live into his or her true identity in very direct yet graceful ways. Without both dynamics working together, you will not see people grow into the people God has created them to be" (2011, Kindle locations 178–80). As a discipler, prepare some time in your own schedule to be available for close relationships with a few disciples who meet regularly for both encouragement and accountability. While this involves a commitment of time and energy, it is well worth the effort. As Robert Coleman declares, "We must decide where we want our ministry to count—in the momentary applause of popular recognition or in the reproduction of our lives in a few chosen people who will carry on our work after we are gone" (1993, 32).

2. Consider your own ministry of discipleship. You do not have to be perfect but simply be available and intentional. Identify the people or group that God has brought into your life to focus your discipleship efforts, recognizing that "discipleship is a relational endeavor depending on broken people living in the grace of God!" (Breen and Cockram 2011, Kindle location 120). Look for potential disciples by considering those who are FAT: Faithful, Available, and Teachable, as defined in light of their own culture. Be selective, pray about the people to invite, then personally invite these people into an intentional discipleship relationship.

3. In your cross-cultural context, consider the following questions: Which of the pairs in table 1.1 needs to be more in balance for your discipleship approach? Which image of salvation is the most appropriate for discipleship in your cultural context? Discuss this with your disciples.

Since discipleship requires intentional focus on a limited few, keep this group of disciples in mind as you work through the activities in the remainder of the book. Ideally, you will meet regularly with this discipleship group for a specific season. Each chapter will have specific activities for you to build on for intercultural discipling. Greg Ogden recommends that you limit the group of disciples to three (yourself and two others) to maximize peer mentoring, leadership rotation, and eventual reproduction of other discipleship groups by the initial disciples (2003, 149). Start with a small group of disciples and then find out how large the discipleship group should be for maximum transformation.

Neither Jew nor Greek

Adapted from Twiss (2000, 32–37).

Chaske was born on a Native American reservation in South Dakota. Living in one of the poorest counties in the country, he saw first-hand the effects of drugs, sexual abuse, and ill health. He also experienced the Native cultural customs, including the communal powwow, purification ritual (*inipi*), intensification ritual (sun dance), and funeral giveaways. As a teenager he gradually experimented with alcohol and drugs, but he felt a deep emptiness inside. Eventually, he left the reservation and began experimenting with several religions, including Native American traditional religion, Hinduism, Taoism, and Buddhism. To his dismay, these did not fill his emptiness, and he concluded that there had to be more to life than he was experiencing.

When he was hitchhiking to get far from home one day, some Christians gave him a ride and talked to him about God, Jesus Christ, and God's plan for Chaske's life. At first he brushed off their words. Two weeks later, however, he was sitting alone on a beach late at night, and an engulfing paranoia overwhelmed him, leading to a strong fear of death or insanity. He tried Eastern meditation and prayers but to no avail. Eventually, he literally cried out at the top of his lungs in desperation, "Jesus, if you're real and can do what those people said you could do, then I want you to come into my heart and life and to forgive me for the wrong I've done!"

To his shock, the fear and paranoia instantly disappeared, and he felt this incredible peace flood his entire body. He felt clean, forgiven, and joyful. He knew that the Creator had revealed himself to Chaske, and he had become a follower of the Jesus way. He was now ready to be trained in the way of Jesus!

Chaske traveled to a ministry training center for discipleship in his newfound faith. With the exception of one African American and a few Native Americans, everyone on the staff was Anglo-American. Chaske started to read theology books and learn how to have an individual quiet time to grow in his faith. The Four Spiritual Laws seemed to make sense, since he could identify with the need to be forgiven of sin and the associated guilt. Chaske's mind was getting clearer, and he could understand the logical reasons behind the need for Jesus to save humans. Chaske was encouraged by the example of others who went through this discipleship program ahead of him and seemed to be living faithfully to serve God. A few months into the discipleship process, though, Chaske began to think back on his Native American heritage and how this should fit into his new Christian experience.

"How I am supposed to relate to my Native American culture now that I have become a Christian?" Chaske asked one of the disciplers.

The discipler opened a Bible and read, "There is neither Jew nor Greek, slave nor free, male nor female, for you are all one in Christ." He explained how cultures should all blend together once we become Christians.

"Chaske, don't worry about being an Indian; just be like us!" the discipler said in a way that seemed to settle the discussion.

Chaske accepted this statement from his discipler like a dry sponge soaks up water. Yet the more he followed this advice, the more nagging doubts lingered in the back of his mind.

"Can I really just leave my Indian culture behind and embrace white culture as the only Christian culture?" Chaske thought.

In order to answer that question, Chaske met another Native American friend who had become a Jesus follower. Larry was still living on the reservation and was excited to hear about Chaske's changed life. The more that Chaske described the discipleship program, the more Larry became excited.

"There is a battle here on the reservation," Larry started. "Bad spirits exist here so I suggest that you stay away from the sun dance, the sweat lodge, and even the powwow. These are not good for your Christian discipleship! If you are not careful, those Indian practices will drag you back into Native spirituality."

Larry became animated now as he recalled, "People asked me to return to a Native way of life, but I told them that I don't care what you pagans want to do—I am not going to enter your ceremonies. They call spirits in there, and you have to be careful what you invite in."

Chaske listened intently and soaked up every word. This made sense to him, since he knew the dangers on the reservation and the presence of evil as well. He appreciated the caution about sliding back into the lifestyle that he was so grateful to leave. The matter seemed settled—until the phone call.

Thomas, a Native friend, called Chaske because he had heard that Chaske was now a follower of Jesus. Thomas had also become a follower of "Jesus on the red road." Thomas had learned an approach that was different from what Chaske had heard and experienced so far. Instead of abandoning Native culture, Thomas encouraged Chaske to consider ways to find the presence of Jesus already in the Native culture.

Thomas asked, "Why would you leave one demon-filled culture (your own) and substitute another demon-filled culture (someone else's) for it? Why not start with your own Native culture and look for ways to express your faith in Jesus?"

Chaske was surprised to hear this approach, and he listened intently. "How do you remain a part of the Native community while not slipping back into Native spirituality?" he asked.

"Since we are an oral culture, you can learn of Christ through the symbols, rituals, stories, proverbs, and dances. Instead of throwing these away, we find evidence of Christ already there and then apply Christian meaning to the local forms. Jesus removes our shame from our past, but he also redeems our past and present. Since the Creator made all things on the earth, we burn the sage that grows in the ground to represent the cleansing of sacred space in our churches. In this way, we do not simply learn about the Creator; we also experience his presence and power. I am not saying that this is easy, but it is taking our own culture seriously and shaping disciples based on our unique realities instead of someone else's reality."

Chaske knew that he had to make a decision. Should he remain in the discipleship program that he had obviously benefited from already (and was affirmed by his friend Larry), or should he leave and follow the approach of his friend Thomas? If he followed Thomas's approach, where would he start? After much prayer, Bible study, and consulting with others, Chaske decided to . . .

Reflection and Discussion

1. In looking at table 1.1, what are the assumptions for the discipleship approaches of the various parties in this case study?
2. What theological perspectives or biblical images may help Chaske?
3. What will it take for Chaske's worldview to be transformed in a way that is biblically faithful and culturally relevant?

Issues That Get Us Stuck

Jiib jeero ale seba by doburim. (The one who carries the load knows how heavy it is.)

—Builsa proverb

Restless Nights

Ahmed wakes up in the middle of the night dripping wet. Sweat beads roll across his face as he awakes from another restless slumber. To make things worse, this is the third night in a row that he cannot sleep. He simply cannot get out of his mind the concern that keeps nagging at him, no matter how hard he tries to calm his nerves. Simply put, he is afraid. He has not traveled very far from his village before, but in two days he will take an overnight, twenty-hour bus ride to the capital city. At first the trip sounded exciting, like a new adventure. As the day approached, however, his fears have continued to increase to the point that he wishes he did not have to go.

Ahmed knows how poor the roads are, both the dirt roads and the paved roads with potholes as big as a hippo. He also knows how the drivers would get tired and get into accidents at times. Just the other week, another accident occurred in a nearby village, causing several deaths. He knows some of the people who lost loved ones. He remembers how they asked the questions about why their loved ones died. Did God not care, or were there other spirits at work? Did someone intentionally mean to do them harm? Did they have enough protection for the journey? Ahmed does not know the answers, but he knows one thing: he does not want to be one of the unlucky ones who returns home in a wooden box.

As much as he has tried to reassure himself that everything will be OK, his fears have continued to rise each day. What started out as a small, nagging concern, like a pebble in his shoe has now overcome his emotions, like a boulder about to crush him. Even though it is in the middle of the night, he has to do something. Anything.

Just as the sun arises from its slumber and peeks over the horizon, Ahmed lifts his groggy body from his sleeping mat. He sets out to get help.

Ahmed is stuck in a spiritual rut and does not know how to break out. He knows that he is carrying a heavy load, but his previous experience has not prepared him to address the intimate issue he is facing. I have described the assumptions that help form our worldview and limit our view of discipleship in the previous chapter; in this chapter I identify the type of discipleship issues that often need to be addressed to get people unstuck. If left unattended, people remain stuck in ruts. Their spiritual journey goes nowhere, like truck tires spinning in the mud without any forward movement. Intercultural discipleship identifies the major issues for discipleship so that the disciple can be released from the ruts. His or her spiritual journey can then move forward once again.

Cross-Cultural Comparison of Religious Belief Systems: Two Tiers versus Three Tiers

Before we identify the major issues for discipleship, it will help to first consider how people tend to put their religious concerns in certain categories. This categorizing varies between cultures. Intercultural disciplers need to know the categories of the culture in order to identify and then address the spiritual concerns of disciples.

Paul Hiebert, R. Daniel Shaw, and Tite Tiénou (1999a) note that Western cultures have a very different religious belief system from majority world

> Our assumption of cultural sameness is what causes cultural incidents. . . . Our expectation, not their behavior, is the real sticking point. . . . The way to prevent cultural incidents is to stop assuming that other people are like us.
>
> Craig Storti (2007, 75–76)

cultures (compare figs. 2.1 and 2.2). They simply have different categories in which to place their questions and concerns. The worldview assumptions of Western cultures discussed in the preceding chapter result in a two-tier religious belief system (fig. 2.1). The worldview assumptions of majority world societies discussed in that chapter, however, result in a three-tier religious belief system (fig. 2.2). Each of these religious belief systems limits what is addressed for discipleship. Once again, monocultural discipleship puts a "straitjacket" on the discipleship process. We will explore this further in order to identify the most important issues/questions that need to be addressed for discipleship.

Figure 2.1
Western two-tier religious belief system

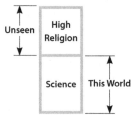

Questions asked of pastors or religious leaders in the Western world are normally answered according to the two-tier system shown in figure 2.1. On the first tier, modern science responds with the empirical data to explain that which can be seen and experienced in this world. This response addresses problems of this world dealing with the natural order or the secular realm (i.e., that which is seen). On the second tier, high religion is left to deal with otherworldly issues such as faith, miracles, inner feelings, and other sacred things that are unseen. The point is that Westerners usually find responses to their religious concerns either in science or high religion.

As the Western world becomes increasingly secularized, the lower tier continues to expand. People increasingly turn to science (and less often to high religion) for answers to issues they face. For example, if in the Western world, Ahmed would likely go to a counselor or doctor to find answers provided by modern science instead of turning to a pastor for answers provided by high religion. The assumption is that science would provide the answers to Ahmed's concerns. A counselor would provide answers from social science, or a doctor would consult medical science to prescribe the proper medication to calm his concerns. In the Western world, people turn to high

Figure 2.2
Majority world three-tier religious belief system

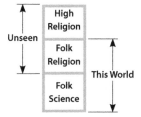

SIDEBAR 2.1

Universal Principles in Cross-Cultural Discipleship

Although in this book we highlight the differences between cultures in order to describe an approach called intercultural discipleship, there is also merit in uncovering universal discipleship principles that can be applied in various cultures. Charles Davis's helpful book *Making Disciples across Cultures: Missional Principles for a Diverse World* (2015) identifies ten universal discipling principles that can be applied in various cultural contexts. He focuses on "theological and cultural assumptions that invisibly shape how those principles become reality in a wide variety of cultures" (10). He then draws the following ten principles from Scripture:

1. Disciples let God lead from the invisible world.
2. Disciples hear and obey.
3. Disciples develop relational interdependence.
4. Disciples do what love requires.
5. Disciples make disciples.
6. Leaders equip disciples for ministry.
7. Disciples live an undivided life.
8. Disciples engage in personal and cultural transformation.
9. Disciples keep the end in mind.
10. Disciples organize flexibly and purposefully.

Kenneth Boa draws on Scripture and church history to construct the following list of eleven discipleship principles:

1. We must be disciples to make disciples.
2. Discipleship is a dependent process.
3. Concentration is crucial to multiplication.
4. People are not our disciples.
5. Reproduction is a mark of discipleship.
6. There is no maturity without ministry.
7. We cannot measure our ministries.
8. Discipleship is more than a program.
9. Discipleship requires a servant attitude.
10. Spiritual friendship is a component of discipleship.
11. Effective discipleship requires more than one method. (2001, 370–76)

Reflection and Discussion

1. Which of the discipling principles is most relevant to your cultural context?
2. How can these principles be communicated and applied in various cultural contexts? Identify those that you recognize will likely be a stretch for you and explain why.
3. While some of the principles appear in both lists, which ones are unique? Why do you think the lists are not identical?

religion only for answers to ultimate questions such as "How can I be sure of salvation?" or "What is the cause of suffering?" The intimate issues are addressed through science.

In contrast to the Western religious belief system, majority world traditional cultures have different categories to address their questions. They have a three-tiered view of reality. When they have questions, they often go to one of three sources to get answers: folk science, folk religion, or high religion.

On the first tier, folk science deals with the questions of this world that can be observed by the senses (i.e., that which is "seen") through interactions with others (e.g., how to fix a truck so that it is safer to drive). On the third tier, high religion deals with the forces and beings in the unseen spiritual "other" world (e.g., how this world was created and where evil comes from). In between these two levels, folk religion addresses forces and beings in the unseen world that affect this world. Ahmed, for example, would visit a local soothsayer, who would ascertain whether there are spiritual forces at work in the unseen world that are causing his fear in this world. He would likely be given a charm or amulet to wear around his neck or wrist in order to obtain power from the unseen spirit world that would protect him from harm in this world.

Note how differently Ahmed's concerns would be addressed in the two-tier world versus the three-tier world. Both systems provide logical responses to insiders, but they seem very strange to outsiders. If Westerners (two-tier) were discipling Ahmed in the majority world (three-tier), they would provide answers to Ahmed's concerns in a way that would entirely miss the category that Ahmed is most concerned about: the middle level. This middle level is so important to discipleship, yet so often overlooked, that Hiebert calls our tendency to ignore it the "flaw of the excluded middle" (Hiebert 1982).

Excluded Middle Issues

This middle tier, folk science, is missing in the Western religious analytical system. Hiebert calls this the "excluded middle," since Westerners typically exclude this tier from their spiritual decision-making process, yet it is "one of the greatest cultural gaps between Western people and many traditional religionists" (1994a, 196). For monocultural disciplers, the excluded middle is simply overlooked. When Westerners make disciples in majority world cultures, the issues in the excluded middle are often ignored or bypassed. The tragedy is that these excluded middle issues are often the daily intimate concerns for which spiritual guidance is desperately needed. Ahmed will need to find an answer—he will not simply roll over and go to sleep.

Surveying majority world cultures, Hiebert, Shaw, and Tiénou identify four key excluded middle issues that typically arise in majority world societies. By identifying these issues, disciplers are one step closer to intercultural discipleship. The four excluded middle issues are the following:

1. Why did someone die/live (e.g., following a sickness or accident)?
2. What is the cause for well-being or misfortune (e.g., wealth, barrenness, crop failure)?

Discipleship Issues for Believers from Muslim Backgrounds

Don Little, in his insightful book *Effective Discipling in Muslim Communities*, notes the challenges of discipleship in Muslim contexts where believers from Muslim backgrounds (BMBs) are under intense pressure to revert to Islam. Little notes, "Far too many of those who are coming to faith in Christ out of Islam today will fall away from Christ unless workers and believers seeking to disciple them learn to disciple well" (2015, Kindle locations 110–11). Drawing largely on his doctoral work, Little identifies eighteen of the most frequently cited obstacles for BMBs to grow in their Christian faith as follows:

1. Pressures from Muslim family; family control especially while single
2. Local Muslim community's hostility, rejection, and/or expulsion
3. Vulnerability due to youthfulness, low social status, weak economic state
4. Fear of all kinds: of problems, suffering, persecution, and oppression
5. Lack of trust between and among BMBs and BMB groups; lack of commitment to one group
6. Challenges for BMB families: child rearing, education, marriage
7. Spiritual nature of Christian faith: it is about the Holy Spirit, prayer, faith, not deeds
8. BMB lack of confidence, complexes, victimization, emotional pain
9. Satanic hold of Islam, demonic and occult bondages, hate, anger, lust
10. Local Christians, churches, and communities do not accept BMBs
11. The love of money; BMBs need to learn to give and be generous
12. Living in a police state where change of religion is not officially possible
13. The discipler's ineffectiveness, poor response, and wrong motives
14. Illiteracy and/or low levels of literacy; oral learners
15. Poor ethics and lack of integrity; must learn new ethics before a holy God
16. Muslim ideology, doctrine, traditions, and so on, all requiring reeducation
17. God is distant and unknowable; difficult to bring God close to BMBs
18. Men especially struggle with sexual issues and lust. (Little 2015, Kindle locations 2466–529)

Reflection and Discussion

1. Compare these obstacles to the definition of excluded middle issues as the "intimate questions and concerns that require unseen spirit power and guidance to effect change in this world." Do they fit under this definition?
2. How will an understanding of these issues affect a discipleship approach to BMBs?
3. What are the likely outcomes if these issues are neglected in discipleship?

3. How do I obtain guidance for an uncertain future (e.g., traveling, marriage, business decisions)?
4. Where do I find justice/protection amid evil (e.g., protection from the evil eye)? (Hiebert, Shaw, and Tiénou 1999b, 74)

These intimate issues are often the ones that disciples need addressed in order to grow in their own discipleship. Instead, Christians framed in Western worldview assumptions will largely ignore the excluded middle issues;

Gospel and cultural engagement is about the conversion of cultures, the turning to Christ and turning over to Christ of all that is there in us, about us and round about us that has defined and shaped us when Jesus meets us, so that the elements of our cultural identity are brought within the orbit of discipleship.

Kwame Bediako (2001, 2)

---

they will replace the third tier of high religion with Christian high religion. Overlooking excluded middle issues greatly hampers the discipleship process in majority world churches.

Hiebert summarizes, "It is clear today that folk religious beliefs and practices remain an unfinished agenda in the lives of young churches around the world" (1993, 258). These excluded middle issues, then, are some of the most critical ones to target for intercultural discipleship.

Excluded Middle in Western Culture

While Hiebert focuses on excluded middle issues for discipleship in majority world cultures, this framework also helps intercultural disciplers understand some of the greatest discipleship needs in Western contexts. Although Hiebert's two-tiered Western framework was very accurate during the period of modernity (characterized in the West by the triumph of reason and science), the relatively recent rise of postmodern thinking in the West has challenged these assumptions, resulting in an openness to experience and feelings. Many Westerners are realizing that they also have intimate issues that are not often addressed through either high religion (at least how it is presented in church) or science. If left unaddressed, these issues stunt the discipleship process, as the following story describes.

When she was in elementary school, Joan was sexually abused by a teacher. She did not tell anyone because she was ashamed of what was happening to her. It lasted for a whole year. Once her parents found out, they felt terrible because they had been unaware of what was happening to their daughter. Joan did not want to talk about it because she knew that it had upset her parents, and she felt guilty for causing them such distress. Following Joan's abuse, the family moved to another city to try to escape the pain.

Since Joan suppressed her emotions and never dealt with what had happened to her, it greatly affected her relationships and behavior as an adolescent. By the time she was fourteen, she was sexually active, and by age seventeen, she was suffering from anorexia. Much of this was because she felt as if she and her body were worthless, since she had been broken by the sexual abuse she experienced in elementary school. At eighteen she gave her life to Christ, but even then she felt as though she could not talk about her traumatic experience, because sexual abuse is just not talked about in the church setting. So she continued to struggle with nightmares about her experience of abuse into her early twenties. It was clear that becoming a Christian had not removed the problem. Deeper healing in Christ was needed.

Joan experienced deep brokenness. Healing is necessary to form healthy relationships and experience freedom. Since sexual abuse is not often spoken about in the church, sexual abuse victims may never get the healing they need. Joan's abuse was not addressed in church, even though it was a major need for

> **Excluded middle issues: the intimate questions and concerns that require unseen spirit power and guidance to effect change in this world.**

her own discipleship. The high religion discussed in church centered on topics such as assurance of salvation and going to heaven when you die. Science did not fully address her intimate concerns either, despite the counseling she had received. Deep down, she knew that God cared, but she did not know how the ultimate God could address her intimate needs. Since issues like this are excluded from the discussions of both high religion and science, and people recognize that they need power from the unseen world to affect this world, I am expanding Hiebert's definition of the excluded middle to include them.

For the Western world, then, excluded middle issues are also some of the primary issues that need to be addressed for discipleship. I define excluded middle issues as the intimate questions and concerns that require unseen spirit power and guidance to effect change in this world. These include concerns of abuse, addiction, transitions, shame, and other intimate issues.

Ignoring Excluded Middle Issues

When monocultural disciplers ignore the excluded middle issues that are important for discipleship, people in majority world cultures do not simply ignore these important issues. Instead, they go to people in the culture who address these issues—largely, traditional healers who practice folk religion.

Definition of Terms for Intercultural Discipleship

Contextualization: the capacity to respond meaningfully to the gospel within the framework of one's own situation. The goal is to enable an understanding of what it means that Jesus Christ, the Word, is authentically experienced in each and every human situation. The Word must dwell among all families of humankind today as truly as Jesus lived among his own kin. The gospel is good news when it provides answers for a particular people living in a particular place at a particular time.

Critical contextualization: a process to implement contextualization that engages culture with Scripture. The four steps of this process include phenomenological study, ontological critique, critical analysis, and missiological transformation. See chapter 6.

Culture: the common ideas, feelings, and values that guide community and personal behavior and organize and regulate what the group thinks, feels, and does about God, the world, and humanity. Cultures shape their models of reality around three dimensions: the cognitive (what do we know?), the affective (what do we feel?), and the evaluative (where are our values and allegiances?). Cultures are also multilayered models of reality. Like a spiral, they move from the surface level of what we call customs through the cognitive, affective, and evaluative dimensions to the level of worldview. Cultural forms are invested with symbolic meanings conventionally accepted by the community. At the core of all cultures is the deep level, where worldviews are generated and stored.

Digitoral: When people gather much of their information via digital means, they start to exhibit the characteristics of oral learners as opposed to print learners. Jonah Sachs (2012) recently coined the term "digi-

toral," while Walter Ong (1982) previously used the term "secondary oral" to describe the learning preference shift that occurred subsequent (or secondary) to literacy, aided by technology. See chapter 11.

Disciple: In the ancient world, the term "disciple" was used generally to designate a follower who was committed to a recognized leader or teacher. Jesus's disciples were those who heard his invitation to begin a new kind of life, accepted his call to the new life, and became obedient to it. The center of this new life was Jesus himself. To "make disciples of all the nations" is to make more of what Jesus made of them (i.e., the existing disciples).

Excluded middle issues: The intimate questions and concerns that require unseen spirit power and guidance to effect change in this world. For folk societies, excluded middle issues include the following: Why did someone die/live (e.g., following a sickness or accident)? What is the cause for well-being or misfortune (e.g., wealth, barrenness, crop failure)? How do I obtain guidance for an uncertain future (e.g., travel, marriage, business decisions)? Where do I find justice/protection amid evil (e.g., protection from the evil eye)? Excluded middle issues are also relevant to Western cultures, particularly when they include concerns of abuse, addiction, transition, shame, and other intimate issues (Hiebert, Shaw, and Tiénou 1999b, 74).

Folk religions: sets of loosely related practices, often mutually contradictory, used not to present a coherent true view of reality but to produce immediate results. They provide answers to the existential questions of everyday life, such as why someone dies/lives, dealing with crises, making everyday decisions, how to have justice/order. Folk religions provide various courses of action for those facing illness, bad fortune, sudden death, and failure in love and marriage, and guidance for those making important decisions.

Intercultural discipleship: the process of worldview transformation whereby Jesus followers center their lives on the kingdom of God and obey Christ's commands in culture, utilizing culturally available genres. See chapter 3.

Myth: While not always based on fact as seen from a rationalist viewpoint, myth is truth from the perspective of people for whom it establishes identity—it is their scripture. Myths provide a sense of identity and place, a history and rationale for beliefs/values. They also communicate cultural lessons/knowledge, validate appropriate behavior, and chastise inappropriate behavior. They are passed down through the generations as oral literature or ritual drama.

Simplex versus multiplex relationships: Simplex relationships occur when people are joined by a single bond, such as a pastor-church member relationship (C. Kraft 1996, 317). They relate to each other in just one context. Their relationship is rather weak, since what they know about each other comes only from what they observe in that one status/role bond. Multiplex relationships, however, exist when people relate to each other in more than one social context. As such, they will have various status/role bonds to connect them, thereby forming stronger relationships. See chapter 11.

Split-level Christianity: a form of Christian expression whereby people go to church to address certain questions/issues in life but go to another source (e.g., folk religion) to address other questions/issues in life. Unlike syncretism, the two sources do not blend; rather, they are isolated and used for different levels of questions.

Symbol: A symbol can be simply explained as "something present that stands for something absent" (Leeds-Hurwitz 1993, 6) or something seen that points to something not seen. Symbols help the disciple to connect the known, visible world with the unknown, invisible spirit world (Turner 1995, 15). Victor Turner (1995) noted three properties of symbols: polarization (a symbol connects a sensory experience with an ideology), unification (disparate symbols can be unified by a common thread of meaning contained in each of the various symbols), and condensation (one symbol condenses or brings together various meanings). See chapter 4.

Syncretism: blending of one idea, practice, or attitude with another. Traditionally among Christians it has been to indicate the replacement or dilution of the essential truths of the gospel through the incorporation of non-Christian elements. Examples range from Western materialism to Asian and African animistic beliefs incorporated into the church. There has been syncretism of some form everywhere the church has existed.

Worldview: a conceptual scheme by which we consciously or unconsciously place or fit everything we believe and by which we interpret and judge reality. In the building of culture, worldview (a) explains how/why things came to be as they are and how/why they continue or change; (b) validates the basic institutions, values, and goals of a society; (c) provides psychological reinforcement for the group; (d) integrates the society, systematizing and ordering the culture's perceptions of reality into an overall design; and (e) provides within its conservatism opportunities for perceptual shifts and alterations in conceptual structuring.

Adapted from Moreau, Netland, and Van Engen (2000)

33

While these young disciples look to Christianity to replace the ultimate questions addressed in the culture's high religion, they still revert to folk religion to address the daily middle-level intimate questions.

In the Western world, if excluded middle issues are not addressed in church, disciples may go to other places that promise to provide answers: palm readers, horoscopes, psychics, or self-help sources such as books, blogs, or popular television talk shows. When excluded middle issues are neglected, the end result is a weakened faith known as "split-level" Christianity.

Split-Level Christianity

Typically, disciplers have not provided spiritual answers to these middle-level questions, hence they have been excluded from discussion. Since Scripture (or at least the way it was presented) did not appear to be relevant to their questions, disciples deferred to local responses. This has been called "split-level" Christianity (Bulatao 1992), since Christianity and another faith system have operated concurrently on two distinct (split) levels. This division has severely limited the discipleship process.

Split-level Christianity can be compared to two parallel railroad tracks. Christian disciples go to the rail of Christianity to answer ultimate questions, while these same Christian disciples follow a totally different rail—namely,

---

To enable people to become disciples we must change whatever it is in their actual belief system that bars confidence in Jesus as Master of the Universe. **That is fundamental and must be taken as an unshakable conscious objective by any maker of disciples.**

Dallas Willard (1998, 307; emphasis in original)

---

folk religion—to answer intimate questions. The two faith systems are not intermingled in church; rather, they are separate and distinct, like two separate and parallel railroad tracks. Each rail of the track addresses different issues.

For example, a woman wants to start a business but is unsure whether this is the right time, place, or even the type of work most suitable for her. Since she does not hear this issue discussed in church, she assumes that this is not a "Christian" matter. As a result, she goes to the place where her dilemma will be addressed. In the majority world, the local shaman may give her the answers that she seeks. In a Western context, she may consult a psychic to find answers to the questions that keep her up at night. While she still goes to church to get Christian answers to ultimate questions, the intimate questions about her business are answered elsewhere.

Syncretism

Another similar but very different problem caused by inadequate discipleship is syncretism. Syncretism can be defined as "the replacement or dilution of the essential truths of the gospel thru the incorporation of non-Christian elements," or simply the "blending of one idea, practice or attitude with another" (Moreau 2000, 924). Syncretism can be compared to two converging streams of water. If one stream is blue in color and the other stream is yellow, the confluence of these two streams will be green (or at least streaked blue and yellow). When the stream of Christianity is mixed with the stream of a folk religion, the resulting practice is a mixture of both such that it is not purely one or the other.

For example, a man takes a Bible and puts it under his bed each night when he goes to sleep. It replaces the talisman that he used to put under his bed. The Bible is now a source of magical protection from the spirit world. While he is using a Christian object, it is mixed with the magical meaning carried over from his folk religion, resulting in syncretism.

Note that syncretism is different from split-level Christianity: the two faith systems are mixed in syncretism, while the two faith systems remain separate in split-level Christianity. This important distinction will help intercultural disciplers understand how to avoid both problems in discipleship.

Syncretism versus Split-Level Christianity

Historically, syncretism has been a danger that cross-cultural workers have guarded against, and rightfully so. The irony is that by guarding against syncretism, disciplers can unknowingly promote split-level Christianity. In our attempts to prevent the local culture from contaminating the gospel, which may result in syncretism, we do not engage the very middle-level issues that are important for discipleship. When we exclude these middle-level issues from Christian discipleship, disciples are forced to go elsewhere for answers—thus we are pushing them to split-level Christianity.

For disciplers, split-level Christianity can be more dangerous than syncretism, since split-level Christianity is not readily detected. The young disciple still goes to church and even behaves like a Christian in church and during Christian activities. It appears that this person is growing and maturing as a strong disciple of Jesus. When an excluded middle crisis arrives, however, the person reverts to folk religion for answers to the questions that are not asked in church. Discipleship is stunted but undetected by disciplers. With syncretism, it is usually very obvious that the two faith systems are intermingled, such that the disciple maker can readily address this issue. Split-level Christianity, though, is not so easily detected and addressed, since it is a limited faith that is appropriate in some areas of life but is replaced with a different system in other areas of life that tend to remain out of sight. Ironically, good intentions of monocultural disciplers to guard against syncretism can result in pushing people into the other extreme of split-level Christianity. Is there any middle ground for disciplers to take that avoids these two extremes? Intercultural discipleship charts the way forward with contextualization.

Critical Contextualization

To protect against the extremes of syncretism and split-level Christianity, integrative disciplers rely on critical contextualization to balance biblical faithfulness and cultural relevance. Darrell L. Whiteman notes, "Contextualization attempts to communicate the gospel in word and deed and to establish the church in ways that make sense to people within their local cultural context, presenting Christianity in such a way that it meets people's deepest needs and penetrates their worldview, thus allowing them to follow Christ and remain within their own culture" (1997, 2). This definition assumes that the gospel must make sense to the local culture. This implies that it must fit within the religious analytical system of the host cultures, whether they have two or three tiers. In addition, the definition states that Christianity must meet the deepest needs and penetrate the worldview level. Intercultural disciplers often identify these deepest needs by looking for the excluded middle issues.

Contextualization can be simply defined as "the capacity to respond meaningfully to the gospel within the framework of one's own situation" such that the "Word must dwell among all families of humankind today as truly as Jesus lived among his own kin" (Gilliland 2000, 225).

Instead of uncritically mixing Scripture and culture (syncretism) or isolating Scripture from culture (split-level Christianity), critical contextualization engages Scripture in a hermeneutical community to critique culture for discipleship. Some aspects of culture will need to be changed or modified. Some aspects of culture will need to be rejected, while other aspects can be accepted and used in Christian discipleship.

While I will discuss this process more thoroughly in chapter 6, an example may help describe this objective of critical contextualization. A few years ago my son purchased a painting in Ghana. After arriving home, he realized that the art was painted on the back of a flour sack. Once the flour sack was emptied, the artist cleaned it, blackened out the words on the sack, and then stretched the cloth across pieces of wood to form an indigenous canvas. The artist worked with the material available in his own culture as the starting point for this unique piece of work. In a similar manner, contextualization begins with the material that already exists in culture. Like a detective searching for clues, contextualization begins with evidence of God's hand at work in the culture. Some aspects of culture need to be rejected or cleansed first. Other aspects of culture need to be modified and stretched across some wood. Just as important, though, some aspects of culture need to be accepted and utilized as the starting point for painting God's glory in culture.

If the artist did not clean the sack and blacken the writing on it, words and colors would be blended, resulting in confusing images on the canvas. Syncretism occurs when there is an uncritical blending of two faith systems, such that Scripture does not critique culture. The artist could have rejected the flour sack altogether and simply painted on an imported canvas. The result would be a painting that is regarded as something from outside the culture and very foreign. Split-level Christianity results when the local culture is rejected or ignored, such that cultural issues are not brought to Scripture for engagement. Critical contextualization, however, stands in the middle of these two extremes, such that Scripture and culture are adequately engaged, resulting in the glory of God revealed in culture—like a painting on the back of an indigenous flour sack.

To describe this a bit further, imagine a road with guardrails that protect cars from falling into the rut on each side of the road. As long as the guardrails are in place, the car can travel freely. If it wanders toward one side or the other, the guardrails remind the traveler to get back toward the middle of the road. If the road is the contextualization process, and the guardrails are scriptural engagement on one side and cultural engagement on the other side, then these two forms of engagement prevent travelers from falling into the ruts of syncretism or split-level Christianity. If contextualization starts to wander toward these two ruts, the guardrails remind travelers to either engage Scripture more (to prevent syncretism) or engage culture more (to prevent split-level Christianity). Figure 2.3 identifies how critical contextualization balances the extremes of syncretism and split-level Christianity.

Figure 2.3
**Critical contextualization balances syncretism
and split-level Christianity**

On the left side of figure 2.3, syncretism results when Scripture does not adequately critique culture. The concern for syncretism encourages the cross-cultural discipler to engage Scripture more in the discipleship process. This dislodges the disciple from syncretism and moves him or her to the right toward contextualization. If disciplers move too far to the right, however, they run into the split-level problem. Split-level Christianity

Personality Preferences Affect Discipleship

Table 1.1 describes how cultural assumptions influence the discipleship process. Similarly, M. Robert Mulholland Jr. (1993) notes that personality preferences affect the discipleship process within cultures. For example, introverts prefer periods of silence, reflection, personal reading, and silent prayer, while extroverts prefer times of group interaction, discussion, collective reading, and outward prayer. A problem results, however, when "we tend to develop spiritual activities that are conducive to our preference pattern and then think that this is the only viable pattern of spirituality for others" (1993, 62). Once other patterns for discipleship are identified, disciplers need to adjust their own preferred discipleship patterns to coincide with disciples' preferences. Later, they balance this with other discipleship practices that are not their strengths. This is true for preferences shaped by personality differences, as well for preferences shaped by cultural differences.

While the effects of personality preferences on spiritual formation have been studied and linked to personality tests such as the Myers-Briggs assessment, what is less well documented is the manner in which cultural preferences affect spiritual formation. Intercultural disciplers will be more effective when they adjust their discipleship patterns to coincide with disciples' preference, both in personality and in culture.

Reflection and Discussion

1. Reflect on the personality traits that tend to be most common or most rare in your home culture. For example, the Myers-Briggs personality trait of sensing is found much more often among people in the United States (73.3 percent of the population tested) than is the personality trait of intuition (26.7 percent), such that the Myers-Briggs personality type ISFJ is the most common (13.8 percent) and INFJ is the least common (1.5 percent), based on a thirty-year study (Lawrence and Martin 2001). How do these personality traits encourage the type of discipleship approaches promoted in US culture?

2. Reflect on the personality traits that tend to be most common or least common in a culture that is different from your own. What adjustments would you need to make in this host culture to promote intercultural discipleship?

---

occurs when cultural issues are not adequately engaged. The concern for split-level Christianity encourages the cross-cultural discipler to consider culture more thoroughly in the discipleship process. This moves the disciple from split-level Christianity toward contextualization. In the midst of this balancing act between Scripture and culture stands critical contextualization, where intercultural disciplers produce disciples who are balanced by scriptural faithfulness and cultural relevance. To achieve this balance, critical contextualization considers the unique discipleship preferences of various cultures.

The Journey Ahead

For the rest of the book, we will visit different cultures and time periods to describe an intercultural approach to contextual discipleship. We will examine societies and religious adherents in Africa, Asia, the Middle East, North and South America, the South Pacific, and Native America. We will also explore cultures in earlier periods of church history when the church experienced substantial growth. Our goal is to learn the discipleship approaches that we may have filtered out from our own individual culture in this particular time and place. By doing so, we will find pathways that promote healthy patterns of discipleship that can be applied to specific contemporary contexts in Western and majority world cultures. The excluded middle issues will be identified and engaged with Scripture to produce contextual disciples, while avoiding the extremes of syncretism and split-level Christianity.

Summary

1. A cross-cultural comparison of religious belief systems identifies two-tiered versus three-tiered religious belief systems. This comparison highlights excluded middle issues, those in which the unseen spirit world affects this world. These issues are key for discipleship, since these are the intimate concerns that disciples wish the ultimate God to address. Unfortunately, these issues are often not addressed in typical Western discipleship approaches.

2. If excluded middle issues are not addressed, one of two results often occurs. The first option is split-level Christianity, where disciples address ultimate concerns through Christianity but go to another faith system (e.g., folk religion) to address intimate issues. The second option is syncretism, where two faith systems are intermixed. Both options weaken the disciple's faith, thereby producing spiritual ruts.

3. Critical contextualization is a better alternative to split-level Christianity and syncretism. In this approach, both Western and majority world cultural assumptions are considered to give new options for discipleship. This practice results in the ultimate God addressing the intimate issues in a manner that is culturally relevant and biblically faithful.

Now that we have discussed "how we got stuck" with the lack of adequate discipleship, and briefly identified the excluded middle issues that often result in spiritual ruts, we can turn to defining and describing more fully the process of intercultural discipleship in the next chapter.

Activity for Discipling

1. Get together with the individual or group whom you identified for a discipleship relationship in the previous chapter. What are the excluded middle issues for discipleship that are often not addressed in church? Discuss this with the individual or group. Pick the one issue that you feel is most important for this discipleship group, such that you will work with this issue throughout this book.

2. If your group members cannot identify an excluded middle issue right away, ask them to consider the following three foundational relationships and then select the relationship that needs the most attention for growth: upward to God, inward to others in their church/family, outward to those not yet in the Christian faith. Breen and Cockram note, "We were created to be three-dimensional beings; when one dimension is missing or is suppressed, the other two do not work as they should. If we do not have all three elements of the Triangle—the Up, the In, and the Out— we are out of balance, and we will wobble through life" (2011, Kindle locations 937–39).

3. Another possible way to initially identify excluded middle issues is to use an assessment tool and then discuss the results together. An example of such a tool is Discipleship Dynamics, available for a small fee at https://discipleshipdynamics.com/about-the-assessment.

4. Breen and Cockram identify *kairos* moments as those times in life when we realize that "we have used someone or something as a substitute for God" (2011, Kindle location 815). Reflecting on these past or present events may provide ripe opportunities for significant learning.

5. At the very least, help stimulate group members' thinking on excluded middle issues by asking two questions every time you meet:
   a. What is God saying to me?
   b. What am I going to do about it? (Breen and Cockram 2011, Kindle locations 2423–24).

Note: I am assuming that the group you are discipling is relationally connected to others in a Bible-believing faith community and participating in the life and worship of the faith community. While discipleship is by nature a relational process, the activities in this book attempt to answer the following questions: "What does a discipler do with the disciple?" and "How does one go about it?"

Tragedy Strikes

Adapted from Moon (2009a, 82–84).

Tragedy struck Immanuel's house. His eighteen-year-old son had been sick for several weeks, but now his death has hit his father hard. This was his only son . . . and now he is gone. He calls the church to help him do the burial and funeral. They gather at Immanuel's house throughout the night and bring comfort to Immanuel and his family as they bury his son. Pastor Kofi conducts the funeral ceremony and also stays with Immanuel until the next day.

Immanuel built his own house a few years ago. His family all became Christians, and they wanted to have a Christian household. As the head of the house, Immanuel can make the decisions concerning the funeral; otherwise, the traditional Builsa elders would have conducted the burial and funeral. Immanuel knows that this would include traditional animal sacrifices to the ancestors. Since he is a Christian now, Immanuel knows that he does not need those sacrifices to help him. Yezu Krista (Jesus Christ) is the sacrifice that Naawen (God) has provided for the Builsa.

"Our fathers have said, 'Fi mabiik dan bo cham zuk, fi kan de teng chain ya' (If your relative is in the top of the sheanut tree, then you do not need to eat the sheanuts that have fallen to the ground)," Immanuel explains to people. "Yezu is the relative who has risen from the grave and now sits at the right hand of Naawen. Since he is at the top of the tree, I can pray to him and he will provide what I need. When others offer sacrifices to the ancestors, they are just gathering the sheanuts that have fallen to the ground—everyone knows that these sheanuts are not nearly as good as the ones at the top of the tree." This makes good sense, and it helps Immanuel to put his confidence in Yezu, the one who sits at the top of the sheanut tree.

After the funeral, Immanuel is confronted by the Builsa village elders, who say, "We need to collect some dirt from the grave and take it home."

Immanuel is not surprised. He knows the importance of funeral rites in Buluk—this is a serious matter for the whole community.

"What will you do with the dirt?" Immanuel asks.

"We need to take it to the *bano* (soothsayer)," the elders explain, "so that he can reveal the reason that your son has died."

Immanuel is unsure what to do. Should he refuse to give them the dirt, or should he comply with their request? This matter has never been discussed in the church. He does not know how to respond.

"I will need to talk to my church leaders before I can allow you to collect the dirt. The elders have said, 'Ba kan kali dai yeng a nak kpeesa a sue yui ya' (They cannot sit in [just] one day and harvest Fra-fra potatoes to fill up a bag)."

This puts off the decision for a few more days until Immanuel can consult with Pastor David. The elders accept this and agree to sit with him another day.

Pastor David arrives shortly thereafter.

"Pastor David went to the Bible college in the capital city, so he must have the answer that I need," Immanuel reasons to himself. As Immanuel explains the whole situation to him, the pastor patiently listens.

"You need to refuse the elders and not allow them to collect the dirt. Don't you see," Pastor David warns, "that they will go to the *bano*, and he will say that the death has come about since the boy followed the path of Yezu Krista? This will only bring about more trouble for the church. You had better refuse them now!"

Immanuel nods his head in approval. "That is what I have been thinking of doing all along," he replies. "Thanks for your help."

Pastor David is not sure himself whether his advice will help. These types of questions relating Scripture to the Builsa culture were never discussed in the training he received at Bible school. He knows that following the path of Yezu Krista is a better way than trying to reach Naawen through the ancestors. As a result, he turned his back on anything related to the ancestors, since he considers it a trap to cause him to backslide into Builsa traditional religion. Even still, he wonders whether there is anything from the ancestors that might be helpful. Do Builsa have to reject everything from the ancestors in order to be fully Christian? Can Builsa Christians retain certain aspects of culture without compromising Scripture?

While Immanuel contemplates this struggle between Scripture and Builsa culture, Pastor Kofi arrives to greet the mourners and offer his condolences. After some time, Immanuel discusses the matter of the "dirt from the grave"

with him, and Immanuel asks for his advice.

Pastor Kofi is not sure how to respond either. He tries to recall what he had been taught in a vernacular Bible training center, but this issue was never discussed.

After some thought, Pastor Kofi replies, "I think that you should allow the elders to collect the dirt. You are not the one who will go to the *bano*, and you will not be the one to bring the sacrifices. You can just allow them to follow the path of the ancestors, and you continue on the path of Yezu. If you totally refuse their request, then this will end up in a fight. It is better to accept their request for now. This will then be over soon, and we can just continue on following Yezu as usual."

Immanuel is confused. He respects Pastor Kofi, and his advice makes sense to him; however, this is the exact opposite of what Pastor David advised.

"The pastors have been to Bible training, and they should know how to advise us," Immanuel thinks. "How can one advise me to reject the elders' request and the other advise me to accept the elders' request? Perhaps Christianity does not deal with these questions, so I should just go along with the elders' request? On the other hand, perhaps I should refuse, since this may weaken my faith in Yezu and cause others to fall away."

Immanuel is still confused. This issue is just too hard to figure out. This type of issue has never been preached about or taught in church, so he has no preparation to know how to deal with it. If the pastors cannot agree on a Christian response, then how can he?

As he is pondering these thoughts, the tribal elders return, as promised, looking to gather some dirt from the grave. Immanuel steps outside to greet the elders and then responds to their request by . . .

Reflection and Discussion

1. What are the excluded middle issues in this case?
2. Which pastor's advice would most likely lead toward syncretism?

Which would likely lead toward split-level Christianity?

3. What advice would you give, or what else may Immanuel need to know/do in order to respond to the elders in a way that is biblically faithful and culturally appropriate?
4. If this case is not handled well, how may it affect Immanuel's own discipleship? His family? His church?

43

What Is Intercultural Discipleship?

If you want to go fast, go alone. If you want to go far, go together.

—African proverb

Is He Really a Christian?

Seminary students are in the midst of a weeklong immersion experience. Spending a week in the inner city with limited showers and unlimited time, they attract all sorts of company. George, a man in his thirties, drops into the seat across from them at the rescue mission. Disheveled and unshaven, this homeless man freely engages in conversation. As the conversation winds down, he unashamedly asks for prayer: "Pray that Jesus will help me overcome my addiction to shoplifting. I just got out of the state pen for shoplifting, and I want to do the right thing. I am asking for Jesus to help me." Earnestness is etched in his face like the wrinkles creasing his forehead.

The seminary students are stunned and confused. Later that night, they discuss George's situation: "Is this man really a Christian? Isn't stealing one of the basics? I mean, it is one of the Ten Commandments!"

Another student protests, "Wait a minute. I think that he is a disciple of Jesus. Don't all of us have issues—it's just that some of them are more visible than others?"

What does it really mean to be a disciple? How can we know whether we are on the right track? What process would you recommend for George? These are the types of questions that I will address in this chapter. Some definitions are needed to clarify terms for the remainder of the book.

SIDEBAR 3.1

Discipleship in the New Testament

Theologian Brenda Colijn discusses the slightly different perspectives on discipleship that each of the Gospel writers provides.

Mark emphasizes discipleship as service, recognizing the difficulties and failures of disciples and their need for restoration by Christ. Matthew highlights the importance of the community of disciples as salt and light in the world. Luke shows the crucial role of the Holy Spirit in empowering disciples to follow Jesus in a life of prayer, compassion and cross-bearing. John views discipleship as a loving relationship with Jesus that expresses itself in action, especially in love for one another. The word for disciple (*mathētēs*) is not found in the New Testament outside the Gospels and Acts. But the concept of discipleship is carried on in metaphorical uses of "following" and "walking," and especially in the idea of imitation. (2010, 77–78)

Throughout the New Testament, the Greek word *sōtēria* is used to indicate salvation, but it means much more than simply conversion. It includes concepts of discipleship related to healing and hope. Colijn observes that

the first century cultures believed that someone's sickness and health were connected not only with the physical state of that individual but also with that person's relationships, and even with

the order or disorder of the cosmos. Treatment for illness should consider its physical, social and spiritual dimensions. Thus healing and salvation could not really be separated. (2010, 127)

She concludes with the following thoughts related to discipleship:

Salvation is not a one-time event completed at conversion. It involves a growth in relationship and in wholeness that is not optional or secondary but essential to what salvation means. . . . God is intimately involved in our lives—past, present and future—and we must depend upon God throughout our life in faith. (2010, 141–42)

Discussion and Reflection

1. Which of the Gospel writers' perspectives on discipleship is most similar to your thoughts and experiences?
2. Consider Colijn's expanded view of salvation to include more than simply conversion but also to entail discipleship. What excluded middle issues do you see in the description of the Greek word *sōtēria*?
3. What relationship do you see between evangelism and discipleship? How may the motivation for discipleship change if it is presented as part of the salvation process rather than an "optional extra" after salvation?

What Is a Disciple?

The word "disciple" in the New Testament comes from the Greek word *mathētēs*, which literally means "a learner," from the verb *manthanō*, which means "to learn" (Vine, Unger, and White 1985, 171). In the world of the Old and the New Testaments, this learning was not an academic exercise; rather, learning was achieved by following a rabbi, such as John (Matt. 9:14), the Pharisees (Matt. 22:16), and Moses (John 9:28). Jesus stepped into this world and appointed the twelve disciples (Luke 6:12–16) to follow him, learn from his teachings, and obey his instructions. In the midst of this relational discipleship, the worldview assumptions of the disciples were transformed. Instead of destroying a worldview, discipleship transforms it through the available genres in culture. This is the goal of discipleship: to transform the worldview, not simply to learn new beliefs or behaviors. The underlying worldview assumptions that lead to new beliefs and behaviors must be transformed (Hiebert 2008, 12).

Bounded Set Theory

To further explain the process of discipleship, we must first ask the question that the seminary students asked at the beginning of the chapter: "Who is a disciple?" In other words, how do we know when someone like George is inside the group or outside? To answer that question, we turn to set theory, based on Paul Hiebert's integration of missiology and mathematics (1994b).

Basically, there are two types of sets: bounded sets and centered sets. In bounded set theory, a boundary line clearly separates who is inside the set. In figure 3.1, objects outside the boundary line are outside the set. The two objects inside the boundary line (closest to the cross at the center) are inside the set. In bounded set thinking, it is very important to clearly and sharply define the boundary line so that there is no doubt concerning who is inside and who is outside the set.

Figure 3.1
Bounded set

Christians have often taken this approach to evangelism and discipleship. The line is clearly drawn by someone who explains the gospel, and listeners are invited to step across the line. Once they do so, they are in—they are saved (regardless of the direction they are headed afterward). In this paradigm, it is very important to clearly define the line so that people can step across it. This line is very fixed. Once you are in, you are in. The need for discipleship, then, is very ambiguous. It is interesting to note that different denominations draw different lines to determine who is inside. For some, it is a prayer; for others, it may be baptism, coming to the front of a church, speaking in tongues, catechism/confirmation, and so on. Along with this anomaly, we note that Jesus never presented salvation the same way twice! Why would he have done this?

Centered Set Theory

To answer this question, let's look at another way of grouping objects called centered sets. In centered set theory, the determination of who is inside the set is based on the direction of movement (see fig. 3.2). Each object is really an arrow pointed in a specific direction. Instead of focusing on proximity to the center, centered set theory focuses on who is pointed toward the center. The three objects that are pointed toward the center are now inside the set. Note that the left object is far removed from the center, yet it is "in the set" since it is pointed toward the center. Also, note how one of the objects close to the center is now "out of the set" since it is pointed away from the center. Unlike bounded sets, which are defined by the distance from the center, centered sets are determined by the direction of movement.

Figure 3.2
Centered set

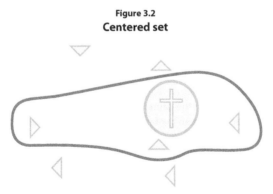

Christian evangelism and discipleship can be regarded this way. The focus of evangelism is to help someone turn away from sin (this is biblical repentance) and turn toward Christ. This results in the person moving toward Christ as the center for his or her life. While people all start at different places with varying degrees of baggage, allegiance to Christ is the central issue (not proximity to the center). Let us return to George's story.

The Rich Young Man and Centered Set Thinking

Did Jesus use centered set thinking? The answer to this question may explain why Jesus never presented the gospel in the same way twice. Even a casual reading of the Gospels reveals that Jesus presented salvation to everyone differently—from the thief on the cross to the rich young man. Could it be that Jesus identified the excluded middle issue that kept each person from seeking first the kingdom of God, and this became the basis for offering salvation? When Jesus said, "Seek first the kingdom of God," he did not mean to make a list of priorities, such as kingdom first, ministry second, spouse third. Instead, he meant that we should place the kingdom of God at the center of our lives such that everything (including ministry, spouse, etc.) points to the kingdom of God. Once Jesus identified whatever prevented a potential disciple from placing the kingdom of God at the center of his or her life, he invited the person to address this issue for salvation. If the person did, then the direction of his or her life was redirected toward the kingdom, resulting in salvation.

The rich young man, for example, was very close to the kingdom due to his obedience to the Ten Commandments (Mark 10:20), like the arrow close to the center. This young man was depending on the fact that he had stepped inside the line by his obedience to the commandments *since his youth.* He was likely referring to a time in his youth when he had made a public commitment (what would later develop into today's bar mitzvah ceremony for Jewish boys when they turn thirteen); therefore, this religious event marked the point when he had stepped inside the set, as shown by the bounded set paradigm in figure 3.1. The rich young man used bounded set thinking.

Jesus, however, saw that the direction of the rich man's life was moving away from the kingdom of God. Jesus then identified the one issue that was preventing the rich man from placing the kingdom of God at the center of his life: he trusted his riches instead of God. Jesus invited him to remove that barrier by selling everything he had and giving to the poor, such that he could become a disciple by turning the direction of his life and following Jesus (v. 21). Jesus used the centered set paradigm in figure 3.2 to depict his faith position based on direction of movement instead of proximity to the center.

Notice that Jesus never presented salvation to anyone else again in this manner. For example, the thief on the cross (Luke 23:40–43) represented someone who was very far from the kingdom of God due to his checkered background, like the far left arrow in figure 3.1 that is outside the set. Surprisingly, the thief redirected his life toward the kingdom in his request "Remember me when you come into your kingdom" (v. 42). Jesus then recognized the direction of his life and replied, "Truly I tell you, today you will be with me in paradise" (v. 43). Jesus used centered set thinking to place the thief inside the set, as depicted by the far left arrow in figure 3.2.

Reflection and Discussion

1. Consider other instances in the Bible where Jesus offers salvation to an individual. Does Jesus use bounded set or centered set thinking? What are the excluded middle issues that Jesus addresses in each case?

2. How does centered set thinking change your approach to evangelism and discipleship? What questions do you ask when using centered set versus bounded set paradigms?

When George pleaded, "Pray that Jesus will help me overcome my addiction to shoplifting. I just got out of the state pen for shoplifting, and I want to do the right thing. I am asking for Jesus to help me," the students asked themselves, "Is this man a Christian?"

From a bounded set approach, the students were doubtful. How can a man claim to follow Christ and still be a thief? From a centered set approach, though, the issue is not about stealing; rather, it is about allegiance to Christ.

We can best improve our thinking about evangelism by construing it as that set of loving, intentional activities governed by the goal of initiating persons into Christian discipleship in response to the reign of God.

Scott Jones (2003, Kindle locations 1849–50)

Is he giving all that he knows of himself to all that he knows of Jesus? If so, then he is pointed in the right direction! Overcoming shoplifting will be a discipleship issue, like any other addiction, and it will take time. But this should not prevent him from turning his allegiance to Christ.

In the centered set approach, evangelism is one part of the discipleship process. Once people turn from sin and turn their allegiance to Jesus, they are in the set. Discipleship is the process of keeping people Christ-focused amid the temptations to turn their allegiance elsewhere. While certain markers will be important for the disciple (e.g., prayer, confession, committing to a church, baptism), these do not form the basis for salvation. The basis for salvation is allegiance to Jesus. Discipleship anticipates the barriers in the path ahead and helps move the disciple in the direction of Christ in order to overcome these barriers. Some of the most obstinate barriers are likely to be excluded middle issues. These are the intimate issues in this world that people need spiritual guidance and power to overcome, such as an addiction to shoplifting.

Discipleship versus Church Leadership

The centered set versus bounded set distinction also helps to articulate the difference between discipleship and leadership training. While all are called to follow Jesus and become disciples, not all are called to be church leaders. The Bible clearly provides guidelines for overseers and deacons in the church in 1 Timothy 3:1–13 and Titus 1:6–9. These criteria form a bounded set: if people do not meet the criteria, they are not eligible for the position of overseer

49

or deacon in the church. However, just because they meet these bounded set criteria does not necessarily mean they should be church leaders. They must also be disciples, which means that they need to be part of the centered set. The Venn diagram in figure 3.3 demonstrates this difference between disciples and leaders. The three disciples are those inside the centered set, while the one church leader arises from the intersection of the centered and the bounded sets.

Figure 3.3
Venn diagram for church leaders

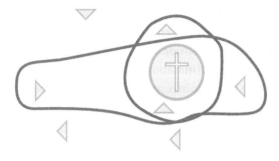

Put simply, all church leaders must be disciples, while all disciples do not have to be church leaders. Without placing burdens on disciples prematurely, the Venn diagram in figure 3.3 also maintains the biblical criteria for church leadership. This distinction keeps the goal of the discipleship process in focus.

Centered Set Discipleship

Using a centered set approach, we understand discipleship as a transforming process whereby people center their lives on the kingdom of God (Matt.

> The present tense of "follow" in Mark 8:34 (in contrast to the aorist tenses of "deny themselves" and "take up their cross") suggests that discipleship is a continuous process that grows out of the definitive choice to deny oneself and follow Jesus.
>
> Brenda Colijn (2010, 76)

6:33), such that they obey Christ's commands in the cultures in which they live (Matt. 28:19–20). In this process, disciples' worldviews are transformed as they apply biblically faithful and culturally relevant responses to issues that attempt to move them away from a kingdom-centered life. This lifelong process helps maturing disciples overcome the dangers of syncretism and split-level Christianity.

Note that this process is lifelong. To maintain a kingdom focus and transform a worldview takes time, as Hiebert notes: "People come as they are with their histories and cultures. We cannot expect an instant transformation of their behavior, beliefs, and worldviews. It is important, therefore, to disciple them into Christian maturity. This includes a transformation not only in the way people think and behave but also in their worldviews" (2008, 12). Recognizing the lifelong emphasis of the centered set approach, Eugene Peterson notes another biblical designation that is important for disciples to bear in mind. Disciples are to be pilgrims, as Peterson explains: "Pilgrim (*parepidēmos*) tells us we are people who spend our lives going someplace, going to God, and whose path for getting there is the way, Jesus Christ. We realize that 'This world is not my home' and set out for the 'Father's house'" (2000, 17).

The centered set discipleship approach also recognizes that discipleship is a daily process that involves engaging the Scripture with culture in order to address excluded middle issues. While these intimate issues may appear insignificant compared to larger ultimate theological concepts, they are critical daily matters that require a Christian response for the disciple to remain centered on the kingdom of God. This centered set process aims at worldview transformation instead of simply targeting beliefs or behavior alone. Hiebert observes, "Transformation is not a once-for-all event. We turn to Christ, and renew our commitment to follow him in every decision we make in our lives. Only when conversion becomes an ongoing process in our lives will there be lasting transformation" (2008, 332).

God Goes before Us in Culture

As discussed earlier, creation theology reminds us that God has created all things and called them good. Despite humanity's subsequent sin and fall, God's original creation was made in God's image. As a result, it would be reasonable to expect to find remnants of God's image existing in every culture . . . somewhere.

John Wesley used the term "prevenient grace" to describe the undeserved love of God that precedes human actions (Olson 2004, 46). In other words, God goes before us in culture, and we begin the discipleship process by continuing the conversation that God has already started. We do not bring God to a culture; rather, God brings us to the culture. Intercultural disciplers start by identifying the stepping-stones that God has already placed in the culture for discipleship, and then they move that conversation Christ-ward.

Redemptive Lore

Don Richardson's book *Eternity in Their Hearts* advocates that God has placed a witness of God's self within each culture (1981, 79). Richardson demonstrates how God's general revelation (which he calls the Melchizedek factor) often prepares the way for people to understand and receive God's special revelation (the Abraham factor). The creator God has provided redemptive analogies within each culture that Christians can use to help explain the good news of Jesus Christ. He calls this "redemptive lore," since it "contributes to the redemption of a people solely by facilitating their understanding of what redemption means" (1981, 59).

Richardson would encourage intercultural disciplers to search for redemptive lore in various cultures since it influences 100 percent of humankind (Psalm 19) and is old (1981, 31). He cites Paul's encounter in Athens (Acts 17:16–23) as an example to follow, since it draws on a well-known and ancient oral tradition. Richardson portrays examples in various cultures whereby redemptive lore has been effectively used to include local stories, proverbs, dances, symbols, customs/rituals, and so on.

He concludes, "The astonishing fact that missionary breakthroughs among the Karen, Kachin, and Lahu tribes came *through* their respective folk religions, rather than in spite of them, has been completely lost upon some scholars" (1981, 99; emphasis in original). For example, when young missionaries expressed a desire to spend more time studying the culture because they were interested in redemptive lore, an older missionary replied, "One does not study Hell. One preaches Heaven!" (1981, 58).

Reflection and Discussion

1. How would you respond to someone who discourages you from studying the local culture because it is a waste of time that removes you from "real" discipleship?
2. Whereas identifying excluded middle issues encourages disciplers to start with the deficits in the group, how could redemptive lore be a good starting place for discipleship based on the assets within the culture?
3. How may redemptive lore interact with excluded middle issues? For example, could redemptive lore be used to address excluded middle issues for intercultural discipleship?

To trace God's stepping-stones in culture, intercultural disciplers draw on the cross-cultural study of religion. Anthropologist Clifford Geertz defines religion, in part, as "a system of symbols which acts to establish powerful, pervasive, and long-lasting moods and motivations in [humans]" (1973, 90–91). Note that Geertz connects religion with symbols. Religions around the world are expressed through powerful symbols. These symbols are then used as building blocks to construct rituals, whereby worldviews are expressed and affirmed.

Understanding the important role of symbols and ceremonies, A. H. Mathias Zahniser, in his groundbreaking book on cross-cultural discipleship, defines discipling as "that ongoing set of intentional activities governed by the goal of initiating people into the kingdom of God through appropriate instructions, experiences, symbols, and ceremonies" (1997, 23). Zahniser notes that cross-cultural disciplers can learn about discipleship from four sources: evidence of the Triune God at work cross-culturally, methods used in the majority world,

---

The goal is not simply to do what Jesus and the apostles did, in terms of their methods of discipleship, but to call on God to birth the kinds of communities that he created in those early years as witnessed in the New Testament documents.

Don Little (2015, Kindle locations 922–24)

---

cross-cultural study of religion and culture, and models/methods from a variety of cultures and religious traditions throughout history (24–27). These sources break us out of the monocultural straitjacket and help formulate an intercultural discipleship approach.

In my own experience living among the Builsa people of Ghana, I observed evidence of God at work in culture through means that were helpful for intercultural discipleship. In addition to the symbols and ceremonies that Zahniser notes, I observed the effective use of proverbs, stories, music, dance, drama, and holistic discipleship. These forms of "oral literature," which "simply means literature delivered by word of mouth" (Okpewho 1992, 3–4), provide fertile material for integrative discipleship. These readily available genres, already present in the culture, can be useful for discipleship.

Defining Intercultural Discipleship

Combining the background and definitions described above, intercultural discipleship can be defined as the process of worldview transformation whereby Jesus followers center their lives on the kingdom of God (Matt. 6:33) and obey Christ's commands in culture (Matt. 28:19–20), utilizing culturally available genres.

Contextual expressions of Christianity use culturally available genres, including symbols, rituals, proverbs, stories, dance, music, and drama. As disciples encounter daily intimate issues within their culture, they respond in a manner that is both biblically faithful and culturally relevant. This lifelong process forms mature followers of Christ who overcome the extremes of syncretism (in which culture is not critiqued, thereby blending two faith systems) and split-level Christianity (in which culture is ignored, thereby pushing people to find solutions to intimate issues elsewhere).

Builsa Funeral Highlights Oral Discipleship Practices

Adapted from Moon (2010, 127–28).

One of the worldview differences noted between Western and majority world cultures is that of oral versus print learning preferences. Oral forms of communication, when used in the discipleship process, can effectively transform young believers into maturing followers of Jesus. Unfortunately, print learners often overlook the value of these oral forms in favor of print methods alone, thereby missing many potent discipleship opportunities within the local culture. This case study briefly describes a Christian funeral among the Builsa people, who mainly live in the Upper East Region of Ghana, West Africa. A Builsa funeral has several stages. After the initial burial and wake-keeping, it may be several months or years until the final performance of the funeral is conducted. This brief description summarizes some aspects of the final performance stage, which has a much different atmosphere from the other stages.

The Builsa people are among the estimated 70 percent of the world's population who are predominantly oral learners (Lovejoy 2007). When observed closely, the funeral describes many of the preferences of oral learners. Contrasting the learning preferences of oral learners to print learners reveals how we have often been looking for discipleship methods in all the wrong places! By viewing the funeral through the eyes of an oral culture, we see that their learning preferences include discipleship practices that are more likely to transform oral learners, including songs, dances, rituals, dramas, stories, proverbs, and holistic development. Each of these genres is then described and applied to discipleship with oral learners. First, though, there is a Builsa funeral to attend.

The fiery crimson sun is sinking, cooling the earth and bringing relief to the dry and scorching savannah. We join a large crowd from the surrounding villages and churches that has gathered outside the house of the deceased. "Boom, boom, boom" beat the drums, vibrating throughout the air. A wide circle forms, filled with people dancing to the rhythm and singing indigenous songs of faith in Jesus. Church leaders from the Bible Church of Africa call out to God for wisdom to guide this important ceremony successfully. A church group arranges a pile of millet stalks in the middle and then lights a match. A brilliant mass of orange light bursts into flame, setting everyone's face aglow. A hush sweeps over the crowd as actors take the dusty stage to begin a short drama. Through entertaining dialogue and movement, the story of the rich man who went to hell is compared to Lazarus, the beggar, who went to heaven when he died (Luke 16:19–31). The pastor retells the biblical story, using picture books that many have taken as their Bible. To explain the story in Builsa terms and metaphors, the pastor uses indigenous stories and proverbs. Around one in the morning, the host family provides a steaming meal of rice and goat meat to all of the visitors. An older church lady then leads a funeral dirge, which honors the memory of the deceased. Prayers are offered for the family and a collection given to them.

The sun begins to peek over the horizon as it rises from its slumber. We begin walking to the well and notice that the "well" is actually a hole dug in the ground with no protective cover or liner. The water resembles chocolate milk. Church leaders comment how this village needs a proper well to prevent further deaths. They agree that this village will be included in the church's hand-dug well project.

As we walk away from the funeral, the woman next to me begins to sing a song of faith from the night before. The urgency in her voice and the tears streaming down her face once again fill me with an overwhelming affirmation of faith . . . a feeling shared by all who participated in the funeral.

This definition incorporates the key concepts discussed above. Instead of considering concepts alone, we can deepen our understanding by also reflecting on the concrete case narrated above, which portrays intercultural discipleship. As you read this case study, keep in mind that intercultural discipleship thrives on a deep engagement of the Scripture with the local culture. The genres used to express discipleship already reside in the local culture—disciplers need to find them. Once found, contextual expressions of Christ in culture can be developed for the critical issues disciples face (including the excluded middle issues). This case study of the Builsa people describes some discipleship practices in oral cultures that print learners may overlook at first glance.

Print-based learners may not recognize it at first, but this funeral ceremony is a significant discipleship event for the church. Discipleship processes for

> **Oral learners are those who "learn best and whose lives are most likely to be transformed when instruction comes in oral forms."**
>
> Grant Lovejoy and David Claydon (2005, 12)

oral learners are vastly different from ones for print learners. Discipleship for print-based learners often depends on written materials covering abstract categories that dissect and systematize Scripture for individual learning. While this approach is not wrong, it is not enough for oral learners, who prefer more concrete, relational harmonizing that connects the past to the present in a corporate retrospection that unites people and aids memory recall.

Socialization and Discipleship

While searching for indigenous Christian discipleship approaches for the ECWA church in Nigeria, Bauta Motty, in his book *Indigenous Christian Disciple-Making* (2013), recognized that the Kaninkon people already had well-established approaches to socialize their children into the ways and culture of the people, such that they would become mature, responsible adults. Motty has concluded that "understanding the socialization process is important for successful indigenous disciple-making, for it provides crucial insights needed for success in the process of helping people of a new society understand and live out the message of the gospel. . . . It is the process of maturing believers in and by the Church to become responsible members of the body of Christ and the society" (2013, 16).

In particular, Motty identifies five socialization practices that can be contextualized for Christian discipleship in the Kaninkon church:

1. Life cycle rituals, particularly birth or childbearing, traditional training on how to be a responsible person in society, marriage, death, and funeral rites.
2. Teaching techniques that emphasize social values and ethics, moral life, rituals of salvation or social acceptance. This includes stories about God through folklore, songs, and proverbs.
3. Ritual processes associated with the role and authority of the local elders, family members' roles, and childhood rituals such as outing. This includes rites for naming, circumcision, initiation, purification, death and funerals, and ancestor-making. All of these practices incorporate people into the community life that involves every person in the society.
4. Social laws or taboos that provide social control.
5. Indigenous traditional education that is oral, family-centered, and group-centered. (2013, 37)

Reflection and Discussion

1. Compare/contrast Kaninkon socialization practices to the Builsa case study. What similarities do you notice? What differences do you see?
2. Why do you think Christian disciplers have often overlooked these socialization practices in the past?
3. What are some of the opportunities and dangers when the local church appropriates these practices?

To help understand these differences, Walter Ong (1982) has noted several preferences of oral learners versus print learners, summarized in table 3.1.

Ong notes that oral learners often learn best by "discipleship, which is a kind of apprenticeship, by listening, by repeating what they hear, by mastering proverbs and ways of combining and recombining them, by assimilating other formulaic materials, by participation in a kind of corporate retrospection—not by study in the strict sense" (1982, 9).

TABLE 3.1	
Comparing Oral versus Print Learning Preferences	
Oral Learners	Print Learners
1. Conceptualize and verbalize knowledge with close reference to human life/world	1. Analytical categories with knowledge structured at a distance from lived experience (statistics, lists, "how-to" manuals)
2. Conservative holism (formulary expressions kept intact and repeated to remember wisdom)	2. Inventive and open to new expression
3. Elderly valued, since they can remember past	3. Elderly not needed to remember past (knowledge is stored in books)
4. Aggregative (harmonizing) tendencies (keep formulaic adjectives with nouns together)	4. Analytical, dissecting tendencies
5. Redundant or copious (to maintain context, since oral utterance vanishes once spoken)	5. Economy of words (can backtrack to recover context)
6. Emphatic and participatory (involved with the speaker)	6. Objective and distanced (knowledge gained without knowing the speaker)
7. Limited vocabulary (1,000–1,500 words)	7. Large vocabulary (e.g., English dictionary has over 1.5 million words)
8. Learn by apprenticeship, mastering proverbs and other formulaic materials	8. Learning is highly analytical, abstractly sequential, classificatory; examination of phenomenon or truths
9. Corporate retrospection, externalized; unites people in groups	9. Individual study and reflection; solitary activity that invites introspection
10. Variation of story due to context and orator	10. Fixed into visual field forever
11. Stitch together story by mnemonics, not memorized verbatim	11. Verbatim memory by referring to text
12. Knowledge must be repeated or it would be lost (library of mnemonic formulas)	12. Knowledge is stored in written texts (library of books), memory is reduced
13. Spoken words have power (magical potency, at times)	13. Written words are labels or name tags
14. Additive sentence structure (string lengthy sentences together with "and")	14. Elaborate and fixed grammar (shorten sentences with careful use of "then," "when," "thus," and "while")
15. Story (usually short) can start in middle of action and not follow chronological order	15. Lengthy novels are possible, usually follow linear plot (e.g., Freytag's pyramid)
16. Speech is performance oriented (doing something to somebody)	16. Speech passes on information
17. Themes of struggle are common	17. Abstractions that disentangle knowledge from human struggle are common

Oral Learners	Print Learners
18. Words have meaning in context (not interested in definitions)	18. Abstract definitions and etymologies of words are important
19. Situational (intelligence is situated in context), operational (favors right-brain thinking)	19. Phonetic alphabet favors left brain, leading to abstract, analytical thinking; meaning is located in language itself
20. Use canniness and knowledge beyond words (often subconscious) to solve riddles	20. Use logic, geometric formulas, and so on, to solve riddles
21. No self-analysis, since self is subconsciously immersed in community	21. Self-analysis and consciousness possible (diaries are product of self-consciousness)
22. Teaching with proverbs invites further reflection by paradoxes	22. Teaching with textbook, catechism, facts

Adapted from Moon (2009a, 204–5).

Learning is so tied to memory that many of the oral learning preferences (see the traits in the left column of table 3.1) enable oral learners to shape their thinking in mnemonic patterns that can be recalled later. For example, repeating aggregative phrases (e.g., "Lazarus, the beggar") makes them easier to remember than dissecting this phrase and trying to remember "Lazarus" or simply "a beggar." Redundancy also enables the oral listener to hear the same thing in different ways such that it forms a well-worn path that can be easily recalled in the future. A close, emphatic, communal participation with the speaker helps the oral learner to connect with the topic in a memorable manner. For print learners, however, many of these preferences are inefficient, cumbersome, unnecessary, or too dependent on others, since these learners can personally recall the material later from written materials. As a result, Ong concludes, "More than any other single invention, writing has transformed human consciousness" (1982, 78). It is not surprising then that print learners often greatly misunderstand oral learners.

A closer examination of the case study illuminates how many of the learning preferences of oral learners are portrayed in the various genres for the discipleship of oral learners. The Builsa funeral provides a concrete example to reveal and explain this discipleship process.

Songs and Dances—"We Become What We Hum"

Oral learners prefer that knowledge be repeated; otherwise it is lost (preference 12 in table 3.1). These repeated mnemonic formulas become a library to draw on, since oral learners do not store information in written sources for future recall. Builsa songs are often just a few lines that are repeated over and over again. In this way, the song is a memory hook to help them remember the theology contained in the song. In the Builsa funeral, note that the people leaving the funeral in the morning still remembered and sang the songs they learned throughout the night. The hook worked, and the song could be retrieved by the oral learner for future recall, similar to the way a book could be retrieved for print learners.

It has been said, "We become what we hum." For many oral learners, their theology is carried in the songs they remember, particularly when the songs are composed by indigenous artists. One of the songs the Builsa composed proclaims,

> Wa chawgsi mu, wa chawgsi mu, wa chawgsi mu.
> Wa chawgsi mu, wa sum jam chawgsi.
> Wa chawgsi mu, Satana yaa de mu.
> Wa chawgsi mu, wa sum jam chawgsi.

Note the repetition of the mnemonic formula *wa chawgsi mu*. If the Builsa remember this formula, then they are well on their way to remembering the rest of the song—and the theology contained therein. The Buli term *chawgsi* means "to wrap up tightly and protect from harm." This term describes how a father catches and wraps up his young son when the boy jumps down from a high place. The Builsa song can be translated,

> He [Jesus] wraps me tightly. He wraps me tightly. He wraps me tightly.
> He wraps me tightly. He really does wrap me tightly.
> He wraps me tightly. Satan wanted to eat [destroy or consume] me.
> He wraps me tightly. He really does wrap me tightly.

This song can be sung the next time that the Builsa disciples are afraid, be it of spiritual forces, enemies, or unknown sources. The song identifies the enemy, Satan, who wants to destroy them. The song also assures them that Jesus surely will wrap them tightly in his arms and protect them from harm. Note how the Builsa song composes theology in indigenous language and concepts that are deeply meaningful to them, as compared to translated songs from another source that simply wrap Western theology in African clothing.

It has been said that Africans sing and dance their theology (Ankele 2011). Oral learners value learning that is emphatic and participatory instead of objective and distanced (preference 6). Through dancing, people participate in the song and feel the theological meaning, not merely gain more head knowledge. This helps the meaning to sink in and transform how the person feels and thinks. James Krabill notes how the Harrist church in West Africa survived in an oral culture, largely through the songs that were composed and passed down by the early church members "from 1913 onwards and transmitted orally with little if any alteration throughout the years in worship contexts up until the present day" (1995, 4). This discipleship form has helped the church to survive over a period of almost one hundred years. Songs and dance are clearly valuable discipleship genres for oral cultures.

Rituals Drive Meaning into the Bone

Another powerful discipleship genre for oral cultures is ritual. Rituals are often used to help people transition from one stage to the next. In the funeral, for example, the church must now transition through the absence of the deceased person. Deep emotions and spiritual questions will likely result. The funeral ritual helps the community of believers cope with the grief, loss, questions, and new social condition by providing a corporate retrospection.

Oral learners prefer that this group retrospection be externalized in a ritual so that they will be united as a group (preference 9). When done well, the ritual can bond the community members to one another and also to their corporate faith. Note how the various Builsa churches were drawn together for the funeral so that the entire funeral ritual reinforced group solidarity. Young disciples are then bonded to other disciples. In addition, they are bonded to their faith. Print learners, however, prefer individual study and reflection via solitary activity that invites introspection. As a result, print discipleship methods often emphasize individual reading and reflection.

Anthropologist Arnold Van Gennep (1960) noted the three stages of a ritual: separation (removed from the routines of daily life), transition (in-between state of uncertainty and liminality), and reincorporation (reenter the social order at a higher status than before). In the middle, or transition, stage there is confusion, uncertainty, liminality, or what Turner (1995) calls "anti-structure." The existing social structure is suspended for a time, and participants now have equal status, accept pain/suffering, simplify life, and accept communal decision making. Turner describes how this condition makes the participants ready to bond to one another as a tightly knit community, a condition he calls *communitas*. As they bond to one another, the participants then are also ready to bond to the faith of the group.

Note how liminality is expressed in the Builsa funeral. This is an all-night event with food at one o'clock in the morning, along with drama, dance, songs, and other community-wide activities. This is very different from the ordinary daily routine of the Builsa, who are hard-working subsistence farmers. Everyone dances around a circle, regardless of age, gender, education, or social status, indicating the equality of people in the group, unlike in ordinary daily life, when social status and roles are important. To forgo sleep is also a painful experience, particularly when the next groggy day arrives.

The end result of this liminality is that young disciples form a strong attachment to the Builsa church. They now experience *communitas*. Combined with disciples' cognitive understanding of Jesus and the church, the ritual will "drive meaning into the bone" (Grimes 2000, 337), such that the disciples are bonded to Jesus and the community of Jesus's followers. The ritual process then becomes a strong discipleship form for oral learners, particularly since oral learners tend to subconsciously immerse themselves in the community instead of self-analyzing as print learners do (preference 21).

Drama Stands the Word of God on Its Feet

Oral learners often enjoy speech as oral art. How something is said is just as important as what is said. As a result, speech should be a performance, where something is done to somebody instead of just passing on information (preference 16). Drama becomes a valued genre that can be useful in the discipleship of oral learners.

In the Builsa funeral, the dramatization of Lazarus the beggar and the rich man created a rich performance that everyone enjoyed. When Lazarus walked across the burning millet stalks, the crowd exploded, thereby creating an unforgettable image. Instead of presenting abstract discussions of heaven and hell, this drama created very vivid and understandable images. Through this performance, the Builsa took the Word of God and "put it on its feet."

Dramas encourage the contextualization of Scripture, since the indigenous believers act this out using local materials (e.g., millet stalks), language (Buli), and contexts (outside a local mud house) that the people are familiar with. This is an important step for the growing disciples—they have to know how to apply the Scripture to their own daily life situations. Since oral learners conceptualize and verbalize knowledge with close reference to the human life world (preference 1), dramas take them one closer step to contextualizing the Scripture within their own worldview.

God Presents Salvation in Story Form

Storytelling is closely related to drama. While drama tends to have more of a memorized script, storytelling in oral cultures relies on mnemonics to stitch together the story without it being memorized verbatim (preference 11). This allows the storyteller to then contextualize the story to fit the audience and the teller (preference 10).

Since Jesus used storytelling extensively for his oral-learner audiences (Mark 4:34), it makes sense that this would be an appropriate genre for the discipleship of oral learners today. In the Builsa funeral, the biblical story was effectively retold. Pictures were shown to the audience to help them visualize the story and also as a mnemonic aid for the storyteller to keep on track. Many of the Builsa church members obtained a copy of the picture book. I have observed oral learners studying the pictures at length, looking for details and connections, in much the same way a print learner would read a book. This picture book then became an oral Bible for many Builsa disciples.

While everyone likes a story, stories tend to be used by print-preference audiences merely to illustrate a point. For an oral-preference audience, though, the story is the point. Instead of pastors dissecting the story and making three-point sermons out of it, oral audiences prefer to hear the entire story

---

It is significant that God does not present us with salvation in the form of an abstract truth, or a precise definition or a catchy slogan, but as story.

Eugene Peterson (2004, 69)

---

as a harmonized, intact whole (preference 4). Then they can remember it and draw on aspects of the story throughout the week. While print learners often construct long stories with a linear, chronological plot (start at the beginning and move to the climax and resolution), oral learners often start at a different place—the place with the most action. In this way, the audience is hooked and will listen to the end, since the listeners want to hear more. If the storyteller cannot hook an oral learner at the beginning of the story, the learner may not be motivated to listen to the end. The starting place for telling the story (usually short instead of long stories) for oral learners may not be in the chronological beginning; rather, it may be in the middle or even the end (preference 15).

Instead of abstract teaching on the theological concepts of suffering, faith, salvation, heaven, and hell, the story of the rich man and Lazarus the beggar portrays these themes in concrete terms amid human struggle (preference 17). It is no wonder that oral learners prefer stories to abstract learning. Perhaps this preference explains in part God's prolific use of stories in the oral cultures of the Bible.

A Proverb Is Worth a Thousand Words

In oral cultures, proverbs often serve as the summation of a story. A short proverb provides a concise formula to help the oral learner remember an entire story. Oral cultures preserve these formulary expressions so that the wisdom of the elders can remain intact and be passed on in a conservative holism (preference 2), as opposed to print cultures, which value inventive new expressions or slogans. If a picture is worth a thousand words in print cultures, then a proverb is worth a thousand words in oral cultures.

When a short proverb is used, it brings to mind the entire story for the listener. This then helps the listener follow the thought patterns of the speaker.

For oral audiences to get from the riverbank of what they know to the other side of what they do not know, proverbs are like stepping-stones carefully placed in the river to help the listener walk firmly across. While print audiences prefer thinking patterns that use analytical, abstract, and sequential classifications/definitions/lists to examine truth claims, oral learners master proverbs and other formulaic expressions in order to process their thoughts (preference 8). Oral learning is very logical; it just relies on a very different logic than print learners use. One Nigerian pastor explained to me, "If you do not use proverbs in speaking, then I cannot follow you for very long" (Moon 2004, 163).

The use of proverbs during the Builsa funeral confirmed to the believers that the message preached that night was from God and not just from a human source. This furthered the disciples' trust in the Bible (spoken in the Buli mother tongue) as the best representation of God in culture. Clearly, local proverbs are pregnant with potential for the discipleship of oral learners such that they will understand God in patterns that are faithful to Scripture as well as culturally relevant.

Holistic Development Connects Words and Deeds to Promote Faith

A funeral brings to the fore intimate questions that disciples have concerning God's care and protection, the causes of life and death, and other such deep-seated concerns. The Builsa church recognized that their water supply was inadequate and causing sickness; therefore, they felt compelled to install a new well. The church's water project helps to restore God's creation to its original purpose of wholeness, health, and completeness (described in the Old Testament as *shalom*). As Christians participate with God in this process of restoring creation, they recognize that their salvation transforms not only them personally but also their place to provide healing and hope. The kingdom of God is revealed as disciples become leaven or mustard seed to transform the land where they live (Matt. 13). This is a form of discipleship for oral learners, who prefer to learn via participation (preference 6) and corporate retrospection that unites people in groups (preference 9).

The Micah Network calls this process "integral mission," since it integrates both the proclamation (words) and the demonstration (deeds) of the gospel to reveal God's glory. The Micah Network's "Declaration on Integral Mission" (2001) states, "Our proclamation has social consequences as we call people to love and repentance in all areas of life. And our social involvement has evangelistic consequences as we bear witness to the transforming grace of Jesus Christ."

The church's well program provides an example of holistic discipleship, as the following account of my experience at the Builsa funeral illustrates.

As the sun awakes from its slumber after the all-night funeral, the hosts offer me a drink of water. As I stare into the calabash of water, the color of the water reminds me of chocolate milk. When we ask to see where the water was drawn from, they direct us to a traditional well that is unprotected from surface contamination.

I think to myself, "Now I know why there was a death here."

The church leaders gather and discuss how the church's hand-dug well program can help. In over seventy other locations, the church has mobilized the community to dig and protect a new well, using local materials and labor. These new wells are designed to protect the groundwater from surface contamination. Once a new well is constructed, hope for better health is also restored. Using water wells, holistic discipleship is fostered as disciples see God's provision for their overall health. Holistic development connects words and deeds to promote faith.

In addition to water development, another form of holistic discipleship is expressed in hospitality. Note how the family shared their food and home with the guests. One African explained to me, "Hospitality combines both faith and works into one." Both the receiving of hospitality in the Christian community and the offering of hospitality to others can be powerful forms of holistic discipleship.

Crossing the River Requires Help

There is a story about a fool who was sitting by a broad, deep river one sunny afternoon (Maguire 1998, 137–38). With a furrowed brow and forlorn eyes, he gazed at the river, desperately needing to get to the other side. The problem was that he could not swim. Suddenly a wise-looking man walked briskly past the fool, stepped out on the water, and quickly walked right over to the other side. The fool sat there stunned and perplexed . . . until another wise man hurried right past him and did the same thing. In shock and disbelief, he rose to his feet—only to be brushed aside by a third wise man, who promptly walked across the surface of the water.

The fool thought to himself, "That didn't look so hard. What am I afraid of? If they can do it, then so can I." Confidently, he rushed into the water.

Screaming and waving his hands, he quickly sank beneath the surface.

One of the wise men looked back and said to his companions, "If only we'd known he wanted to cross, we could have told him where the rocks are!"

Many disciplers are trying to help their churches across the river to land on the shore of mature discipleship. To move from the riverbank of new belief to the other bank of maturity in Christ is a challenging process. Our wise and loving God desires disciples to move from the point of young faith to mature, kingdom-centered life. As a result, God has gone before us in culture and placed rocks for us to use as stepping-stones. Wise intercultural disciplers take the time to find where the stones are placed in the culture. Unfortunately, many monocultural disciplers are either discouraged or failing since they often rely on print methods alone to swim through oral contexts.

The Builsa funeral reveals discipleship forms that are placed in oral cultures, like stepping-stones, to guide them—songs, dance, rituals, dramas, stories, proverbs, and holistic development are a few key stones in the river to facilitate discipleship in oral cultures. While these stones may be unnoticed or overlooked by print learners, who favor written materials, they are effective forms that teach and transform the lives of oral learners. Since oral learners

> Discipleship, the widely accepted term that describes the ongoing life of the disciple, . . . has a nice ongoing feel—a sense of journey, the idea of becoming a disciple rather than having been made a disciple.
>
> Bill Hull (2006, 35)

prefer redundancy to aid memory (preference 5), the combination of these forms increases the transforming effects for discipleship. When all the above forms emphasize the same theme, as described in the funeral, the Builsa disciples move safely cross the river. This cross-cultural encounter affected my own discipleship journey, as the following description of my impressions after the Builsa funeral shows.

I finally arrive home from the all-night funeral. The songs of faith still resound in my ears like a beating drum. As the vivid images of the drama flash across the movie screen of my mind, my memories of the proverbs and stories make me laugh once again, reminding me of the preacher's message. These all reveal to me new aspects of Builsa culture and Scripture that are sure to remain with me for a long time. I am humbled by the generous hospitality that I have received, and this challenges me to express my faith more through hospitality. Best of all, I now feel a stronger commitment to the Builsa believers and our common bond of faith in Jesus Christ. I am beginning to realize how this funeral, viewed through the eyes of oral learners, helped us all become better disciples—with the help of stepping-stones placed carefully along the way.

Intercultural disciplers recognize the benefit of *both* oral and print discipleship methods. Instead of being limited to one alone, both are useful. The African proverb reminds us, "If you want to go fast, go alone; if you want to go far, go together." For the long journey of discipleship, oral and print methods need to be together. Coming from a predominantly print culture, we can explore how oral discipleship practices can provide balance to our methods.

Those from oral cultures can also benefit from print methods. Intercultural discipleship strips off the straitjacket of monocultural approaches.

Finally, we return to the definition of intercultural discipleship: the process of worldview transformation whereby Jesus followers center their lives on the kingdom of God and obey Christ's commands in culture, utilizing culturally available genres. This intercultural approach is useful in Western and majority world cultures around the world. Others from print cultures have written extensively on the biblical instructions to use in discipleship by suggesting various important topics and Scriptural guidance (Eims 1976, 1978; Cosgrove 1988). Instead of repeating the information found in these fine materials (produced from a print culture), the remainder of this book will compare various cultural stepping-stones placed in various time periods in order to identify experiences, symbols, rituals, and other oral literature that are helpful for discipleship. Examples from both Western and majority world cultures will demonstrate the usefulness of these stepping-stones.

In the next chapter, we will discuss one of the major stones that resides in cultures around the world: symbols.

Summary

1. Christian discipleship is a relational journey whereby learners obey the commands of Jesus, such that their worldview is transformed.

2. A centered set approach demonstrates that the direction of movement is more important than the distance from the center. While disciples all have unique starting points in the discipleship journey, allegiance to Jesus is the key concern. The excluded middle issues that may push a disciple away from kingdom-centeredness are important issues for discipleship.

3. Leaders must be disciples, but not all disciples are leaders. This distinction maintains the biblical standards for church leadership without placing premature requirements on disciples.

4. God goes before us in culture, providing means for discipleship. Various genres in culture provide fertile ground for discipleship, including unwritten forms of expression (oral literature), such as symbols, rituals, proverbs, stories, music, dance, and holistic means.

5. Integrative discipleship is the process of worldview transformation whereby Jesus followers center their lives on the kingdom of God and obey Christ's commands in culture, utilizing culturally available genres.

6. If we want to go far in the discipleship journey, then Western and majority world approaches (e.g., print and oral methods) should be used together.

Builsa Funeral

Review the description of the Builsa funeral in this chapter. Then reflect on and discuss the following questions:

1. What excluded middle issues are addressed in this discipleship event?
2. How will this discipleship event empower the Builsa believers to better center their lives on the kingdom of God and obey Christ's commands in their culture?
3. If critical contextualization is not carefully applied, how might the uncritical use of indigenous genres unknowingly slide the church into errors, such as syncretism or split-level Christianity?
4. Can you imagine other genres available in this culture that may be readily available for discipleship? For example, consider the creative arts and architecture. How would you start to identify, understand, appreciate, and then contextualize them for discipleship?

Activity for Discipling

1. Based on centered set thinking, ask your disciples questions such as: Are you moving closer to God or farther away? What is preventing you from focusing your life on the kingdom of God? Then explain centered versus bounded set thinking.
2. Ask your disciples to complete the Learning Preference Assessment at https://wmausa.org/wp-content/uploads/2016/12/Orality-Assessment-Tool-Worksheet.pdf. Discuss their experiences with oral or print-based discipleship approaches.
3. Which oral genres will be most useful to explore for your disciples in order to address their excluded middle issue(s)?

4

Symbols Speak When
Words Can't

Emphiempango ekukwatwa nilobho ihango. (Big fish are caught with big hooks.)
—Kerewe Tanzanian proverb (Durand and Nkumbulwa 2012)

Smoke from Burning Sage Grass

A cloud of burning sage smoke settles in the room as he gently brushes the haze across his body with his fingers, gathered together like a feather. He closes his eyes. The distinct, sweet aroma opens his senses to a host of memories and emotions. In his culture, sage symbolizes the cleansing of sacred spaces. Like every other morning and evening, today this growing disciple of Jesus "bathes" himself with sage smoke to help him overcome his addiction to pornography. He has tried other self-help methods, but he has found that God gives him strength through this symbol. Why is this symbol so powerful in helping him address an excluded middle area? How can symbols be used effectively in the discipleship process?

What Are Symbols?

Humans create meaning of the world around them. Symbols are used to grasp and express this reality. In religious events, symbols connect the known, visible world with the unknown, invisible spirit world (Turner 1995, 15). They also connect "the world of exterior realities to inner mental worlds" (Hiebert, Shaw, and Tiénou 1999b, 232). A symbol can be simply explained as "something present that stands for something absent" (Leeds-Hurwitz 1993, 6) or something seen that points to something not seen. How do you see concepts such as "sacredness" or the presence of the Holy Spirit? For the Native American Christian described above, the smell of burning sage helps him to connect to the sacredness that he can't touch. When the sage smoke

Understanding and Interpreting Symbols/Signs

Various perspectives have been put forth on how to interpret signs and symbols. Technically, symbols are a subset of a larger category called "signs." Charles S. Peirce ([1940] 1955) calls symbols unmotivated or arbitrary signs, meaning that they do not necessarily resemble the reality that they represent (i.e., they are not obviously related). Two approaches to interpret signs/symbols are helpful to compare.

Ferdinand de Saussure (1983) was a pioneer in semiotics (the study of symbols/signs). He explained the meaning and interpretation of signs by dividing signs into inner mental images and outer, experienceable forms. Thus meaning is totally constructed in a culture and is only in the mind. Taken to its logical conclusion, this notion leads to a cognitive relativism in which meaning is totally subjective to the one receiving it.

Peirce ([1940] 1955), a contemporary of Saussure, did not accept this approach to signs; instead, he affirmed that meaning is derived by a triangle to include signifier (the sign), mental image (the signification), and reality (that which was signified). In this view, a sign is a bridge to connect the inner thought world to the outward realities that exist. This affirms the existence of an external objective reality and does not leave the inner meaning totally subjective in the mind. Paul Hiebert finds this position more attractive from an evangelical standpoint. Instead of meaning being totally subjective, Hiebert

notes that this triadic model "holds that all knowledge has both objective and subjective dimensions to it" (1999, 72–73). He uses this model to advocate an epistemology of critical realism, as opposed to instrumentalism (implied by Saussure's model of signs) or naive realism (signs are exact representations of reality). The topic of epistemology is important enough that we will consider it further in chapter 11 when discussing discipleship in postmodern contexts. For now, though, it is useful to recognize that our framework for interpreting the meaning of a symbol will greatly affect how we approach and use symbols.

Reflection and Discussion

1. If Saussure is correct that symbols have no meaning except that which individuals assign to them, what are the opportunities and limitations of using symbols for discipleship?

2. If Peirce is correct that a symbol is a bridge to connect an inner mental image (in the mind of the receiver) with an outer objective reality, what are the opportunities and limitations of using symbols for discipleship?

3. Why do you think that Protestant churches tend to be skeptical of using symbols in the church? Could a proper interpretive framework be helpful to alleviate some of these fears?

---

fills the room, it reminds him of the Holy Spirit filling the room with power and protection—even when his eyes cannot see it.

Words alone are often not enough to communicate deep values and emotions. In fact, words may be the least effective communicators of deep values and emotions. For example, a certain degree of value and emotion is communicated when a young man says to his girlfriend, "I love you." It is quite another thing entirely, though, when he gets down on his knee and extends a diamond ring to her. Without uttering a word, the symbols drive home a deeper level of value and emotion than words alone could communicate. As the young man is about to speak the words, "Will you marry me?" the Tanzanian proverb whispers in his ear, "Big fish are caught with big hooks." Symbols fill the gap when words are not enough to catch the big fish.

Symbols Construct Religion and Worldview

In the last chapter, we discussed Geertz's definition of religion as a symbol system. In an attempt to point to divine realities that are unseen, religions around the world depend on symbols to communicate when mere words fail. Theologian Paul Tillich describes how symbols "open up levels of reality which otherwise are closed" and notes that they "open up levels of the human mind of which we otherwise are not aware" (1955, 109). Sacred symbols, then, are

---

Even the plainest symbols . . . are magic portals into the other world where the truth of one's religion is visible, felt, and far overshadows the inconsistent ordinary.

Robert S. Ellwood (1983, 66)

---

crucial to help construct a religion and an underlying worldview, as described by Hiebert, Shaw, and Tiénou, who note that "they [sacred symbols] integrate and give expression to a people's worldview—the mental picture they have of the way things in reality actually are (the cognitive dimension); the tone, character, and aesthetic quality of their life (the affective dimension); and the moral standards that set their ideals and govern their relationships (the evaluative dimensions)" (1999b, 247).

The value of symbols in communicating the unseen religious world and constructing a worldview cannot be overstated. Consider, for example, how the Israelites were being formed as a "kingdom of priests and a holy nation" (Exod. 19:6). During a brutal four hundred years of slavery, an oppressive worldview formed through generational poverty/suppression, which affected their identity and faith. It would take forty years for God to reshape this worldview (i.e., form disciples). It has been said that it took one day to get Israel out of Egypt, but it took forty years to get Egypt out of Israel. What does God use to reconstruct their worldview from that of slaves to that of a kingdom of priests and a holy nation? Symbols are at the heart of the tabernacle that God instructs Moses to build in order to symbolize the heavenly realities. Elaborate and detailed instructions are given for the multitude of symbols. For this discipleship process, symbols are used to open the Israelites to another world, like magic portals. Why are symbols so important in constructing a religion and a worldview? What properties do symbols have that would serve cross-cultural disciplers well in transforming the worldview of maturing disciples?

Three Properties of Symbols

Victor Turner, living amid the Ndembu people in East Africa, identified three properties of symbols that help to explain why they are so powerful in religious rituals: *polarization, condensation,* and *unification* (1967). Once we understand these properties and apply them for the selection of symbols, they become powerful building blocks for rituals in the discipleship process.

POLARIZATION: SYMBOLS HELP YOU WANT TO DO WHAT YOU SHOULD DO

A well-placed symbol connects two very distinct aspects of our lives: the sensory side and the ideological side. Table 4.1 describes these two polar opposites.

TABLE 4.1	
Contrasting Two Poles United by a Symbol	
Ideological Pole	Sensory Pole
Beliefs	Feelings
Norms	Needs
Values	Appetites and desires
Head	Heart
What you SHOULD do	What you WANT to do

While these two poles describe opposite aspects of our lives, symbols have a unique way of connecting them. Turner calls this the *polarization property* of symbols. The symbol places the sensory pole at the service of the ideological pole. The end result is that a symbol helps stir the desire (sensory) within you to do what is right (ideology). Put more simply, symbols help you *want* to do what you *should* do. This is crucial in discipleship. Often disciples know what they should do (the ideological pole); however, they just do not want to do it due to other pressures (sensory pole). Additional instructions are not enough to motivate and stir the disciple—symbols fill the gap to produce the desire to do what he or she should do.

The young man who uses sage to overcome his addiction understands the power of the polarization property. The aroma and smoke of burning sage connect deeply with him such that he is empowered to do what he should do. More than simply words, this symbol connects his deep feelings/desires to the proper values/beliefs. The polarization property of symbols is evident in more than private, intimate settings.

When describing the African worldview, Jean-Marc Ela observes, "All things speak, [and] signs play an important role in every socio-religious practice" (2009, 34). We certainly see this in larger public settings, as described by the following story.

> The blistering sun beats down on the villagers crowded around a well in a Muslim dominated village in Ghana, West Africa. Children peer through the legs of the adults gathered around the well, inching towards the front to witness this important event. It is the final stage of the dedication ceremony for a new hand dug, concrete-lined well. As a missionary pulls the rope to draw out the first bucket of water, he prays God's blessing upon the entire village and thanks God for providing the blessing of clean water. All eyes focus on the bucket as the water is poured into a calabash and then handed to the village chief and the Muslim cleric. They drink deeply from the calabash, letting the clean water wash down their dry throats. Then, the calabash of water is handed to the church leaders, who also drink gratefully and then pass it on. Eventually, the entire village takes a turn tasting this new blessing of clean well water. (Moon 2012d, 146)

The sharing of water from the missionary to the chief, from chief to Muslim cleric, from Muslim cleric to church leaders, and finally from church leaders to everyone in the village communicates that this well is for everyone, regardless of faith. Trust and respect are communicated in a way that words alone could not. Note how the calabash of water connects two poles. On the

---

[By neglecting the use of symbols in discipleship,] Protestant disciplers . . . left a void that believers filled with magical practices and folk cures inherited from their traditional religion. It seems clear, then, that effective cross-cultural discipling requires working with symbols. . . . Symbols must be basic to our cross-cultural discipling.

Mathias Zahniser (1997, 75)

---

sensory pole, people want to quench their thirst from the harsh sun, and also wanted health and hope for their family survival. On the ideological pole, the people value trust, respect, sharing, and thankfulness to God. The calabash of water becomes a symbol that connected these two poles.

Symbols encourage discipleship. Consider how the symbol of water plays a significant role in the discipleship of believers in this young church. While Christians in a Muslim village will likely face persecution and social ostracism, this symbol in the calabash helps to mitigate such suspicion, at least for the moment, in a way that words cannot provide. Each day, as people draw water from the well, the well "speaks" to them concerning the benefits of the church being in the village. This symbol connects the sensory and ideological poles in this village when words alone would not be readily accepted. Perhaps some young believers in the village are following Jesus secretly but fear social rejection by coming to the church. For these young believers, the symbol of the well may connect the sensory and the ideological poles by giving them courage to do what they should do: be a part of the local church. The story in this village continues.

> Early the next day, a villager walks the dusty, pot-holed mile to the local missionary's house. The villager sits down, pauses, and receives a drink of water.
>
> Eventually, he reveals what is on his mind, "I had eight children but six died due to diarrhea. Since this well has been here, my two remaining children have not had diarrhea. I am now hopeful that my two children will live. I thank God that He sent the church to our community to help us."
>
> The symbol, a calabash of water, used in the community development ritual effectively communicated to this Muslim that he should thank God for the presence of the church. As a result, he desires to do what is he should do—thank God for the well and the church, aided by the use of symbols in rituals. While he is not ready to openly proclaim allegiance to Jesus this day, he is now one step closer to understanding how God demonstrates His loving care for him and his family through the church. In the centered set approach, you could say that he is still in the process of turning to make Christ central to his life. While not fully there yet, he and his village are slowly being changed. (Moon 2012d, 146)

CONDENSATION: ONE SYMBOL CONDENSES VARIOUS MEANINGS

In addition to polarization, symbols effectively aid communication in rituals by their second property, which Turner calls *condensation*. Symbols are multivocal, meaning that they speak many messages at once. Consider for a moment what the color red symbolizes. Over the past century in the Western world, red has symbolized death, stop, blood, danger, fire, debt, communism, and more. The condensation property recognizes that one symbol condenses or brings together these different meanings. This property of symbols can be used very effectively in rituals to communicate differently to people, based on their varying needs and concerns. For example, the condensation property is evidenced in the use of a white cloth worn by pilgrims in Mecca for the Muslim pilgrimage called the hajj:

Leaving their air-conditioned cars and buses, pilgrims step back to an ancient time as they arrive at the mosque in Mecca. Sweat makes the back of this pilgrim's shirt stick to his body as the blistering heat stifles the American. Sticking out like a sore thumb, his Western shirt and slacks, which seemed so normal back home, now make him appear very out of place. He joins the other pilgrims as he enters the changing room. Stripping off the clothing and culture [of] where he came from, he emerges from the changing room a different man. Leaving his button down shirt and slacks behind, he dons only a pure white cloth that wraps around his body. This feels strange at first since this also strips him of his identity as a respected Western journalist that he has spent his entire career establishing. Not only is the cloth humbling; it also reminds him of a simplicity that is overlooked amidst a complicated world. This simple and essential cloth stirs him to think of the simple and essential aspects of life. The pure white reminds him of the holy nature of this journey to Mecca. Lost in his thoughts, he hardly notices that everyone else is wearing the same garb. Slowly, this awkward American starts to blend into the crowd, like one more leaf in a pile of gathered leaves. He starts to feel like he is one of them. (Koppel 1997)

Several different meanings are condensed into this one symbol. The white cloth represents humility, simplicity, holiness, and unity with others. This symbol helps to transform an awkward stranger into an acceptable insider in order to prepare him for a religious experience. While individual symbols are powerful in themselves, the effects are multiplied when various symbols are gathered together.

UNIFICATION: VARIOUS SYMBOLS UNIFY ONE MEANING

While condensation gathers various meanings of an individual symbol into one message, Turner identifies a third property of symbols, *unification*. In a ceremony, various symbols are often used. The disparate symbols can be unified by a common thread of meaning contained in each of the different symbols. For example, think of the different symbols that can be used to express communism. The color red, an image of the hammer and sickle, a picture of Mao, and a statue of Stalin are all symbols for communism. The difference between the properties of condensation and unification can be expressed simply:

Condensation = **One** symbol communicates **many** meanings (fig. 4.1)
Unification = **Many** symbols communicate **one** meaning (fig. 4.2)

The unification property of symbols is evident during the *inipi* ritual, one of the seven sacred ceremonies of the Lakota Sioux (J. Brown 1989). It is often called the "sweat lodge" due to the intense heat involved. In my personal account that follows, notice the various symbols used in this ceremony:

Figure 4.1
Condensation: one symbol and many means

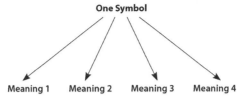

Figure 4.2
Unification: many symbols and one meaning

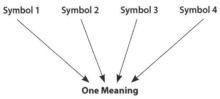

Stripped down to their shorts, the men walk past the fire, which makes the rocks glow red in preparation for the ritual.

"After this," the ritual specialist exhorts, "you will never take for granted air and water again."

Approaching the enclosure in single file, they stoop down and crawl on hands and knees to enter one at a time in circular fashion. Once inside, the flap is closed, and there is no visible light—it is pitch dark such that you cannot even see your hand in front of your face. Gradually, hot rocks, glowing red, are ushered into the enclosure and placed in the center, amid the anxious bodies huddled around them.

"Ssssssssss," the rocks cry out, as the water splashed on them turns to steam and heats the room. Sage is placed on the rocks to provide a distinct and familiar aroma. Soaked with sweat, the participants eventually leave the enclosure, once again on hands and knees.

This intense ceremony intends to provide purification and renewed strength to emphasize one meaning: we are in need of help, and the Creator provides the strength we need. Note how the following symbols indicate weakness and the need for help: the humbling of the participants in stripping down, crawling on hands and knees, entering into darkness, enduring heat, and sweating profusely. The symbols also communicate that the Creator provides what is needed through the creation of fire, rocks, plants, water, steam, and finally air. The meaning of the *inipi* ceremony is driven home by the various symbols as they are unified in a common meaning, like a nail that is continually hit by a hammer.

Symbols in the *Inipi* Ceremony

The Lakota Sioux consider the Black Hills of South Dakota sacred ground. Carved out of a mountain there, the Crazy Horse memorial towers high above the ground, several times larger than the more famous (and nearby) Mount Rushmore memorial. A museum next to the Crazy Horse memorial contains a mock *inipi* enclosure with a plaque containing the following words, accredited to Lakota spiritual leader Black Elk, as he describes the meaning of the symbols used in the *inipi* ceremony:

> The fire . . . represents the great power of *Wakan-Tanka* which gives life to all things. It is a ray from the sun. . . . The eternal fire always burns; through it we shall live again by being made pure; and by coming closer to your powers. The rocks represent the everlasting creation of the Great Spirit. In placing these sacred rocks at the four quarters we understand that it is you who are at the center. When the rocks are taken into the purification lodge, sacred plants are severally sprinkled on them, . . . and everything is made sacred; and if there is anything in the lodge that is not good, it is driven away by the power of the smoke. When we drink the water we are made pure. The water helps us to pray. When we drink the water we know that all life depends on the water; it is the water of life. When we use the water in the sweat lodge we should always think of *Wakan-Tanka* who is always flowing, giving its power and life to everything; we should even be as the water, which is lower than all things, yet stronger even than the rock. The steam and the heat make the body and mind pure. The prayers and the sacred songs help in cleansing the mind. . . . When we leave the sweat lodge we are purified; we leave behind all that is impure, that we may live as the Great Spirit wishes, and that we may know something of that real world of the Spirit, which is behind this one. (adapted from J. Brown 1989, 31–43)

Agreement on the meaning of the Lakota term *Wakan-Tanka* is not unanimous. Some translate it as "Great Spirit" or "God" (Bucko 1998, 89). Others translate it as "Great Mystery" (Hassrick 1964, 245). While the unseen Creator is not easy to define, a common meaning unifies the various symbols for participation with the Creator.

Reflection and Discussion

1. Why are so many different symbols used in one ceremony?
2. How do the various symbols reduce the potential for misinterpretation of one symbol?
3. What memories may be triggered when participants later see some of these symbols elsewhere (e.g., sacred plants such as sage grass, rocks, fire, steam)?

Symbols as Building Blocks for Rituals

If the properties of polarization, condensation, and unification are considered when we select symbols to construct a ritual, these symbols are potent building blocks for powerful rituals. The symbols connect the senses with an ideology so that participants want to do what they should do. One symbol will speak a shade differently to each individual such that the individual concerns of all participants are addressed. In addition, the various symbols are unified in a common meaning, such that the point of the ritual is driven home and remembered for a long time. Intercultural disciplers understand the value of symbols and use them abundantly because they speak louder and longer than mere words alone. Before we investigate the use of rituals for discipleship

---

Without teaching with words, disciples cannot grasp the meaning of the gospel. Without symbols and ceremonies, it will be much harder, as Clark Pinnock insists, for them to access God's presence.

Mathias Zahniser (1997, 2)

---

in the next chapter, there is one more piece to the puzzle that intercultural disciplers need to understand: the role of myths.

Myths as Sacred Stories

Despite the popular connotation of the word, "myth" does not mean falsehood. Quite the contrary, scholars use the term "myth" in religious studies to refer to the sacred stories of a people that form their identity and explain where they came from, how the world was created, how they reached their present situation, and their hopes for the future. These are the ultimate realities that undergird a religious belief system. Myth scholar Mircea Eliade notes,

> In short, myths describe the various and sometimes dramatic breakthroughs of the sacred (or the "supernatural") into the world. It is this sudden breakthrough of the sacred that really *establishes* the World and makes it what it is today. Furthermore, it is as a result of the intervention of Supernatural Beings that man himself is what he is today, a mortal, sexed, and cultural being. . . . Myth is regarded as a sacred story, and hence a "true history," because it always deals with *realities*. (1998, 6)

In anthropological terms, myths are at the core of the worldview that serves to shape reality and help people interpret the world around them. Hiebert notes,

> A myth is the overarching story, bigger than history and believed to be true, that serves as a paradigm for people to understand the larger stories in which ordinary lives are embedded. Myths are paradigmatic stories, master narratives that bring cosmic order, coherence, and sense to the seemingly senseless

experiences, emotions, ideas, and judgments of everyday life by telling people what is real, eternal, and enduring. (2008, 66)

To understand the role of myths in religion, it may help to think of myths as the operating system of a computer. This operating system makes sense of all the other actions performed with the computer. Without it, the computer cannot make meaning of the data that is typed on the keyboard. The operating system takes software applications and makes them meaningful for users to help people in their daily lives. The operating system is always in the background, unseen and quietly at work. It is very important as the underlying basis for creating meaning. Likewise, myths are the underlying meaning-making mechanisms that help people make sense of life around them. While unseen and always quietly at work in the background, myths serve as the underlying basis to form a worldview.

Interconnection between Myth, Worldview, Symbols, and Rituals

For intercultural disciplers, the connection between worldview, myths, symbols, and rituals is very important. If disciplers do not address these areas, the problems of split-level Christianity or syncretism will persist.

Figure 4.3 shows the connections between these elements (Hiebert 2008, 316). A tree has three distinct but connected parts: leaves/branches, trunk, and root ball.

In figure 4.3, there are three levels to consider:

- *Level one*: When gazing at a tree, the leaves and branches are most evident. This is what is typically used to identify the type of tree. This observable part of the tree is compared to the behavior/ritual level of discipleship. The rituals are composed of symbols.
- *Level two*: The trunk of the tree is what moves nutrients and water from the ground to the leaves and branches. This part of the tree is compared to the belief level of discipleship.
- *Level three*: Underlying the trunk, however, is the part of the tree that is not seen. It is the most important part, since the tree would have never started growing without it. The root ball underlying the tree is compared to the worldview level of discipleship, and the individual roots are likened to the collection of myths.

Starting Discipleship at Level One

Disciplers often start at level one, the level of behavior and/or ritual. The disciple is taught to stop drinking/smoking, start to read the Bible, pray, go

Figure 4.3
Connection between ritual, beliefs, worldview, and myths

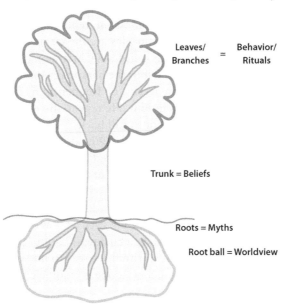

Leaves/
Branches = Behavior/
Rituals

Trunk = Beliefs

Roots = Myths

Root ball = Worldview

to church, memorize some Bible verses, get baptized, and so on. While this is helpful, if the beliefs are not changed this discipleship approach can easily result in syncretism. As described in chapter 2, an African destroyed his idols and protective charms; however, he also put a Bible under his pillow at night. Since the underlying belief system is unchanged, the Bible has now become a good-luck charm that magically manipulates the spirit world for him. This is an example of syncretism in the majority world as Christian and traditional religious beliefs are intermixed.

In the Western world, syncretism also results when discipleship focuses on the behavior/ritual level alone. For example, an American went from church to church in order to find the church that was just right for her. She left when the church did not meet her needs. "Church shopping" makes sense in a hyperindividualistic, consumer-driven culture. J. I. Packer warns, however, that worship is not pleasing to God when "the focus of the worshiper is on himself or herself rather than on God, and the worshiper's interest is in the quality of experience" (*The Music* 2011). If her underlying beliefs are not challenged, she blends together assumptions from her hyperindividualistic consumer culture with Christianity such that syncretism results. A focus on behavior/rituals alone is not sufficient for transforming disciples. This is one of the reasons that contemporary Christianity has often been described as a mile wide and an inch deep.

Starting Discipleship at Level Two

Some disciplers focus on level two, the level of beliefs. Disciples are taught to believe the right theology of sin, confession, repentance, salvation, sanctification, church, and so on. If these topics are the exclusive focus without addressing the other two levels, then split-level Christianity can result.

For example, a new pastor moved into the parsonage that the church provided for him. Within the first few weeks, he frequently received calls from the psychic hotline, offering to help him. He repeatedly told the caller that he did not need these services and not to call back.

Finally, one day in frustration, he asked, "Why do you keep calling me?"

The simple answer was, "The lady who used to live here called us often."

What happened? We can only speculate that the previous pastor (or pastor's spouse) had intimate excluded middle issues that were not addressed in the church. While the ultimate issues were addressed with biblical beliefs, she may have wanted answers to questions such as, "Why did this person die?" or "When is the best time to start a business?" Split-level Christianity results when people go to different spiritual sources to find answers or help for different questions. A focus on beliefs alone is insufficient for transforming disciples.

Starting Discipleship at Level Three

When intercultural disciplers start at level three and transform a person's worldview, changes will occur in beliefs and behavior, just like healthy leaves, branches, and trunks result from a healthy root system. For an example, in the following personal account, let's hear Peter's story as he visited me one day in the village of Fumbisi in Ghana.

> While sitting on the porch one Sunday afternoon, Peter comes to visit. Instead of his usual jovial self, he has a serious look in his eyes. Slowly but deliberately, he shares his problem: "I would like you to destroy the idols that my parents made for me. They are still in my house, but I do not need them anymore. Can you destroy them for me?"
>
> Peter was growing in his newfound Christian faith. When he was growing up in the Builsa culture, his parents had made a personal idol for him that he could consult for guidance and protection. He had feared this idol his entire life. Today, though, it was different.
>
> "What happened to make this change?" I asked.
>
> "Well, I have been thinking about it. Today at church, we again talked about the power of Jesus, who overcame death and Satan, and now he sits at the right hand of God. Since I have Jesus to guide and protect me, I do not need this idol anymore."

I was overjoyed. We discussed how his faith in Jesus had brought him to this point. His faith will also be needed to destroy not just the physical idol but also any spiritual connections to it.

"I am available to stand by and assist you, Peter," I respond, "but you need to do this act as a response of your faith in Christ. Are you ready for this?"

"Yes, I am, with God's help!" he joyously responded.

This was a significant marker in Peter's discipleship journey. As his worldview was changing, his changed belief system then guided him to change his behavior. This ritual act of destroying his personal idol was a crucial event for him. His faith in personally destroying the idol demonstrated the power of Christ (not the power of the missionary/pastor) to protect him.

In the seminary classroom one day, graduate assistant Osias Segura Guzman sketched figure 4.4 to portray how symbols are interconnected with rituals and myths in discipleship.

Figure 4.4
Ritual reenacts myth

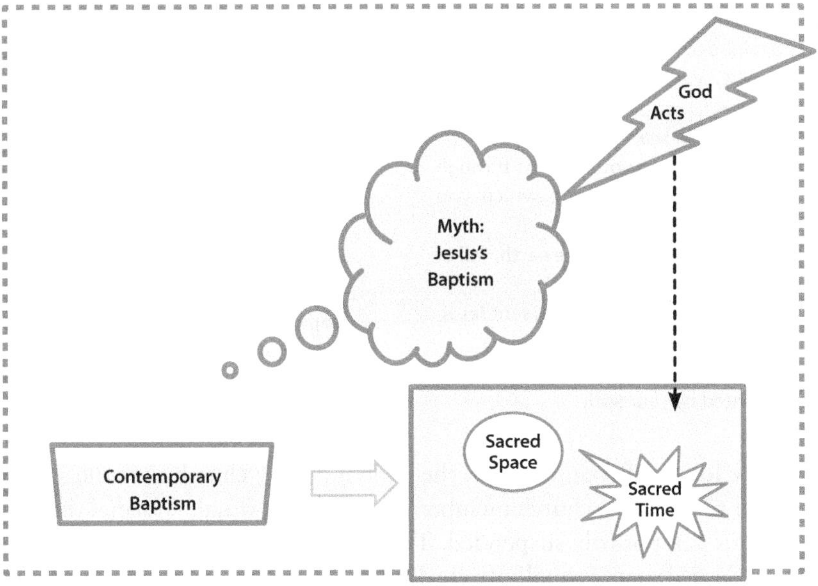

In the upper right-hand corner, note that God has acted in history. When the ritual is performed in contemporary times, God acts again today to transform people, similar to the way God acted before. For example, God's act is recorded in Jesus's baptism (Mark 1:9–11). This historical event shapes the Christian reality as a fundamental sacred story or myth.

Interplay of Symbol, Ritual, and Myths

The interplay of symbol, ritual, and myths is evident in *The United Methodist Hymnal*, which contains the following prayer to be offered just prior to baptism. Notice how the biblical sacred stories are recalled to establish the basis for the baptism ritual. Through this ritual, sacred time and space are entered so that God will work again as God has done in ages past.

Eternal Father:
When nothing existed but chaos, you swept across the dark waters and brought forth light.
In the days of Noah you saved those on the ark through water.
After the flood you set in the clouds a rainbow.
When you saw your people as slaves in Egypt, you led them to freedom through the sea.
Their children you brought through the Jordan to the land which you promised.
Sing to the Lord, all the earth. Tell of God's mercy each day.
In the fullness of time you sent Jesus, nurtured in the water of a womb.
He was baptized by John and anointed by your Sprit.

He called his disciples to share in the baptism of his death and resurrection and to make disciples of all nations.
Declare his works to the nations, his glory among all the people.
Pour out your Holy Spirit, to bless this gift of water and those who receive it, to wash away their sin and clothe them in righteousness throughout their lives, that, dying and being raised with Christ, they may share in his final victory.
All praise to you, Eternal Father, through your Son Jesus Christ, who with you and the Holy Spirit lives and reigns forever. Amen. (Job 1989, 36)

Reflection and Discussion

1. In addition to the story of Jesus's baptism, which major biblical stories does this liturgy draw on?
2. How does the symbol of water tie these biblical stories together?
3. How do these sacred stories act as the "operating system" to explain how God acted in history such that the contemporary participants can expect God to act again via the baptism ritual?

In the lower left-hand corner, the contemporary church uses the symbol of water to baptize a church member. Through this ritual, "normal time and space" are temporarily suspended. The participants enter "sacred time and space." Sacred space is qualitatively different from "normal space" in that the power and presence of the divine God are more acutely felt. A prime example of this is found in Exodus 3:5, where Moses is told to take off his shoes when approaching the burning bush, since it is holy ground. Sacred time is also qualitatively different from "normal time." Sacred time, instead of being linear and progressing forward, is "indefinitely recoverable, indefinitely repeatable" (Eliade 1959, 69). Chronological time is suspended, as if the two-thousand-year gap between the time of Jesus's original baptism and today did not exist. The time is symbolically brought to the present during the ritual.

In summary, myths form a worldview of how God has acted in history. Contemporary believers then use symbols to construct rituals in order to "act out" the myths in sacred time and space. When this is done well, God acts again today, as God has done in the past in order to transform people. This combination of symbols, rituals, myths, and worldviews is thus useful in helping disciples experience God again for transformation.

These elements are important for intercultural disciplers to transform disciples' worldview. Where rituals already exist in the church, the value of symbols, sacred time/space, and myths can be emphasized to drive home the ritual more deeply. Where there are no existing rituals for dealing with excluded middle issues, symbols should be selected and utilized to construct rituals that will address these discipleship needs, as described in my personal account below.

It is early Sunday morning, and the unusual quietness in the house reminds me that the children are all still fast asleep. No one is scurrying about to rush out the door. The bathroom counter is even empty of hot curling irons, hairbrushes, and toothbrushes. The busy week of school, homework, sports, and visiting friends has left the children all exhausted. Finally, this is the one day of the week that they can sleep late. You can call it Sunday, Lord's Day, Sabbath, Day of Worship, whatever . . . the children want to call this a "Stay in Bed" day.

Into their blissful dreams, I, their dad, need to rouse them from their slumber and remind them to get ready to go to church. Like a cat approaching a sleeping watchdog, this undertaking is a setup for eventual conflict. I have told the kids many times how our family chooses to worship on this day. This is our weekly Sabbath, and it is a day to put other distractions aside so that we can worship God. On Sunday, we focus on our relationship with God together as a family. I insist that we attend Sunday school together and then go to the worship service as a family. After the service, we have a meal together. Gathering for worship with others at church is an important part of their discipleship.

Begrudgingly, they agree, and eventually we make it to church, have a meal together, and enjoy the day—until next Sunday morning, when I need to rouse the sleeping dog once again. The problem is that they know they should go to church and worship as followers of Jesus, but they simply do not feel like it. Like the sleeping disciples in the Garden of Gethsemane, "The spirit is willing, but the flesh is weak" (Matt. 26:41). Can a symbol help?

My wife and I decide to try an experiment. I start off by lighting a candle in the center of the kitchen table one Sunday morning. Without saying a word, amid the spoons plunging into their bowls as the children gulp down cereal, they all gradually notice the flame and inquire. I explain that God told the Israelites to keep a fire burning in the tabernacle as a sign of God's presence.

Since this is a day set apart for worshiping God, I want this candle to serve as a reminder. We do not light a candle at the breakfast table on any other day except Sunday. This day is set apart for worship. Each Sunday, then, I light the candle as a symbol of this day being set apart.

Some Native American Christian friends eventually gift me with an abalone

> **At the center of a culture are its sacred symbols. . . . The study of their sacred symbols, in particular, provides a window on a people's understanding of ultimate reality.**
>
> Paul Hiebert (Hiebert, Shaw, and Tiénou 1999b, 122)

shell, a feather, and some herbs (sage, sweet grass, and cedar). While the kids are still sleeping, I light the herbs and walk throughout the house, praying for the Holy Spirit to cleanse, renew, and guide us this week. One room at a time, I wave the feather to blow the smoke into their rooms. Each of the herbs has a distinct and pleasing aroma. As the kids are stirring, the smoke reaches their noses—a simple reminder that this day is set apart from the others. There is no need to complain or fuss; this is the only day when Dad brings this aroma to their rooms, which means that it is time to arise from their slumber and go to church.

The fragrant herbs become a good and pleasant reminder. As a result, this smell helps them want to do what they should do. It helps them want to get up from bed and get ready for worship, as they should. While this is not to say that some Sunday mornings are not more challenging than others, what I have observed is that the burning herbs provide a powerful symbol to connect the sensory and the ideological poles for these growing disciples. Throughout the day, the abalone shell with the feather and burnt herbs lie quietly on the table—constantly speaking to us that this day is set apart from the rest. Symbols fill the gap for discipleship when words alone are insufficient.

Summary

In this chapter we focused on symbols, which form building blocks for rituals. Several important aspects of symbols make them ideally suited for intercultural discipleship.

1. Religious *symbols* open up unique doors to help disciples feel the intimate presence of the ultimate God.

2. The *polarization* property means that symbols connect an ideological pole with a sensory pole. A well-placed symbol encourages the disciple to want to do what he or she should do.

3. The *condensation* property means that one symbol draws together different meanings. Symbols, then, will connect various meanings and feelings to make the discipleship experience more personal.

4. The *unification* property means that many different symbols can communicate one meaning. Disparate symbols, then, can speak the same meaning to make the experience more memorable and impactful.

5. *Myths* are sacred stories that form the basis for a worldview. While myths are not always articulated in daily conversation, they function in the background like an operating system on a computer.

6. When *rituals* enact the myths, sacred space and sacred time are ushered in such that God acts again, as God has done in the past. Symbols are a key to constructing these sacred rituals.

7. Symbols can play a crucial role in addressing excluded middle issues for discipleship. Where words alone are insufficient to catch the big fish, symbols can provide the necessary hook.

In the next chapter, we focus on how rituals are used by religions around the world (and in history) to disciple people from one level of faith to another.

Activity for Discipling

1. Identify some of the root causes of the excluded middle issue that you previously chose to address with your disciples.

2. What biblical stories can serve as sacred myths to help address this issue and its underlying root causes?

3. What symbols may be used to communicate deep value and emotions when words are not enough? Begin by considering the following questions:

   a. What meaning do you want to communicate? What symbols will stir the desire to reinforce the spiritual significance that you want to convey? The better you know the disciples, the more carefully the symbols can be selected to connect deep emotions and commitment to the ideology being expressed (i.e., polarization).

   b. What familiar symbols in the culture communicate various meanings? Look for symbols that condense various meanings. Since symbols are multivocal, they can speak to different people based on their particular concerns and needs.

c. Which symbols can be combined with others to reinforce the same meaning? Making such connections drives home the central message in an impactful and memorable way. Memory is key in oral cultures, since learning is directly connected to memory (Ong 1982, 33–34). Unifying various symbols through a common thread of meaning makes the ritual a more memorable discipleship experience.

String Tying Ritual in Thailand

Adapted from De Neui (2005).

Banyat was born and raised in Bangkok. Although the majority of the population of Thailand is Buddhist, his parents were Christian. They did not participate in many local rituals because of their faith. From time to time the pressure to participate in Buddhist customs with friends would cause Banyat internal conflict. Was he a good Thai if he did not participate in these events? When he came home from college wearing strings on his wrists from the welcoming ceremony (*sukhwan*) from the upper classmates, his parents told him to take them off right away: "We are Christians. How will people know that if you look like everyone else?" From then on he never had a desire to participate in *sukhwan* rituals, even though it was practiced at weddings and other social gatherings. For most of the time he could simply ignore such things. And then he met Ying.

He first saw her at church, when she had just moved to Bangkok. Ying grew up in a small village in rural northeast Thailand, but her Christian parents had encouraged her to continue through university studies. After graduation she landed a good job in Bangkok and found a church home. She considered herself a strong Christian; however, she preferred the term *Luk Pra Chao* (the term found in John 1:12 for "child of God"). Her village church regularly practiced *sukhwan* for many occasions in the life of the community with the explanation that it visually symbolized the love of Christ in a tangible way. For her, the sending-off ceremony to come

to Bangkok, when all the church members and local friends had come to tie her wrist with spoken blessings, was particularly meaningful. She wore the strings for a long time when she first arrived, which Banyat thought was strange, but since nobody ever said anything about it, neither did he.

Banyat and Ying were attracted to each other and shared their hopes and dreams of marriage. Finally the time came, as was the custom, for the *phu yai* (family members and pastors) to come together to discuss engagement. After some negotiation, the proposals were accepted by both sides with much celebration and a feast at Ying's home church. As the months went by, plans were made for the wedding, which was to be held at the larger church in Bangkok, with both pastors officiating. Everything was going along quite well until it came to one final detail of the wedding. Ying's family assumed that the ceremony would conclude with the *sukhwan* ceremony, when the entire community could come and bless the couple by tying a string on their wrists. When Banyat's pastor heard this, he politely disagreed: "We are Christians. We want everyone who is coming to know this. We don't want them to think that we are falling back into traditional practices. *Sukhwan* is used to call on spiritual powers. We don't want to open ourselves up to that."

Ying's pastor had faced this response before and was ready with an explanation. "Yes, in northeast Thailand we use the string tying ritual for many things, major comings and goings, giving birth, new house celebration, healings, and yes—weddings! And it is also true that very few churches are willing to use it because it does look like the old ways from the outside."

He went on, "But most Thai people who practice *sukhwan* don't know what it means. For some Buddhists the three strands of cotton strings knotted together represent their belief in the power of the Triphidok [the Buddha, the Dharma teaching, and the community of Buddhist monks, the Sangha]. Normally those strings are taken to a local spiritual leader to *puk sekkatah* [consecrate with spiritual power]. After that they are added to the *don bai sri* [flower arrangement] and brought to a ritual assembly on a specially selected auspicious day to bless someone or some couple who is in transition. All that is in the *don bai sri* indicates blessing: the gold flowers, the love flowers, the everlasting flowers, even the dry rice in which the whole things stands reminding us of the blessing of food. Every part of the ceremony is designed to bless."

Ying's pastor continued: "As children of God, there are certain parts of the tradition that we use and other parts we do not. The flowers, the white strings, the way we gather are all beautiful and give glory to God. For us, the three strings represent the Father, the Son, and the Holy Spirit, three in one. But there is no need for special consecration of the strings because the power is already available in what Jesus has done for us. Every time we do the ceremony, we explain to everyone that no *puk sekkatah* has taken place. This is just ordinary cotton thread that God has given us to symbolize an internal reality in an external way. We depend on God's power to help those we want

to bless, and anyone can share in giving that blessing. In typical tying ceremonies, people must pay money to bless, but we don't do that in the church. Anyone can come and take a string from the bouquet and tie a blessing on to those who are being honored that day. The strings are temporary. They will not last for a long time, and this is intentional. As Christ followers, we explain that the string itself will break, but the love of Christ that it symbolizes will never break and will never leave us."

The pastor ended with these words: "Ritual moments are very powerful. They are teachable moments. They bring us closer together and help us to understand what God's love means to us today. We always include them in our weddings when a new relationship is formally beginning."

More discussion followed, particularly between the two pastors. The rural pastor explained that God commands ritual as one means, among many, to express God's heart, to identify with people, to demonstrate God's purposes, and to reveal God's self. The string-tying ritual was nowhere commanded directly by God as were the other rituals; however, according to scriptural records, God accepts the offerings of the joyful and willing heart in whatever forms or amounts they may come (Isa. 42:3; 2 Cor. 9:7–11). He added that many of the Western traditions found in so-called Christian weddings were not commanded in the Bible either but were adapted from practices previously not Christian.

Banyat's family had learned a great deal about *sukhwan* symbols and ritual and how one Christian fellowship had contextualized it. This was also a learning experience for their Bangkok pastor, who had never been taught that such rituals could be used within the church context. He had never experienced the ritual himself either. At this point, the decision was up to him. Both families were waiting for his opinion on the matter, since the wedding would be held in his sanctuary. He had to think about his church congregation, who had never done this before. How would he explain it to them? What would this mean for the future of his ministry in Bangkok if other pastors found out what he was allowing to happen? At the same time, he wanted to honor this new couple as members of his church. After reflecting on the issues, the pastor finally decided to . . .

Reflection and Discussion

1. How are the three properties of symbols evident in the use of the symbols in the *sukhwan*?
2. How much of the meaning of the symbols in *sukhwan* ceremony do you feel needs to be changed in order to incorporate this ritual into a Christian wedding? How can this happen successfully?
3. If you were the Bangkok pastor guiding the families of Banyat and Ying in this decision, how would you counsel them?

5

Rituals Drive Meaning
Deep into the Bone

Pein dan kan joya, di voorika an tua. (If an arrow has not yet entered deeply, its removal is not difficult.)

—Builsa proverb

Transforming an American Teenager

With tears streaming down his cheeks, the seventeen-year-old American boy patiently awaits his turn in line. Normally a self-composed and even-keel guy, this "football player" type is not prone to public displays of emotion. Now, however, he is openly expressing his emotions amid sixty other teenagers. As he approaches the camp leaders, they anoint his forehead with oil, lay hands on him, and pray over him. The oil drips down his forehead and onto his nose, eventually finding a resting place near his lips, touching his sense of touch, smell, and taste along the way.

"As I was anointed with a cross on my forehead, I felt God's presence very strongly upon me," he explains.

This anointing ritual, during a weeklong Christian camp, becomes an important discipleship experience to move youth from one level of faith to another. Over two months later, he candidly recalls the experience:

> Coming into the camp, my spiritual walk with Christ was good, but I felt I still lacked what I needed to have to become a stronger Christian and a leader figure for the campers who attended. I had been used to cutting people down to gain favor in other people's eyes, when I really needed favor in only God's eyes. There at camp, I learned how to stick up for younger kids who I knew weren't too popular in other kids' eyes. . . . All week we were talking about how the Holy Spirit works and how powerful it is. . . . Through this Lake Poinsett camp, it gave me another look of what the Holy Spirit is capable of doing. . . . To wrap it all up, I would say my spiritual walk with Christ has elevated during this last summer,

and I'm more eager than ever to walk in my Lord God's footsteps to help me make good choices that will glorify him.

In this story of a personal experience shared with the author, why was this camp and ensuing ritual so powerful in this teenager's discipleship process? While he will still have other barriers to overcome along the way, what is unique about the ritual process that helps elevate his spiritual walk?

Overcoming a Bad Name

For some, the word "ritual" stirs up images of something that is boring, repetitive, or a meaningless performance. Those who grew up in a nonliturgical church tradition may be skeptical about the necessity of rituals, since reliance on the Bible is sufficient. Others may be concerned about misplaced

---

Evangelicals can be reluctant to consciously focus on ritual as a means of discipleship. By doing so, however, they overlook the simple fact that many of their discipling activities (small group Bible studies, corporate worship, one-on-one discipleship, devotional time) are inherently ritualistic. They have lost sight of how we were created as ritualistic beings.

Scott Moreau (Moreau, Campbell, and Greener 2014, 275)

---

faith through rituals that may lead to idolatry. While these concerns need to be considered, it can be too easy to overlook the value of rituals in everyday life (e.g., handshakes, pledging allegiance) and in religious formation (e.g., Communion, baptism, pilgrimages). When observing religions around the world, we find that rituals are often at the heart of the discipleship process. Rituals help to express commitment to God for both the sake of individual participants and the entire faith community.

Paul Hiebert notes that creating living rituals is an important part of transforming worldviews, since the rituals help to restructure and express the new worldview.

We need to overcome our fear of rituals. The answer to dead traditions and idolatrous rituals is not to do away with rituals. It is to constantly consciously examine and re-create our rituals to keep them vibrant and to transform us through participation in them. Without living rituals, we have no appropriate ways to affirm our deepest beliefs, feelings, and morals, which lead to new lives in a new community and in the world. (2008, 324)

Rituals can be defined as a prescribed set of actions that employ symbols to reenact the deepest beliefs, feelings, and values of a people (Kimball 2008, 48; Hiebert 2008, 98). Religious rituals have "reference to divine or transcendent beings" (Bowie 2005, 32) by bringing the past into the present through sacred time and space, as discussed in the preceding chapter. Ronald Grimes describes how rituals have the unique ability to drive meaning "deeply into the bone" (2000). If the meaning of Christianity is not driven deeply to the bone, then disciples can too easily fall away, as the African proverb reminds us: "If an arrow has not yet entered deeply, its removal is not difficult." For intercultural disciplers, rituals provide important opportunities to address excluded middle issues for growing disciples so that the ultimate God becomes deeply intimate and close in their personal and communal lives (Zahniser 1997, 33).

Three-Stage Ritual Structure

Arnold Van Gennep (1960) studied rituals from around the world and observed a common structure in ritual performance that included three distinct stages. While he was largely studying the rites of passage during life-cycle events, this same ritual structure also appears in other types of rituals, such as festivals, pilgrimages, retreats, celebrations, and calendrical rituals. The three-stage structure is diagrammed in figure 5.1.

Figure 5.1
Three-stage ritual structure

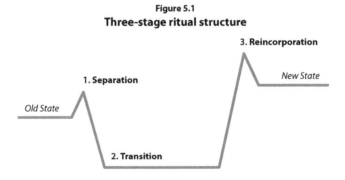

To describe this ritual structure and how it relates to intercultural discipleship, I will use the example of the most powerful tool of discipleship in Islam: the hajj. All devout Muslims are exhorted to take this pilgrimage to Mecca once in their lifetime. After returning from the hajj, they are often more committed to their faith. How does the ritual process work to drive meaning to the bone in discipleship?

1. Separation

The first stage removes the participants from the daily chores and patterns of life. This requires a physical separation, such that there is a clean break from these normal activities and responsibilities. Muslims leave their homes far behind as they travel to Mecca. This sharp break from the routine of life prepares pilgrims for the next stage. There may be a going-away party that further heightens the expectations and blessings of those who have sent the pilgrim on his or her way.

2. Transition

This important stage is marked by uncertainty, confusion, and chaos. Turner (1995) describes this period as "anti-structure," since it is markedly different from the normal routines (structure) of life. Participants do not know what is about to occur. As a result, they are always off balance and unsure what

---

Important Definitions for Rituals

Liminality: "the transitional period or phase of a rite of passage, during which the participant lacks social status or rank, remains anonymous, shows obedience and humility, and follows prescribed forms of conduct, dress, etc." Turner also uses the term "anti-structure" to differentiate this period from the normal flow of life (structure).

Communitas: "the sense of sharing and intimacy that develops among persons who experience liminality as a group."

http://dictionary.reference.com

---

is waiting just around the bend. Turner also uses the term "liminality" to describe this feeling of being "betwixt and between." "Liminality" is derived from the Latin term *limen*, which means "threshold." Participants are not in or out; rather, they are in a middle transition state that is uncomfortable, as portrayed by the following pilgrim:

> As Michael arrives at the mosque, he promptly removes his khaki pants, brown button-down shirt, and fancy leather shoes. Replacing these "normal clothes" with only two white cotton unstitched pieces of cloth and a pair of sandals, he admits to feeling naked and frail. The simple attire strips away his sense of

93

identity as an American, and his work as a journalist. Instead of his normal confident stride, he walks slowly and gently amidst the unknown surrounding. Walking to the water fountain, he stoops to wash his face, hands, and feet. Leaving the building, he joins the throng of other white-robed pilgrims. (Koppel 1997)

Turner describes this liminal feeling or state of "anti-structure" by comparing it with the normal structure of everyday life:

TABLE 5.1	
Characteristics of Liminality versus Structure	
Liminality	**Structure**
Equality	Inequality
No property/wealth	Property/wealth
Humility	Pride of position
Transition	State of stability
No status, rank	Social status/rank important
Foolishness	Seriousness
Simplicity	Complexity
Accept pain/suffering	Avoid pain/suffering
Communal	Individual
All look the same	Distinct clothing

Adapted from Turner (1995, 106–7).

This transition phase produces liminality, thereby stripping away Michael's individuality and uniqueness, to be replaced by a communal identity. He now feels like a brother and is proud to stand shoulder to shoulder with others in the throng. Turner (1995, 96) identifies this unique bond that occurs during the transition phase with the term *communitas*. The unique conditions of liminality during the transition period of the ritual process are ripe for the fruit of deep bonding with other people. In addition to the bonding of fellow pilgrims with one another, this condition is also ripe for participants to bond with their faith in a unique way. As a result, it is a powerful tool for discipleship that religions around the world use.

During the five-day journey when Michael walks several miles under the hot sun to sacred sites, he will reenact the mythology of Islam. For example, he walks up and down a long hallway, culminating in a drink from a well to reenact Hagar's wandering in the desert in search of water as she fled from her mistress, Sarah. This experience drives home more deeply what it means to be a follower of this faith system.

3. Reincorporation

After completing the hajj, Michael returns home to be reincorporated into society. Now, though, he reenters at a higher level of spiritual maturity; he is even given a new name, Al Haji. This marks him as a Muslim disciple who has gone on the hajj. The reincorporation is important for the faith community (which now recognizes his commitment) and also for the individual

> Religion the world around relies upon symbols and rituals to address the intimate middle issues that Hiebert has identified. But, because theologians and social scientists have not given them the serious attention they deserve, symbols and rituals have received little attention from Christian disciplers.
>
> Mathias Zahniser (1997, 53)

(who may have new responsibilities). The reincorporation may be celebrated with others, including sharing a meal or some other means of celebration. Ultimately, this ritual serves as a powerful discipleship tool for bonding the disciple to his or her faith and to other disciples.

Early Church Use of Ritual

The early church relied on the ritual process to deepen the bonding of the faith community to other community members and to their faith. Amid persecution and the threat of martyrdom, Christianity grew from a small sect to the dominant religion in the Roman world in a few hundred years. The ritual process had a significant role in the discipleship of the early believers. Drawing from the Apostolic Tradition of Hippolytus around AD 200, Thomas Finn notes, "Christians survived in Rome to a large extent because they developed a dynamic ritual process for the making of Christians, technically called the 'catechumenate'" (1989, 69).

The ritual process that the early church developed in its first few hundred years followed the ritual structure schematized in figure 5.1.

Separation: In the first stage, sponsors accompanied those wanting to be part of the community of faith to a formal inquiry. They were asked personal questions concerning their motivations, occupations, status, and so on. The main function of this inquiry was to "gauge candidates' willingness to distance themselves from the reach of society" (Finn 1989, 72).

Discipleship in Taiwan

"From a discipling standpoint, the church in Taiwan is in crisis," observes Jim Courson (1998, 301). He cites both the low rate at which new believers are incorporated into the church and the high loss rate among new Christians. Searching for answers to raise the rate of church incorporation and lower the losses out the "back door," Courson recommends a discipling approach based on a rite-of-passage structure modeled after the early church catechumenate process (described herein) utilizing the three-stage ritual structure.

Courson recommends a rite of separation in the church to include a sponsor who accompanies the initiate through questioning about personal morality and ethics and discussions of filial piety/family responsibility and occupational issues. This stage would then lead to the liminal stage, which would include instruction related to the believer's status relative to ancestors, gods, and ghosts. Courson notes, "Traditional practices will need to be addressed. Functional substitutes for practices such as burning paper money at ancestral shrines must be explored, providing inquirers with visible forms for expressing filial piety that are culturally appropriate, yet Christian" (1998, 309). The middle liminal stage may take between two and three years.

The final stage would include a rite of incorporation, including a fast from Friday to Sunday, followed by a baptism and a celebration feast to which the family members of the new believers are invited. He concludes, "This is a time for new believers to share their newfound faith, for the non-believing community to witness the vitality of the community of faith, and for the community of faith to share its message of hope with those willing to hear" (1998, 311).

Reflection and Discussion

1. What similarities do you see between Courson's recommended discipling approach for the Taiwanese church and the catechumenate ritual process used by the local church? What differences do you observe between the two? What suggests these differences?

2. Compare/contrast the church in Taiwan to the contemporary church in your area. What can you learn from the church in Taiwan to help you in discipling in other locations?

Transition: Following separation, the candidates moved into the transition stage by receiving oral instruction, prayer, and the laying on of hands. This transition period often lasted three years, culminating in a period of exorcism. Following the period of exorcism and subsequent fasting/prayer, the candidates were anointed with oil and prepared for baptism.

During the transition time, however, the candidates were not allowed to participate in Communion. In addition, they did not receive the customary kiss of peace and embrace, nor did they mingle with church members. It was considered a capital offense in the Roman Empire to be identified as a Christian at this time, so there was the constant threat of people being "discovered." Since the candidates were not fully a part of the church body, yet they were not fully a part of Roman society either, they were in a state of "betwixt and between," or liminality. This liminal condition provided a fertile environment for deep bonding with fellow candidates and their faith.

Reincorporation: The candidates were now considered "the elect" and ready for baptism in the third stage. They were led to the water, where they were immersed three times. Emerging from the water, they were anointed with the oil of thanksgiving. They then quickly dried off and dressed for entry into the church assembly. The newly baptized members received Communion for the first time, along with the kiss of peace and embrace. The church members now recognized the new status of the newly baptized and treated them as part of the family of faith.

The catechumenate ritual process worked. Inquirers were moved from one level of faith to another as an integral part of their discipleship. Not only did they bond more deeply with their faith; they also bonded deeply with other Christians. Finn concludes his study of the early church with this assessment: "The impact of this ritual homecoming is difficult to overestimate. The newly baptized were initiated into a practical kinship network of telling effect. . . . The inescapable conclusion is that the survival of Christianity before Constantine depended heavily on the development of an effective catechumenate, a powerful ritual process" (1989, 78–80).

Use of Rituals for Contemporary Discipleship

Can the ritual process be used to transform the worldview of contemporary disciples? Can the church recover what was forgotten from the past and apply rituals for discipleship in our present time? If we apply our understanding of symbols and the ritual structure, two discipleship opportunities present themselves to contemporary disciplers:

Where no ritual exists: Identify a contemporary excluded middle need in culture that is not being addressed. Construct a ritual that addresses the

---

Discipleship that focuses on the headiness of cognitive information often misses the power of symbols and ceremonies and seldom transfers well from one cultural context to another.

Darrell Whiteman (in Zahniser 1997, ix)

---

root issues with a faith community (a process demonstrated in this chapter). The end result is to help growing disciples address intimate issues, thereby removing obstacles that prevent disciples from centering their lives on Christ.

Where rituals already exist: Identify an existing ritual in culture. Uncover the function that this ritual plays in culture and use the critical contextualization process to communicate Christian meaning (a process demonstrated in chap. 6). Again, the end goal is to help growing disciples experience the ultimate God in cultural forms that keep them centered on Christ.

Where No Ritual Exists

Remember that excluded middle issues are those intimate questions and concerns that require unseen spirit power and guidance to effect change in this world This is where the physical world is affected by the spirit world. As discussed in chapter 2, these intimate issues are often overlooked in the church; hence, people are forced to go to other sources for help. This can stunt the growth of disciples, as described below in my personal recounting of Sarah's story:

Sarah, a seminary student who normally has a very cheerful countenance, is very reserved and sullen. She was selected for jury duty this week, and the case that she has to try deals with the tragic death of a baby. For hours that turned to days, she has had to sit through the gruesome details of this horrendous case. By the end of the trial, she is depressed and confused. Her faith is challenged with questions such as, "How can God let a young baby die so cruelly? What if the decision of our jury was wrong? Why do I feel so weighed down?"

Noticing that she is not her usual spunky self, her friends gather around to hear her story. As she describes her feelings, the other seminary students quickly notice that this intimate issue is not usually addressed in the church or seminary classes. Yet these are nitty-gritty concerns that might dull her faith and calling by God, if not addressed. Times of tension or transition are the fertile soil for rituals. Here is the ritual that her friends construct.

As Sarah speaks aloud her questions and feelings to her friends, she is asked to put a rock in her backpack for each one. Fun at first, this quickly turns into a heavy load. Increasingly, she can feel the pain in her lower back as each rock is piled into the backpack. Eventually, she runs out of questions and concerns, symbolized by the rocks filling the backpack. After giving encouraging words and sharing Scripture, her friends then ask her to go to the top of a bridge overlooking a river. She is to visualize the backpack full of her concerns, feelings, and questions. When she is ready, her friends remove each rock one at a time. Reaching into the backpack to remove the first rock, the friends pray a blessing over Sarah, and then hand the rock to Sarah for her to release into the roaring river below.

WHOOOOSH!

The rock plummets twenty feet, suddenly splashing into the river, with water spraying in all directions. Quickly, the waters surround the rock as it disappears below the surface . . . never to be seen again. The remaining rocks are released in the same manner, one by one.

Tips for Constructing Rituals

Tom F. Driver advocates the use of rituals for addressing contemporary issues. He provides the following advice for constructing the middle stage of the ritual process (1991, 212–15):

- Active participants should outnumber passive ones.
- Art is play done workfully, but ritual is work done playfully. Be creative and integrate playfulness with solemnity.
- Christian ritual is liminal and authentic when the people of God receive the Spirit of God into their midst.
- Whereas magic attempts to manipulate the spirit powers to do what they would not do otherwise, faith invites God to do what God already wants to do. The inviting of God's presence may be symbolically communicated (e.g., lighting a candle).
- To be boring is to bear false witness. . . . [When it is not boring,] the ritual becomes less like a scripted drama and more like a well-hosted party.
- Ritual loves not paper. Discard written bulletins and speeches in favor of participatory events, symbols, and creative playfulness using generous amounts of oral literature.
- In ritual, words shift from being mainly descriptive or informative to become, in one degree or another, carriers of transforming power. Choose carefully the few words that are spoken. These words are meant to be gifts to help the disciples as they reenter society.
- While too many words weary the audience and diffuse its attention (Clarke 2011, 28), a few carefully chosen words or phrases can last a lifetime.

Reflection and Discussion

1. Consider a ritual that you have observed or read about (e.g., Sarah's story). Which of these tips were implemented well?
2. Which of these tips for good ritual construction tend to be overlooked?
3. How may the discipling impact of rituals change if the ritual specialist tries to incorporate tips like these into rituals?

Standing on the bridge, her friends pray over her and accompany her back to the dorm. Later that night, Sarah feels released from the emotional toll. With the aid of her faith community, using a simple symbol, in a simple ritual, she feels reassured of God's presence. Once again, she is focused on God's call for her life. She later recalls that this was a life-changing moment.

While intimate issues like Sarah's may sound insignificant to some, these may be the very concerns that people need to address in order to progress in their discipleship. In the centered set approach to discipleship (discussed in chap. 3), discipleship must address whatever issues may push the growing disciple away from remaining focused on Christ and his kingdom. These important discipleship issues vary from person to person, and they vary throughout a person's lifetime as well. Because of this variation, we need a handmade approach to discipleship that is tailored for the particular person during a particular stage of life, instead of an assembly-line production approach.

Rituals Maintain Continuity amid Transition

Particularly during times of crisis or transition, disciples need to be reminded that the ultimate God cares about their intimate needs. During these times, they feel frail and vulnerable. They want to experience God's presence amid their own confusion or doubts. Rituals are used to maintain continuity during the transitions of life (Van der Hart 1983). Rituals help people clarify their experiences. Rituals allow space for them to talk about their feelings and learn coping strategies. Disciples also come to appreciate anew the community of faith, which bonds them more deeply to this community. At the same time, they are ready to bond afresh to their faith, which will sustain them. These important discipleship opportunities are often overlooked in programmed, assembly-line production approaches. Yet these intimate issues are crucial for discipleship.

It is not hard to anticipate some of the major transitions in the human life cycle. Kingsland Baptist Church in Katy, Texas, has identified seven life stages it calls milestones (Haynes 2009). During each of these stages, the specific teaching needed to help parents in the discipleship of their children is identified. Each of the milestones culminates in a ritual at the church or home, including a mixture of symbols, vows, and actions. The goal of this approach is for the church to equip parents in the discipleship of their children from birth to adulthood. These preventive rituals for children are meant to ward off future problems in adulthood. The seven milestones are

1. Birth of a baby
2. Faith commitment
3. Preparing for adolescence
4. Commitment to purity
5. Passage to adulthood
6. High school graduation
7. Life in Christ

The ritual process is ideally suited for these times of transition. When society does not provide rituals for these transitions, rituals can be created to help the growing disciple maintain his or her focus on Christ. Societies around the world focus particularly on the passage to adulthood. Young people want to know when they have become young men or women. If society does not provide this ritual passage, youth tend to create their own markers. Unfortunately, these markers are often destructive, involving a car, a dangerous substance, or a sexual encounter. The church and the family can recognize

---

Contemporary [American] society is typified by a poverty of vibrant rituals—ceremonies that are connected to the deeper realms of human existence, the realms traditionally touched by mythology, . . . [resulting in a] bankruptcy of meaningful ritual in American homes.

David Feinstein and Peg Mayo (1990, 42)

---

this transitional period as a discipleship opportunity. A ritual created for and uniquely suited to the young person will include the three stages of separation, transition, and reincorporation. Symbols are used to speak during and after the ritual so that the youth and community recognize that this young person has now become a young man or a young woman. While resources are available to help faith communities develop rituals for youth (Lewis 2007; Farrel and Hanna 2009), the following story describes a portion of a "preparing for adolescence" ritual for an American family:

Jeremy has waited a long time for this day. His dad said that the day would arrive when he would take him away on the motorcycle and teach him the secrets of manhood—when Jeremy was ready.

Just a few weeks ago, his dad approached him with a firm but caring look in his eye as he said, "I have been watching you, and you are showing signs of maturity. You are now ready to learn the secrets of becoming a man."

Today, they pack the motorcycle to drive to an undisclosed location. Surrounded by his mom and siblings, Jeremy waves good-bye to his family, his home, and his childhood.

Pu pu pu pu pu pu. The motorcycle drones along the bumpy road for an hour, jostling every bone in his body, as well as the sleeping bags and food tied to the back.

"Where are we going? What are we going to do? Will this be painful?" Jeremy wonders, his curiosity piqued.

The motorcycle takes an unexpected turn and winds up a mountain. His body is weary as he dismounts the motorcycle, but Jeremy looks around with curiosity. He is attentive to everything that is done and said. When his dad sits down and discusses the secrets of being a young man, Jeremy is all ears. When his dad is revealing the new privileges and responsibilities about to be placed on him, he is also keenly attentive.

Long into the night, the mixture of play and discussion keeps him off balance. Eventually, they fall asleep.

As the morning sun showers their bodies with warmth, Jeremy notices a small object nearby.

His dad hands him the Swiss army knife and explains, "This knife can be used for great harm or great good. You are also getting stronger, and your body

---

When a person brings dishonor (or shame) to the ingroup, the only way to restore purity or expunge shame is through some type of ritual that will erase the impurity and restore the relationship. . . . Christians who live in honor societies will tend to search for ways to be restored to a pure state through cleansing (Heb. 9:14) and restoration of relationship (John 1:12–13). They will look for rituals to do this rather than rely on simple declarations of innocence.

Scott Moreau (Moreau, Campbell, and
Greener 2014, 7:197–98)

---

can be used for great harm or great good. I am trusting you to use your body to help others and make sure that girls never feel threatened by your presence. As a result, I am now trusting you to use this knife for good."

Jeremy ponders his new responsibilities and privileges as the knife weighs down his pocket. Deep inside him, this simple ritual drives the meaning of adulthood deep into the bone—he is now a young man, as recognized by his father.

His movement through adolescence is eased by a simple ritual and a symbolic gift. Both the memory and the gift stay with him long after the weekend is over.

Jeremy's story summarizes a ritual for a period of life that can be anticipated. There are times, however, when unexpected events occur. Once again, rituals help to smooth the transition.

Rituals for Unexpected Transitions

Transitions are also important discipleship opportunities. Rituals can be developed for events such as a first pregnancy, a move to a new home/job, going to the hospital, or job loss/transfer/advancement. Any issue that threatens to prevent the growing disciple from maintaining a kingdom-centered life is an important discipleship opportunity. If the issue is not addressed, the person's discipleship can become stunted.

Weekend Rituals

When people do not successfully move through the transitions of life, they can get stuck in a spiritual rut. Their spirituality can become weak and in need of revitalization. Weekend events such as Upper Room's Walk to Emmaus (http://emmaus.upperroom.org/resources) and Chrysalis (http://chrysalis.upperroom.org/about) utilize the ritual process to help disciples renew their faith. Participants are taken away from their home area for a retreat to mark the separation stage of the ritual process. Liminality is heightened during the transition stage by the removal of clocks and schedules and the addition of "surprises" along the way. Finally, the weekend ends with a reincorporation event. When the participants return home, this ritual process has renewed them to a higher level of faith commitment.

Comments from participants (see "Introductory Video" in: http://emmaus.upperroom.org/resources) include:

"I discovered . . . I had my priorities out of order and I became a deeply committed Christian by the time the weekend was over."

"It really refreshed my spirituality. I felt I was recharged, refreshed, and revitalized."

[I made] "a recommitment to not be a passive Christian but to be an active Christian within the church and in my community."

The ritual process helped these disciples gain a kingdom-centered focus for their lives. When no rituals exist, construct appropriate ones to engage intimate issues in culture with the Bible amid the faith community.

Intercultural disciplers draw on the experience of the early church and other cultures to construct meaningful rituals that help disciples experience Christianity in culture.

Reflection and Discussion

1. Why can one weekend be so powerful compared to the normal weekly church service/activities?
2. How can ritual events be incorporated into the discipleship approach for an entire church?

During a two-week intensive class that I have taught over the last ten years, I have observed students develop Christian rituals for the following important discipleship events. Note the intimate nature of many of these events, yet they are rarely discussed or addressed in any discipleship program.

1. Teenagers preparing to obtain a driver's license
2. Youth transitioning to college
3. People leaving a promiscuous lifestyle
4. Unwed mothers entering a church
5. Children of divorce creating a blended family
6. Adults transitioning through a divorce
7. Adults working through childhood sexual abuse

8. Women leaving the sex trade
9. Families adopting children
10. Families dealing with the death of a child
11. Military spouses who return home, reunifying and reintegrating
12. Third-culture kids (e.g., missionary children) returning "home"
13. People welcoming international students to a US seminary
14. People welcoming a refugee family to a church and a community

During each of these rituals, symbols were carefully selected with a ritual specialist to guide the participants through the three-stage ritual process. Sacred space and sacred time were created as the participants drew on biblical stories to address their intimate issues. At the end of the two-week course, participants enacted the rituals. Several students told me later that they followed up on these rituals with dramatic results. The end result was that the disciples experienced the presence of the ultimate God once again, such that they maintained a kingdom-centered life amid the intimate transitions of life.

Constructing Rituals

To construct meaningful rituals for discipleship, consider the following steps:

1. Identify an excluded middle issue that the disciple needs to address. This implies that there is a trusting relationship between the disciple and the discipler. It also means that the discipler must listen to hear the disciple's heart issues. When the disciple is unable to clearly articulate her or his need, it helps at times to ask, "Can you give me a metaphor that describes how you feel?" The person may respond, "I feel like the house is on fire and no one is doing anything," or "I feel like a hamster on a wheel. I'm running hard but not making any progress." Metaphors can open up discussion and help the person identify discipleship issues. In addition, these same metaphors are useful as the discipler later thinks through what symbols to use for the ritual.
   a. As the disciple is describing the need, try to identify the possible root causes of this concern. This may take time, but it is important to address the underlying issues (see sidebar 5.4).
   b. Consider what function you want the ritual to serve. Is this a status-elevation ritual, such as the adolescent rite of passage? Is this an intensification ritual, such as a summer camp? It helps to clearly identify what you would like to happen in the life of the disciple as a result of the ritual. Driver reminds us, "A ritual is a 'transformance'—a

performance designed to change a situation" (1991, 212). Focus on the power of the ritual to be used by God to weaken the grip of oppressive powers/habits, empower the disciple with new strength/hope, and transform individuals and communities.

2. Identify primary roots to address. Out of all the root issues that you have identified, try to pinpoint the main one that needs to be addressed by this ritual. The discipler is sorting out truth from perception at this stage. Relevant biblical themes and stories serve as a plumb line to guide the truth-revealing process. Resist the tendency to drift toward two extremes: uncritically accept everything as truth or critically reject everything that is said.

3. Evaluate individual roots. Scripture, not individual preference, evaluates each of the root issues. Consider the following:

   a. Does Scripture affirm the underlying issue? The ritual will then be created to intensify the disciple's faith.

   b. Does Scripture modify the underlying issue? The ritual will be created to alter or modify the disciple's behavior or thinking.

   c. Does Scripture reject the underlying issue? The ritual will be created to permit the disciple to denounce or break from sinful habits that are preventing him or her from living a Christ-centered life.

   d. Who else is affected by this root issue and how? In constructing the ritual, you may include these stakeholders.

   e. What will happen if we ignore this need? This consideration may promote a sense of urgency, giving the disciple needed energy and desire for the change.

   f. What functional substitutes could be used? If something is to be removed during the ritual, what could replace this? For example, in chapter 4 the sage smoke became a functional substitute for the Native American to overcome his addiction to pornography.

4. Choose symbols. Consider Turner's (1967) properties of symbols in order to select symbols to build the ritual. Taking the effort to consider which symbols work most effectively for a particular person dignifies the participants. Mathias Zahniser calls this the "dignity of effort." Participants in a ritual feel dignified and valued by the effort disciplers exert to choose the best symbols for a well-constructed ritual. Start off by considering:

   a. *Polarization*: What meaning and feeling do you want to communicate? How can the ritual be constructed so that the desire is stirred to reinforce the spiritual significance you want to convey? What symbols will aid in connecting the sensory and ideological poles? The better you know the participants in the ritual, the more carefully the symbols can be selected to connect deep emotions and commitment to the ideology being expressed.

b. *Condensation*: What familiar symbols in the culture communicate various meanings? Since symbols are multivocal, carefully selected symbols can speak to participants based on their varying concerns and needs. Cultural outsiders cannot select these symbols alone; rather, it requires collaboration with local insiders to gain the insiders' perspective.

c. *Unification*: Try to use more than one symbol in the ritual. If an abundance of symbols all speak the same meaning, this drives home the central message in an impactful and memorable way, like a hammer repeatedly pounding a nail on the head. Memory is key in oral cultures, since learning is directly connected to memory (Ong 1982, 33–34). Unifying various symbols through a common thread of meaning makes the ritual a more memorable learning experience.

d. A special gift may be offered for its symbolic value. This gift is carefully selected to help the disciple as he or she reenters society, as Jeremy's Swiss army knife demonstrated. Following the ritual, the gift becomes a steady reminder to trigger the disciple's memories and commitments made during the ritual.

5. Select the biblical themes and stories that you want to emphasize in the ritual to serve as the true myths. These will help to reshape the "operating system" to transform the disciple's worldview.

6. Carefully select the ritual specialist. This person should be someone who is trusted and respected by the individual and the group. While the liminal stage appears chaotic and out of control to the disciple, the ritual specialist is calmly in control, guiding the process smoothly.

7. Create sacred space and sacred time. This means taking the effort to prepare a special location to conduct the ritual. An ideal place is one that is removed from the everyday flow of life. There should be no rush for time. The ritual will conclude only when the intended result is achieved; therefore, a clock will not be used to determine the ending point.

8. Incorporate the three stages of the ritual process.

a. *Separation*: Physically remove the disciple from his or her daily responsibilities. A definite "break" can also be symbolized by using special clothing, shaving the head, having a formal send-off party, and so on.

b. *Transition*: Enhance liminality so that the person does not know what will occur next. You can increase liminality by removing watches, cell phones, schedules, and ordinary conveniences. Some struggle,

Do You Want to Be Healed?

After a lengthy conversation on the plane flight from Africa to the United States, my newfound friend, Femi, leans forward to share a story that he knows is about to rock my world.

"There was a lady in Nigeria who was sick," he starts. "She went from hospital to hospital, but they could not heal her. Finally, she came to our church. We laid hands on her and started to pray."

I am getting excited now. The Nigerian church is dealing with excluded middle issues such as sickness. I expect this story to end with an instantaneous miracle. The story takes a surprising turn, however.

Femi continues, "When we laid hands on her to pray, God spoke to the church leader, 'Ask if she wants to be healed.'"

The sick lady was taken aback by the question at first and disrupted the prayer meeting. She hesitated and then sheepishly responded, "No."

As if the first shock was not enough, she now shared the rest of her story: "When I am well, my husband does not pay any attention to me. When I am sick, he stays with me and speaks kindly to me. I would rather be sick and have my husband's affection than be well and miss it. That is why I do not want to be healed."

Femi concludes, "God being so good, we counseled with the husband, and he promised to take good care of his wife if she got healed. God then healed her, and she is now fine. God also healed the marriage. It is true; we need to take time to consider the roots."

Adapted from Moon (2009a, 5:199–200)

Reflection and Discussion

1. What are the intimate excluded middle issues in this situation?
2. How does an awareness of these root causes change the discipleship approach?
3. How can this information be used to construct a ritual for the excluded middle issues?

challenge, or confusion is helpful. The ritual specialist is careful to make sure that no one gets hurt.

    c. *Reincorporation*: The disciple needs to reenter society but at a different level. This is important both for the individual and for the larger faith community and family. Often the reincorporation is marked by a special meal with family and friends.

Summary

In this chapter we focused on the use of rituals for discipleship. When no existing ritual exists to address excluded middle issues, a disciple can get sidetracked or stuck in her or his faith. When we create meaningful rituals, the disciple's worldview is slowly changed toward a Christ-centered life. The guidelines in this chapter can be used to construct a ritual that addresses an excluded middle issue for discipleship.

107

In the next chapter, we will discuss what to do when rituals already exist in a culture but have not originated from a Christian worldview. Instead of simply rejecting or accepting the ritual, we will explore the careful process of critical contextualization of existing rituals for discipleship.

Activity for Discipling

Concerning the excluded middle issue that you selected to address in chapters 2 and 3, bring together the pieces that you have been working on to construct a discipleship ritual for your disciples. Use the eight steps described above.

In Need of a Ritual

Adapted from Moon (2012d, 141, 149).

The sun grows hot on their backs, as the young missionary family searches for a good location to build their house in the village. They are eager to find the "right place" for ministry in this community as well as a location to raise their four children. The local chief has already been consulted and has given his blessing for the family to live in his village. For several days, the African church leaders have introduced the missionaries to families in their mud homes and to women under the shade tree as they have pounded the millet into powder for the daily meal. After winding through the dusty trails that snaked through the village, they finally agree on a piece of land adjacent to friendly neighbors and located not too far from the market.

The negotiations take several days. It seems that everyone wants to be in on the discussion of how much and what type of gifts should be exchanged. Fortunately, the African church leaders patiently wait through the process and even seem to enjoy the banter and jokes that result. Eventually, chickens are tied up and passed into the hands of the local chief along with some money. The same occurs with the local neighbors who own the land. In exchange for the gifts, the missionaries are given a ninety-nine-year lease to build on the land, since the neighbors are not technically selling the land away. By the end of the negotiations, all parties seem pleased that a new family is moving into the neighborhood.

Construction proceeds along fine—at first. After several weeks of construction, the concrete walls of the building were coming along fine. One night, though, violent winds blow through the village and shake buildings to the core. As the light peeks over the horizon the next morning, the missionary family drives up to the construction site to see the effects of the winds through the night.

Before they can even open the car doors, the local landowner rushes over for a chat. His ruffled clothing and unkempt appearance alert them that something is not quite right.

"I didn't sleep at all last night!" he starts. "The wind was so strong that my whole house was shaking. I was scared for my life."

"Yes, we were concerned as well," the missionary responds. "I have not heard that kind of wind in a long time!"

The neighbor responds, "I was wide awake and suddenly I heard a loud CRASH in the middle of the night. I ran outside to see what it was. That is when I saw this."

He points to the missionaries' house. Sections of concrete blocks are strewn along one side of the house, as one long concrete wall has been forced down by the wind.

Disappointed but not totally overwhelmed, the missionary surveys the damage. He understands that the lack of steel reinforcing bars and temporary horizontal bracing allowed the wall to collapse. He also starts to calculate how long it will take to reconstruct it, as well as the amount of money/materials needed.

The local neighbor, though, is not finished with his story. Actually, it is just beginning,

"Since the wall came down so violently, I rushed to the *bano* last night to find out why this happened. I couldn't sleep until I knew why this occurred and what should be done to protect us all," he exclaims. The earnest look on his face reveals that this is no trivial matter. It is a life and death issue for the whole community.

The missionary glances at the African church leader who has also arrived at the scene. His face becomes very serious, as if he is bracing for another violent wind. He knows that the local medicine man will likely find some spiritual cause for this event. The unseen spirit world always affects the seen physical world.

The local neighbor finally comes out with the real reason for arriving so early to the construction site: "The *bano* told me why the wall fell down. He said that the cause of the problem was due to the evil wood used to make the buildings' window frames. If the window frames are not burned and remade with new wood, then he claims there will be further problems in the construction process. I urge you to burn the window frames today."

The missionary and the African church leader have not heard of this before. It is all news to them. None of their theological training has addressed this type of concern. Furthermore, this is a discipleship issue for all involved.

"How can we respond in a way that is honoring to the God that we serve, as well as satisfying to the local neighbor who fears for our safety?" he confides in the African church leader.

Thinking it through, they reason that they could explain why the wall fell down by demonstrating sound building principles. The wall should have had steel reinforcing and temporary braces—that should be easy to show. They would make sure that this construction technique is changed. However, the neighbor is convinced that there is a spiritual danger that needs to be addressed. If not, things will only get worse.

Eventually, the missionary and church leader decide to construct a ritual to address the roots of the excluded middle issues. They walk together to speak with their neighbor, and they explain their rituals as follows . . .

Reflection and Discussion

1. Explain the excluded middle issue. What are the root concerns?
2. What are some of the sacred stories from the Bible that could be used to address the root concerns?
3. What symbols would you use to construct this ritual?
4. How, where, and when would the ritual be performed? What type of rituals could be performed both before and after construction?
5. How will this ritual affect the discipleship of all the parties involved?

6

Contextualization Process—Tailored Pants Fit Just Right

Borrowed pants: if they are not tight at the ankle, they are loose at the thigh.

—African proverb

Intense Encounter of Jesus

Standing in shorts and bare feet, participants tentatively wait in a single-file line. Quietly, they approach a stick with an eagle feather tied at the top, blowing gently in the wind.

"If you have any animosity or resentment toward someone, you must confess it here," Randy explains. "Then you are ready to go inside the sweat lodge. We will wait until you are ready." His voice trails off. As each person approaches the feather, his or her face reveals deep reflection and honest soul-searching.

Some take longer than others.

As each person enters, Randy offers burning sage to those who desire to "bathe" themselves with the smoke. The smoke reminds them of God's presence, which cleanses sacred spaces. They are about to enter a sacred space amid sacred time.

Bending down, they each crawl on hands and knees to find a spot to sit inside the small circular enclosure. With the entrance still open, light peeks through, revealing anxiety on the faces of the participants. Will I be able to endure the heat? Will I be freaked out by the darkness? Is it safe here? Such questions run through their minds.

Having concluded the separation stage, they prepare for the transition stage.

FLLLPPP. The entrance flap is closed. It is pitch dark. Huddled close to one another, some of the women instantly grab each other's hands for support. This is instantaneous *communitas* created by this liminal condition. After hot rocks are ushered into the middle of the floor, Randy starts with a song. The small tentlike enclosure is filled with praise. Following a few choruses, he gives the opportunity for anyone to offer a song to God.

Round two. More rocks come in. More heat. More steam.

"Pass this dipper of water to the person on your left," Randy explains. "When you receive it, drink all of it. Then you can offer some words to the group. The only stipulation is that they must be words that have come from your heart," he whispers.

Veiled by the darkness, deep thoughts and feelings emerge from the participants, one by one. These feelings have been bottled up for a long time. Perhaps they went Sunday to Sunday, hoping to share them with someone at church but never having the opportunity. These excluded middle issues do not simply go away.

The last person drinks the water.

Round three. As more rocks are brought in, the heat and steam accumulate. Sweat pours from the participants' bodies. Randy now offers words of encouragement and advice. Using Scripture and wisdom accumulated over the years, he addresses the intimate issues that people have revealed earlier. The liminal condition prepares people to listen closely without distractions. They take the

> **Cross-cultural communicators . . . can overlook rituals altogether. At best they may work to contextualize liturgical New Testament rituals such as communion and baptism. However, they are likely to ignore or suppress important indigenous rituals that may be adaptable to church life, such as rituals for conflict resolution, life transitions, and socialization—in other words, rituals important for discipleship.**
>
> Scott Moreau (Moreau, Campbell, and Greener 2014, 275)

words to heart. It has been ten years now, and I can still remember the words that Randy spoke to me!

FLLLPPP. The flap is opened again. Light and refreshing air flood the enclosure. One by one we crawl out of the enclosure, ready to move to the next stage.

Reincorporation. Catching our breath and drinking water like horses, we slowly stagger toward the house. A potluck meal is ready for everyone. Sitting at the table, I notice how we feel much more connected to one another. Like a family that has been through tough times together, we now feel bonded. While this *communitas* wafts throughout the atmosphere like the smell of fresh coffee, I realize that I have just had a powerful encounter of Christian community. I have also just experienced a deep and personal touch with God concerning an excluded middle issue that has been in the back of my mind for a long time.

Deep community.

Deep transformation.

I overhear the group discussion:

"I now feel stronger in my faith—God met me in the sweat lodge," one participant exclaims.

"I had my most intense encounter of Jesus in the sweat lodge!" another affirms.

I realize that I am not the only one who has experienced a significant discipleship event as a result of the contextualized sweat-lodge ritual. (adapted from Moon 2015, 172–74)

The Native American ritual described above, commonly known as the sweat lodge, is an intense ritual of purification. Chapter 4 describes the symbols used to construct the *inipi* ritual of the Lakota Sioux, and others have written about this ritual as well (J. Brown 1989; Bucko 1998). This chapter considers how existing rituals like this one can be contextualized for discipleship.

Could a ceremony like the sweat lodge help to express faith in Jesus in a way that is culturally relevant and biblically faithful for Native Americans who place their faith in Jesus? Is this an aspect of culture that the Creator God provided before the gospel came in order for Native Americans to understand and receive the truth of Jesus? How then can existing rituals like this be contextualized for disciples to keep them kingdom-centered and culturally relevant?

Contextualization of Existing Rituals

Rituals are often abundant in cultures outside the Western world. When these rituals are present, they are often opportunities for contextualization. Instead of simply ignoring the cultural rituals (which leads to split-level Christianity)

> **Wise missionaries will be observant of rituals in their new culture and will constantly think of ways such rituals can be used for evangelism, discipleship, or social transformation.**
>
> Scott Moreau (in Pocock, Van Rheenen, and McConnell 2005, 341)

or simply adopting the existing rituals uncritically (which leads to syncretism), the process of contextualization helps the disciple maintain a Christ-centered life in culture.

Before we discuss the process of contextualizing existing rituals, it will be helpful to understand the dangers that can occur when contextualization does *not* occur. An African people group had a ritual that marked when a woman was pregnant for the first time. To signify her new status, her head was shaved and white powder was applied to her face. The church knew that there were other aspects of this ritual that did not agree with Scripture, so they banned the ritual altogether. By totally eliminating the ritual, however, they overlooked the function that it provided in culture. When the older women noticed a woman with a shaved head and white face, they freely encouraged her and offered advice to the nervous mother-to-be. In addition, people excused the expectant mother from heavy labor (e.g., carrying water, collecting firewood), since they all knew her condition. Without the outward symbols, however, people did not know when a Christian woman was pregnant for the first time. As a result, she missed the encouragement and counsel of the older women, as well as the rest usually granted expectant mothers. Instead of total rejection of the pregnancy ritual, a better way forward is to critically contextualize this ritual to maintain the cultural function while retaining biblical integrity.

Caution: Magic versus Faith

At the outset, it helps to clearly caution intercultural disciplers against the danger of crossing from faith to magic. Because of the powerful nature of symbols and rituals, it is important that an interpretive community take time to carefully critique existing rituals in the contextualization process. We should not be naive and overlook how power can too easily be abused in rituals if proper care is not taken. Symbols can also slip from being representations of reality to becoming the reality itself, as in the case of idolatry or magic, where symbols are considered efficacious.

Faith invites the presence of God to do what God already wants to do. That is, we pray in Jesus's name to invite Jesus to do what he already wants to do in that person's life. We cannot presuppose that we know exactly how Jesus will answer that prayer. In faith, we pray, though, and invite Jesus's presence among us. Faith puts hope in the power of Jesus but not in the objects themselves.

Magic, on the other hand, is an attempt to manipulate the spirit world to effect what would not occur otherwise. For example, a person may put a talisman or charm around his or her neck for protection. This is an attempt to manipulate the spirit world to provide protection. Magic puts hope in the object itself being efficacious, as the object itself is considered to have power residing in it.

Maintaining this distinction is an age-old struggle. God instructed Moses to make the tabernacle, including the ark of the covenant (Exod. 25–26). This symbol was a visual reminder of the presence of God among the Israelites, inviting them to approach God in faith. In time, though, the Israelites turned this faith into magic as they supposed that the ark would magically protect them in battle (1 Sam. 4). They assumed that the power of God resided in the ark and that they could use it to manipulate the spirit world (they eventually realized that, tragically, they could not). Faith invites God to do what God already wants to do, whereas magic manipulates the spirit world to do what it would not do otherwise.

Intercultural disciplers must keep this distinction in mind. Contextualization is driven by faith, *not* by magic. It is important to caution against the slide from faith to magic. Instead of abandoning rituals altogether for fear of magic creeping in, critical contextualization is a process whereby existing rituals can be critiqued and modified. In this way, the function that the ritual provides in culture can be retained or infused with Christian framing, while biblical faith is promoted. Instead of throwing the baby out with the ritual bathwater, we can view some existing rituals as another example of the prevenient grace of God, preparing people to understand and experience the presence of God.

The Goal of Intercultural Discipleship: Worldview Transformation

The goal of intercultural discipleship is to transform the worldview of the disciple so that he or she stays centered on the kingdom of God, as described in chapter 3. In chapter 4 we discussed how worldviews are formed via the interrelationship of behavior/rituals, beliefs, and myths. Figure 6.1 demonstrates how worldviews are expressed in culture.

Figure 6.1
Forms are given meaning to express worldviews in culture

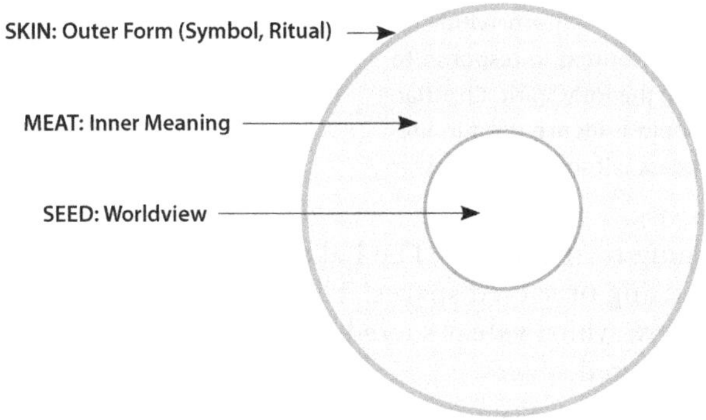

SKIN: Outer Form (Symbol, Ritual)

MEAT: Inner Meaning

SEED: Worldview

The analogy of a peach (or mango) demonstrates how cultural forms are given meaning in the culture to express the worldview. The skin of the peach/mango is the outward, observable part. Likewise, forms are the outward, observable parts of culture. For example, sage smoke prior to entering the sweat lodge is a form that participants see and smell. The forms, though, have no inherent meaning in themselves; rather, societies

Adding on to the Three-Self Church: "Self-Discipling"

In the mid-nineteenth century, Henry Venn and Rufus Anderson first developed the concept of a "three-self" church that would be indigenous to the local cultural context by exhibiting three characteristics: self-governing, self-propagating, and self-supporting. The objective was for missionaries to plant churches that naturally fit into the cultural context and did not rely on or exhibit the characteristics of a foreign culture.

Allen Tippett later expanded the three-self church formula by adding self-image, self-functioning, and self-giving. Later, Paul Hiebert added self-theologizing, and Charles Van Engen added self-missiologizing. Bauta Motty recently expanded the definition of indigenous churches even further by calling for the church to be self-discipling:

> The new model of making disciples among, and by, local believers is Christian socialization or "self-discipling." This model seeks to help an indigenous Christian grow into maturity within his or her cultural context in response to the leading of the Holy Spirit. Christian maturity should evidence itself in lifestyle that bears witness to the power

and the uniqueness of the gospel. The Church should encourage every tribal group . . . to formulate their own indigenous Christian discipling model for local believers. (2013, 299)

Motty advocates contextualization of the Kaninkon peoples' folklore for discipleship. In particular, he notes that "the indigenous traditional rites can be transformed and adapted for church services. Some rites like *huhu, siyoh mantok* and *Siyon* grouping, now have new meaning as they can now serve to disciple Kaninkon Christians" (2013, 300). Note that the case study at the end of this chapter describes one of the traditional rites mentioned by Motty.

Adapted from Terry (2000, 483–84)

Reflection and Discussion

1. Do you agree that "self-discipling" should be added to the criteria for indigenous churches? What difference does your answer make concerning intercultural discipleship?
2. Can you identify traditional rites from various cultures that have been contextualized for discipleship?

ascribe meaning to the forms. The Lakota Sioux ascribe meaning to the sage: the cleansing of sacred spaces. This meaning arises from the Lakota Sioux worldview, which values sacred plants that are given by the Creator God to create sacred spaces.

Note how the form is given meaning by the society based on its worldview. For intercultural disciplers to transform worldviews, then, they must identify existing forms in the culture into which they can instill a Christian meaning in order to shape a Christian worldview. This means that cultural forms should not be rejected outright (e.g., symbols such as sage or rituals like the sweat lodge), since they are useful for expressing the meaning of elements of a relationship with Christ in order to shape a Christian worldview. This is the process of contextualization.

Principles to Guide the Contextualization Process

Principles to guide the contextualization process are needed in order to avoid the dangers of syncretism and split-level Christianity (described in chap. 2). We can identify at least five important components: (1) hermeneutical community, (2) Holy Spirit–led and inspired, (3) emic and etic perspectives, (4) mother-tongue Scripture, and (5) evidence of God in culture. We'll touch on each briefly in turn.

Hermeneutical Community

For rituals to be significant discipleship tools, proper contextualization must be performed in a community, interpreting both the context and Scripture. Usually this process begins in a small group and widens gradually. It could start with church elders, then gradually expand to include other local pastors, with eventual input from regional and perhaps global church voices. The goal is to listen to the perspective of those close to the culture *and* to the perspective of those more removed from the culture (i.e., outsiders, who provide the etic view, discussed below). The point is that the community is the interpreter/theologian, not simply one person or one family making all the decisions (Schreiter 1985, 16).

Holy Spirit–Led and Inspired

Contextualization is ultimately a process of inviting the Holy Spirit to speak concerning areas of the gospel and culture. This requires a period of waiting. Usually it includes fasting and prayer. Instead of regarding contextualization as a good academic exercise, we should consider it an opportunity for the Holy Spirit to speak into culture, breathing life and clarity into areas that God has wanted to reveal for a long time.

Emic and Etic Perspectives

Kenneth Pike (1954) used the terms "emic" and "etic" to describe how people learn language and also culture differently, depending on whether they were born in the culture (emic, derived from the term "phonemic") or outside the culture (etic, derived from the term "phonetic").

The emic perspective is portrayed by the Builsa proverb "Nichaano ze zabuura nyiamwa" (The visitor does not know that the millet water offered him comes from the seeds meant for sowing). The visitor has assumed that it was just another meal, but the family knows that this meal was made from the seeds that they were saving to plant for next year. It would be too shameful, however, not to feed the visitor, so the family suffers while the visitor consumes the meal happily. In the emic perspective, insiders have knowledge that outsiders simply do not notice.

The etic perspective is portrayed by the Builsa proverb "Yala nuru ale a nya waiik zuk pein" (The man at a distance sees the arrow in an antelope's head). While those inside the house assume that this is another good day, the one outside the house sees that enemies are already shooting arrows at them. The etic perspective emphasizes that outsiders have knowledge that the insiders simply do not notice.

Both perspectives offer important insights (seeing what the other misses), and both also have limitations (missing what the other sees). For intercultural disciplers, the value of combining both perspectives cannot be stressed enough. When both the emic and the etic perspectives are understood, gross mistakes in contextualization can be avoided.

One of the core values of the United Methodist Church, for example, is that it is a connectional system: United Methodists worldwide are connected to one another. As such, decisions for the denomination cannot be made unilaterally by one conference alone. For issues that deal with the gospel and culture,

---

Given the capacity of ritual to convey meaning to the Taiwanese, it seems highly improper to attempt to plant and sustain a form of Christianity devoid of meaningful rites.

Jim Courson (1998, 312)

United Methodists around the world must listen to their various perspectives prior to voting. The combination of the emic and the etic perspectives helps the United Methodist Church arrive at sound decisions by avoiding the limited perspectives of one culture alone.

Mother-Tongue Scripture

The Bible, when translated into the mother tongue of the people, becomes the "interpreter of all culture and tradition" (Bediako 1999, 1). The hermeneutical community must use the mother-tongue Bible to interpret aspects of the ritual that are to be accepted, modified, or rejected. Once the Bible is available in the mother tongue of the people, it is fully a part of the fabric of culture, since it in the language of the people. It is also fully of God, since it is God's word to us.

Evidence of God in Culture

A creation theology reminds us that God is pleased with creation. God created humankind in the image of God; subsequently, humans created societies that bear marks of God's image. The cultures that humans inhabit, then, are not inconsequential; rather, they are determined by God "so that they [humans] would seek him and perhaps reach out for him and find him, though he is not far from any one of us" (Acts 17:27). Amid the stain of sin, God has left signposts of God's presence to point disciples to Christ. Intercultural disciplers look for this evidence of God in culture.

Discipleship Examples

The more we look for God's signposts in culture, the more they can be found. In particular, look for intimate or excluded middle moments when a ritual helps to maintain continuity amid transition. This could be as simple as a ceremony to celebrate when a baby first smiles, around three months of age (Charles 2013), or blessing the farm tools, seeds, and workers during the planting season (Neeley 2013). A group of seminary students identified the following rituals in various cultures that could be appropriately contextualized for discipleship:

1. *Quinceañera* adolescent girl rite of passage
2. Masai adolescent male rite of passage
3. Lakota vision quest
4. Ugandan marriage ritual
5. Mi'kmaq wedding ritual
6. Turkana *akinyonyo* postwedding ritual for Christian transformation and identification
7. Native American Midewiwin society *madoodiswan* lodge ceremony
8. Reconciliation ritual for North Korean defectors entering a South Korean church
9. *Guru diksha* ceremony used for Christian baptism and initiation of Hindus in India
10. *Musalaha* reconciliation rituals for Bedouin people
11. Buddhist death rituals for bereaved Japanese families
12. Fasting of formerly Muslim Bengali believers for Ramazan (often transliterated "Ramadan," Ramazan is the transliterated pronunciation common in south Asia [Friedman and Toon 2008, 5])
13. Female puberty ritual in Tanzania

All these rituals were enacted in the classroom as preparation for contextualization in the future. As an example of the contextualization of rituals, here is an excerpt from "The Liminality of Ramazan in the Context of the 'Isai Jamat," by Matthew Friedman and Jonathan Toon (2008, 9–11).

Winding his way back through the bazaar carrying his large pot of delicious *halim* (stew), Hassan found his way to the door of Mannan's building, and then struggled up the two flights of stairs to the now-familiar door, and rang the bell. He was glad to have made it; he really wouldn't have wanted to miss taking *iftar* (the fast-breaking ritual at sundown during Ramazan) with everyone. Yusuf answered the door with a big smile and took the clay pot from Hassan, his face beaming that much more widely as he smelled its contents.

He greeted Hassan with a vigorous "*As-salaam wa-laikum,*" receiving back a hearty "*Walaikum as-salaam, wa rahmatullah!*"

Yusuf was, like Hassan, a fairly new member of the *jamat* (local word for the Greek word *ekklēsia*), and he was also here for his first Ramazan as a follower of Isa (Jesus). Hassan entered and saw through the crack in the kitchen door that Mannan's wife was making last-minute preparation for the *iftar*. Yusuf quickly handed the *halim* pot to Mannan, who carried it into the kitchen.

The other eight members of the *jamat* were already seated in a circle and ready as Mannan invited Hassan to go wash in preparation for the meal and prayers that would follow. He quickly washed, placed his *tupi*, or prayer cap, on his head, and took his seat with the others. By now the food was coming out, and each one showed the day's weariness and anticipation of the fast-breaking to come. Finally, they could hear the *azan*, or call to prayer, from the mosque just a block away, and each one took a date and then a long, cool drink of lemonade. They then quickly polished off the fried vegetables, fruit, and other snacks, and when the *halim* was brought out, Hassan beamed with pride as Mannan announced that he had brought it for everyone.

The food finished, they each filed into the bathrooms and washed their mouths and hands, and then lined up to pray as they had always done, ever since they were children.

"*Allah hu Akbar!*" Mannan chanted as they went through their paces of the *namaz* liturgy.

With the second round, however, instead of verses from the Qur'an in Arabic, Mannan chanted the first three verses of Yohanna in their mother tongue,

> In the beginning was the Word,
> And the Word was with God
> And the Word was God
> He was with God in the beginning.
> Through him all things were made; without him nothing was made
> that has been made.

"*Allah hu Akbar!*" came the chant again, and they all bowed, foreheads pressed to the ground.

After the *namaz* was finished, they rearranged themselves into a circle, and this time Ali, who had been a follower of Isa for more than seven years, was asked if he had something that he wanted to share. He smiled and told again a story which they had all heard at least once, of how Isa had appeared to him in a dream, and how not long afterwards he had met another believer in the bazaar. After three weeks of conversations with Bilal, the urgency of their discussion fueled by the vision, Ali had put his faith in Isa. He had struggled afterward with some ostracism from his family, and had almost lost his wife, Zarina, in the process, but she sat contentedly across from him, now his sister in faith as well as his wife and the mother of their four boys, who were playing in the other room.

The praises began again, with Yusuf contributing a *qawwali* he had composed about Isa's love for his people, and more *zikr* (a remembrance) based on various verses in the *Injil* (New Testament), which were becoming more and more familiar to Hassan as they met daily. Finally, after nearly an hour of

---

Symbols and ceremonies, the discipling tools of religion, represent crucial resources for effective discipling. . . . The system of symbols is typically narrated in myths and dramatized in rituals.

Mathias Zahniser (1997, 63)

---

songs, prayer for one another, and *zikr*, Mannan's wife brought out a chapati, unleavened flat bread, and a cup of juice. With Mannan leading, they chanted one final *zikr* about their Isa, who died and rose from the dead, as they dipped pieces of chapati into the juice.

As he said his final salaams and walked home, Hassan marveled at how spiritually "full" he felt in this month of fasting, and how excited he was even for the next day's fasting, for it would be capped by fellowship as wonderful as this had been. The shared meal had brought them together as brothers and sisters, and as they prayed, chanted, worshiped, and ate together, they were becoming a family in the mercy of Al Masih.

Notice how "at home" this ritual is for the Muslim-background believer. Because it resonates with a part of his culture, it feels familiar. It also fills an important need in his life as he is voluntarily observing the fast (outward form). Instead of the usual meaning that he learned as a child, though, this ritual form is ascribed Christian meaning that is now transforming his worldview. Since there is the danger that this approach could slip into syncretism, however, a careful process of critically contextualizing existing rituals should be observed.

Steps for Critical Contextualization of Existing Rituals

Hiebert has developed the process of critical contextualization to contextualize appropriate existing rituals for discipleship (Hiebert 1987), using the following four-step process.

Phenomenological Study

Meet with other disciplers in the cultural context and describe what is occurring. Try to identify the cultural forms used and the possible meanings that the culture ascribes to these forms. Study each of the symbols, carefully considering the multiple meanings connected to them. Consider primary and secondary meanings. During this period of brainstorming, temporarily withhold judgment. This restraint prevents the hermeneutical community from reacting too quickly with knee-jerk responses. A phenomenological approach requires that participants be like reporters in describing what they see. They should do their best to portray the event using the indigenous terms and categories of thought. One way to understand the function of the ritual is to ask insiders, "What would happen if this ritual were no longer practiced?" Ideally, both the emic and the etic voices will be heard.

By way of illustration, we can look at a few aspects of the contextualization process for *iftar*, the fast-breaking described above. The intercultural disciplers described the symbols involved, including the *halim* stew, customary greetings, *tupi* cap, *zikr* (practice of chanting a devotional formula), waiting for the *azan*, and ritual washing. They also identified how this ritual connects with an important theme in Islam concerning *baraka*:

> The power of *baraka*, or blessing in the sense in which it becomes an intangible power, [is] akin to what anthropologists often refer to as *mana*. . . . The person who joins a group in breaking the fast together (and likely joining in group liturgical prayer following) adds to the *baraka* already present in the group and is seen as well to benefit from it. (Friedman and Toon 2008, 6)

These insights are useful preparation for the following steps in critical contextualization.

Ontological Critique

Based on the reflections and discussion of step 1, try to determine the underlying issues in the culture that have prompted this ritual. That is, what needs does it satisfy, what values are emphasized, and what feelings are promoted? Which of the possible roots identified is really prompting/requiring this ritual? Which of the root issues identified is secondary? Consider the symbols involved, and try to identify the primary meanings that are emphasized in the ritual. This process will take some time due to the multivocal nature of symbols.

Is this ritual serving a godly function in culture? To answer this question, consider what Scripture has to say about the roots identified. Look for relevant biblical themes, biblical stories that relate to the root issues. Try to guard against proof texts, individual Scripture texts taken in isolation from the overall context of Scripture. Resist the tendency to drift toward two extremes: uncritically accepting everything as valid or critically rejecting everything as un-Christian.

For the *iftar* fast-breaking observance described above, the cross-cultural disciplers observed that the month of Ramazan is of great importance to devout Muslims because they believe that God began to reveal the holy Qur'an to Muhammad during this month. For Sunni Muslims, the Qur'an represents the uncreated, eternal Word of God. This is contrasted with Scripture, where Jesus is the eternal Word of God (e.g., John). The fast is often broken with others in communal gatherings. The liminality of the fast creates *communitas* among the participants. This bonding is an important function of the ritual that could assist the church. The intercultural disciplers also noted that participants observe the fast breaking in order to maintain one of the five pillars of Islam, required for the accrual of merit or simply to avoid hell. This is also contrasted with the grace of God (cf. Galatians, Romans). While the *zikr* chanting is a strong mnemonic device, it is sometimes done to work the devotee into a state of trance or ecstasy. These forms will require some transformation prior to their contextualization.

Critical Evaluation

Based on steps 1 and 2 above, the hermeneutical community now critically evaluates each of the root issues, symbols, and ritual functions. The mother-tongue Scripture is like a plumb line that is used to determine when cultural pieces are out of line. Consider these questions:

1. Does Scripture affirm the issue/symbol/function? Consider ways to affirm this in the discipleship ritual.

2. Does Scripture modify the issue/symbol/function? Consider modifying or altering this aspect for the discipleship ritual.

3. Does Scripture reject the issue/symbol/function? The ritual will be created to denounce or break from sinful habits that are preventing the disciple from living a kingdom-centered life.

4. Who else is affected by this root issue and how? In constructing the ritual, you may include these stakeholders.

5. What will happen if we ignore this need? This question may promote a sense of urgency, giving the disciple needed energy and desire for the change.

6. What functional substitutes could be used? That is, if something is to be removed during the ritual, what could replace this?

7. Are other aspects/people of the culture affected by this? How should they be considered when accepting, modifying, or rejecting aspects of the ritual?

For the *iftar* ritual, the cross-cultural disciplers affirmed the symbols of the *halim*, the *tupi*, greetings, prayer form, and ritual washing. They also modified the *zikr* chanting, as well as the function of the ritual to promote Christian bonding, and the meaning of the ritual to focus on Jesus as the eternal Word of God. In addition, they rejected the compulsory nature of the fast, which strives to gain merit with God, yet affirmed the place of fasting as a part of spiritual life and discipline that can facilitate drawing closer to the Lord communally as well as individually.

Missiological Transformation

Take the reflections from the steps above and decide from among the viable options which path to take. Choose the symbols that affirm Christian meanings that will transform the participants' worldview. Select the most potent biblical stories/themes that address the important root issues. Decide on functional substitutes to replace symbols or other elements that were rejected. Decide how to involve the church, the community, and individuals in the ritual.

1. When choosing the symbols to accept, modify, or reject, consider:
    a. *Polarization*: What meaning and feeling should this ritual communicate? How can the ritual be adapted so that the desire is stirred to reinforce the spiritual significance that you want to convey? What symbols will aid in connecting the sensory and ideological poles? The better you know the participants in the ritual, the more precisely you can select the symbols to connect deep emotions and commitment to the ideology being expressed.
    b. *Condensation*: Carefully consider the various meanings communicated in the symbols and the ritual. Are there unintended meanings that we need to be careful of? Since symbols are multivocal, this step will take time and counsel.
    c. *Unification*: Try to use more than one symbol in the ritual. An abundance of symbols that all speak the same meaning drives home the central message in an impactful and memorable way, like a hammer repeatedly pounding the nail on the head. Unifying various symbols through a common thread of meaning makes the ritual a more memorable learning experience.
2. Consider the role of gift giving and how it is used to initiate and reinforce relationships.

3. Select the biblical themes and stories that you want to emphasize in the ritual. These will help to reshape the "operating system" to transform the disciples' worldview.

4. Carefully select the ritual specialist. This person should be someone who is trusted and respected by the individual and the group. While the liminal stage appears chaotic and out of control to the disciple, the ritual specialist is calmly in control, guiding the process smoothly.

5. Create sacred space and sacred time. This requires making the effort to prepare a special location to conduct the ritual. An ideal place is one that is removed from the everyday flow of life. There should be no rush for time. The ritual will conclude only when the intended result is achieved; therefore, a clock will not be used to determine the ending point.

6. Consider how the three stages of the ritual process are carried out in the ritual. Do you need to pay more attention to one particular stage? Consider questions such as, Is there sufficient liminality to promote *communitas*? Is there sufficient participation, play, and creativity? Is the presence of the Holy Spirit experienced? Is sufficient care taken to promote faith and avoid magic? What important words or phrases are spoken that must be retained or modified?

For the *iftar* ritual, note the gift of *halim* that Hassad brought to the gathering. Many other symbols were retained, since they connect both a sensory and an ideological meaning in the ritual. The *zikr* was modified to help oral learners memorize John 1:14 in order to focus on Jesus as the eternal Word of God.

The intercultural disciplers noticed that the ritual followed the three-phase ritual structure. Separation starts when the fast is initiated. The liminality created by the fasting can result in strong Christian bonding. Reintegration occurs during the evening fast-breaking celebration. In order to stress that the fasting is not a means to earn merit with God, they emphasized that this is a voluntary fast as part of the Christian struggle to overcome the flesh. This joyous offering to God is not, however, required of Christians.

The disciplers realized that this fast breaking is theologically parallel to Christmas. It recognizes the eternal Word of God coming to earth. Culturally, it is the most joyous local celebration and an annual time of giving gifts to children and friends. This joyous aspect of the ritual was maintained with new Christian meaning.

Status Reversal

Iftar is an example of a ritual that is celebrated every year, like Christmas and Easter. Such rituals are called calendrical rites, meaning that they are planned

Celtic Christianity

George Hunter (2000) delightfully describes how Patrick, from England, engaged in intercultural discipleship to the Irish in the late fourth/early fifth century. Among other things, Patrick understood the culture and ways of the Irish such that he employed their oral literature, including "parable, story, poetry, song, visual symbols, visual arts, and perhaps, drama to engage the Celtic peoples' remarkable imaginations" (2000, 21).

Hunter notes that Patrick prayed for sick people, exorcised demons, counseled people, mediated conflicts, and even blessed a river so that people could catch more fish (2000, 21). Gradually daily rituals were developed to accompany mundane activities such as getting dressed, starting the morning fire, washing clothes/dishes, going to work, healing diseases, and finally going to bed (33).

By engaging "right brain thinking," Patrick used symbols, such as the "Celtic knot" (denoting God's protection, eternity, progress of the pilgrim life) and the cross with a circle in it—denoting the integration of creation and redemption (Hunter 2000, 74).

Hunter observes that "Celtic Christianity preferred continuity rather than discontinuity"; therefore, the Celts often "retained, and 'Christianized,' some of the prior religion's holy days, festivals, and ceremonies" (93).

This discipleship approach worked, as Hunter concludes, "In two or three generations, all of Ireland had become substantially Christian" (2000, 35).

Reflection and Discussion

1. What are the excluded middle issues that Patrick identified and addressed? How did he do this?
2. What was the role of symbols, rituals, and other oral literature in the Celtic discipleship approach?
3. Hunter believes that Christians can "regain the West . . . again" by using the Celtic model. What can intercultural disciplers learn from the Celtic model of the fourth/fifth century that can be applied to discipleship today in other cultural contexts?

by the calendar, in contrast with life-cycle rites (e.g., the early church catechesis, adolescent rites of passage) and crisis rites (e.g., sweat lodge, healing). Table 6.1 summarizes the characteristics of the rituals that we have discussed (Hiebert 2008; Turner 1995; Van der Hart 1983; Zahniser 1997).

		TABLE 6.1	
		Taxonomy of Rituals	
	Calendrical Rituals	Life-Cycle Rituals	Crisis Rituals
Function	Continuity	Transition	Transition
Frequency	Regularly	Once	As needed
Scheduling	Planned (by calendar)	Planned (when ready)	Unplanned (when needed)
Change sought	Intensify present status (may use temporary status reversal)	Status elevation	Status restoration

	Calendrical Rituals	Life-Cycle Rituals	Crisis Rituals
Overcome	Forgetfulness	Stagnancy or immaturity	Threats to shalom
Group size	Large group	Small group	Individuals
Examples	*Iftar*, Ramazan, White Sunday, Easter, Christmas, Halloween, Sunday church service, Communion, April Fools' Day, New Year's Eve	Catechesis, birth, puberty, marriage, death, hajj, baptism, walk to Emmaus	Sweat lodge, healing, reconciliation

One important aspect of calendrical rituals that we have not yet discussed is the occasional presence of temporary status reversal. Status reversal occurs when the participants who normally occupy the low-status positions in society are temporarily given power over those who normally have higher status. This may appear, at first blush, to be counterintuitive and strange, but status reversal has a very powerful function in society.

Ill will or tension accumulates in a society throughout the year. Those not in power have little voice to change the status quo, so they have to "stuff it down." To discharge these ill feelings, calendrical rituals sometimes encourage status reversal. This acts as a safety valve to relieve the pressure. At the end of the prescribed ritual, the society is once again rejuvenated and the structure of society is reaffirmed.

SIDEBAR 6.3

Jesus's Contextualization of Rituals

Jesus identified the existing rituals of Israel and then contextualized them for new meaning. James and Jeannette Krabill note,

> Jesus understood the importance of rituals when he took common practices already "ritualized" in Jewish culture—like washing feet, eating bread, and drinking wine—and invested them with additional meaning by commanding his disciples, whenever they gathered, to "do this in memory of me." . . . When faith communities, following the model of Jesus, do the creative work of embedding Christian rituals in already existing, culturally appropriate societal patterns, the meaning of such practices

is deepened in the minds and hearts of believers. (2016, 83)

Reflection and Discussion

1. Consider the various rituals that Jesus observed and contextualized. Where do they fit in table 6.1?
2. How did Jesus's contextualization of the rituals affect the status of the disciples: intensification, reversal, elevation, or restoration?
3. Compare these rituals to the ancient Israelite rituals. What did Jesus affirm, modify, or reject in each one?
4. How can Jesus's example be a model for intercultural disciplers in relation to ritual today?

127

Status Reversal Reinforces Structure?

A simple example of a status-reversal ritual that reinforces structure is the April Fools' Day observance in the West. For one day of the year, participants are allowed to play tricks on one another. They know that they cannot go too far with the tricks, since the day will be over and those in power will once again regain power. But this ritual allows ill feelings to be discharged for a short period of time. At the end of the day, people reaffirm the structure: "I am glad that we do not trick each other every day. It would be a crazy place to live if we could not trust each other."

The status-reversal ritual functions, ironically, to reinforce the structure of society. By encouraging people to go against the norms for a short time, it affirms that the norms of society are proper and good. Following the ritual, people reenter society with the norms of society reanimated and reinvigorated.

It is important to maintain this function of status-reversal rituals. If the ritual is rejected outright, the function of the ritual is lost as well. If a functional substitute is not found, society is worse off. Halloween also falls into this category of status-reversal rituals. Children are warned by their parents not to eat too much candy throughout the year. The children are tempted to disobey this rule. One day in the year, they go to their neighbors with a bag full of candy and ask for *more* candy! At the end of the day, the kids eat too much candy and feel sick. They then realize that it is not good to eat too much candy—thanks to this status-reversal ritual. The structure is reinforced by the presence of anti-structure in the status-reversal ritual, which can also be applied to intercultural discipleship.

White Sunday, a Status-Reversal Ritual

The White Sunday ritual performed by the church in American Samoa is an example of a status-reversal ritual that is used for discipleship (Roach 1988). One Sunday of the year, each child in the village is given a new white church outfit. Wearing these outfits proudly to church that day, the children conduct the church service. They lead the prayers, read passages from the Bible, sing hymns (many are memorized especially for this service), recite Scripture passages from memory, and enact dramas. By performing the duties normally reserved for the pastor and the adults, the children temporarily reverse status with the adults. For the first time, perhaps, the children start to appreciate how much effort is involved in performing a church service.

Following the service, a lavish meal is served. On this day, the adults serve the children first, unlike during the rest of the year. Usually, the children serve the elders first, followed by the adults, which means that the children eat what is left over. "The order in which people are served food in Samoa, for instance, is a fairly reliable indicator of the relative statuses of those present" (Roach

1988, 180). Normally, elders have the highest status, followed by adults, with the children on the bottom. On White Sunday, though, the status is reversed, and the children are served first. Now the adults have to wait patiently on the children, waiting to eat after them. This reminds the adults that they should appreciate the children's service and patience throughout the year.

The status reversal experienced during the calendrical ritual of White Sunday becomes a "ceremonial safety valve" (Roach 1988, 180) that relieves the tensions accumulated over the year. It reinforces and reinvigorates the norms in the church and society. Intercultural disciplers can use status reversal for the discipleship of youth and adults.

Contextualizing Older Christian Rituals

So far we have discussed the contextualization of rituals from other cultures. Older Christian rituals can also be contextualized for contemporary purposes. The following story describes a powerful ritual whereby a senior mentor passed the baton of ministry to the younger generation. The Communion service was contextualized for this occasion as follows (based on my personal recollection).

> Weary from the short night's sleep, I arise early to meet the others at six o'clock in the morning. Stepping out into the blackness of night, I see fifteen shapes huddled together. The cool blast of morning air stirs me awake.
>
> Darrell, our mentor, faces the group.
>
> Like a football quarterback calling a play in the huddle, Darrell looks into the faces surrounding him and explains, "I called you here at this early hour for a special reason. For the next several minutes, I want you to think about the reason that we have come together this weekend."
>
> The looks on the faces of those gathered portray a mixture of bewilderment and excitement. It reminds me of the way the disciples' faces must have appeared when Jesus spoke with them prior to observing the Last Supper.
>
> "Walk with me in silence. If you need to speak to someone, please use a whisper," Darrell continues.
>
> Without another word, Darrell takes off at a quick pace.
>
> Quietly the group follows Darrell down the path and into the woods. I can see his silhouette in the moonlight, but we do not know where he is taking us. No one dares to utter a word.
>
> Silence—for twenty minutes.
>
> Finally, there is a sharp turn in the path. At the top of the hill stands an old stone chapel, where the entourage comes to a halt.
>
> "I brought you here this weekend since I am passing the baton of ministry on to you. I still plan to be active for the next fifteen years, but I want to empower you to do even more than I have done. Please take a seat inside."
>
> Seated inside, the group is "all ears" to hear what is next. The chapel is so silent you could hear a pin drop.

Discipling with Symbols and Rituals on the Emmaus Road

In Luke 24:13–35, we see a picture of Jesus encountering two potential disciples. Even though these two had heard eyewitnesses of the resurrection that morning, look at the direction that they were walking—away from Jerusalem. This indicates the likely direction of their faith as well. In the centered set approach (see chap. 3), they would seem to be walking away from the center instead of toward it.

Even though Jesus had a busy schedule (rising from the dead that morning would qualify as such!), he took the time to listen to the excluded middle issues of these two potential disciples. In the midst of their confusion and disappointment, Jesus surveyed the entire Old Testament to explain what was written about the Messiah. Since the journey was approximately seven miles long, it is likely that Jesus spent over two hours sharing with these two men! Even still, they did not recognize him.

Finally, when words were not enough, Jesus used something else to communicate. The symbol of bread likely triggered a memory of the Last Supper ritual, such that their eyes were finally opened. The symbol connected both their senses and ideology such that they were finally inspired to turn the direction of their lives and rush back to Jerusalem that very night. In short, the symbol encouraged them to "want to do" what they "should do." In the centered set approach, the disciples were redirected to the center through Jesus's discipleship approach. To address their excluded middle issues, Jesus used what wise disciplers of today often use: symbols inside rituals.

Reflection and Discussion

1. Why did Jesus start this discipleship encounter with two questions? What was the initial result?
2. What is the role of words in this encounter? How do symbols fill the gap when words are not enough (even though they were words from Jesus himself)?
3. What can we learn from Jesus's example about the use of symbols and rituals, along with words for discipleship?

Reaching into a bag, Darrell pulls out a metal baton. Inscribed on it are the words "And the things you have heard me say in the presence of many witnesses entrust to reliable men who will also be qualified to teach others" (2 Tim. 2:2).

Darrell begins, "I have been mentored by four key people in my ministry— Eugene Nida, Alan Tippett, Chuck Kraft, and Paul Hiebert. They passed on to me what I have passed on to you. Take this baton and carry it forward for the next generation."

Calling each one forward, Darrell speaks words of personal blessing, encouragement, and challenge. I look over at the others and realize that there is not a dry eye in the house. That explains the moisture in my own eyes. The feeling of being empowered by this man that we know and love is overwhelming.

Breaking the bread and passing the cup of juice, we share Communion together, which unites the group to an even larger community and faith legacy. The cracked and weary beams above my head in this chapel remind me of the long legacy that we are sitting under.

As we step out of the church, the morning sun splashes light on our faces. I look at the others a bit differently now. Tightly bound together as fellow pilgrims, we move toward home.

Was this a dream? I have this feeling that something wonderful just happened in my own life. I feel empowered, affirmed, united to others, and challenged. I have a new appreciation for the Last Supper that Jesus shared with his disciples. I have also been given some direction for ministry. The lightness of their steps and bright glow on their faces reveals that the others in the group feel the same way.

Summary

In this chapter, we focused on the process of contextualization. While a lack of contextualization overlooks the evidence of God in culture, critical contextualization aims to instill the cultural forms with Christian meaning in order to form a Christian worldview. Intercultural disciplers need to apply the principles of critical contextualization:

1. Slippage into a magical use of symbols must be prevented.
2. Contextualization is best done in a hermeneutical community, starting locally and working outward.
3. Time should be allowed for the Holy Spirit to breathe creative insight and discovery. This may also require periods of fasting and prayer.
4. Disciplers must listen to both the emic and the etic perspectives in order to overcome the limitations of each one and leverage the benefits of both.
5. The mother-tongue Scripture is the best interpreter of all culture and tradition.
6. For a good point to start contextualization, look for evidence of God in the culture. Existing rituals and symbols often meet important needs in culture and serve vital functions.
7. The critical contextualization process provides a pathway to contextualize existing rituals:
   a. *Phenomenological study*: Objectively study and describe the ritual, using the indigenous terms and categories of thought.
   b. *Ontological critique*: Discover the root issues that are being addressed by the ritual. Also identify the function of the ritual in culture and the relevant Scripture stories/themes.
   c. *Critical evaluation*: Use Scripture to accept, modify, or reject each aspect of the ritual.
   d. *Missiological transformation*: Decide which options will be implemented to modify the ritual to express Christian meaning in culture.

8. Disciplers should consider the use of temporary status reversal, particularly for calendrical rituals.

For intercultural disciplers, existing rituals in culture are fertile ground for contextualization. When we engage the gospel with culture, evidence of God in culture is revealed. Contextualization is not limited to existing rituals, though. A similar process can be applied to other aspects of culture in order to keep followers of Jesus on a kingdom-centered path. In the next chapter, we will apply the intercultural discipleship method of contextualization to indigenous stories.

Activity for Discipling

1. Reread the leadership-transition ritual with Darrell in this chapter that drew from and contextualized the Communion ritual. Consider constructing a ritual with your disciples that incorporates the elements that have been discussed in the book so far. It would be ideal if you could find a place to take them away from their normal routines in order to increase liminality.
2. During and after the ritual that you conduct with your disciples, look for evidence of change, such as *communitas* and increased commitment to their faith and the faith community.

Becoming a Kaninkon

Adapted from Motty (2013, 173–77).

The day has finally arrived. Magani is finally going to be incorporated into the life of the Kaninkon people. While he has lived here for many years, he was not born among this people. As a result, he has always been considered an *nsuwed* (stranger). He feels excluded from the community life, since he cannot participate in many of the social activities of the people. He has not been initiated into the religious life of the people either. In short, he feels like he is no better than a child!

He has been informed that the conversion ritual for the Kaninkon people is a means to *siyoh a tiyah nisih* (incorporate into the life of the society) that will provide all the rights and privileges of being a part of the Kaninkon people.

Getting to this day has not been easy or quick, though. He remembers the questions lobbed at him from the elders: "How long have you been here? How long do you plan to stay here? Are you willing to remain in the village for life?"

When Magani agreed to become a citizen of the village, the head of the household where he lived was informed, and a date was set for the ritual.

Today, most of the people in the village are gathered together to witness this festive event. Looking around the circle, Magani recognizes all the faces of the people, including the house head, who is front and center. The elders motion for Magani to sit on the ground in the middle of the circle. Nervous, yet excited, he shuffles his feet forward and sits down.

One of the elders steps forward and looks out at the faces gathered around the circle. He then proclaims, "*Rig a zego yeh-ito. Rig nyung-tod. Gbed-modi a tudo nyeh. Toda gun kag nunung.*" (God escorted him to us [our village]. God loves us. Our ancestors sent him to us. We do not reject any person.)

Magani listens to every word spoken as he looks around the circle to see the heads nod in approval.

The elder now faces Magani and continues, "*Wo-a song ito da, diya zhi tod. Wo ye dyih wamod a to ti se wamwi. Tin-too mi. Tod da a tawoo.*" (You have been with us and you know us. You shall be our own and we shall be yours. Welcome. We have accepted you.)

The elder takes a drink of *huhu* (porridge) and then passes it on to the other elders to take a drink in turn. While Magani enjoyed *huhu* before, he knew this day would be different. Today, the *huhu* is mixed with some medicine that is believed to *ring disiyong mani* (meaning, "to make the convert to forget about going away, but to remain permanently with the people"). After all the elders have taken a drink, it is passed to Magani.

Taking a deep breath, he swallows the *huhu* and breathes a sigh of relief.

The elder then sprinkles the *huhu* on Magani's body before sprinkling it over all of the people gathered in the circle. Everyone knows the belief that if Magani now wants to run away, the *huhu* will trap or kill him.

The elder now warns the crowd gathered that no one can call Magani a stranger anymore. If anyone is caught doing so, they will be fined. Magani is now like any other person of the society. The ritual has removed all foreignness in him. He can now be circumcised, if he was not before. He can also marry any female in the village, and he will be given farmland. Furthermore, he can be initiated into the culture of the village and tribe. Magani must observe all religious beliefs and practices, as well as adhere strictly to all social and value systems of the society.

The pastor of the local church was also in the circle of people gathered around Magani. He witnessed the entire ritual and was touched by it. He has known Magani for some time, but now he looks at him differently.

"He is really one of us now!" the pastor muses.

The ritual has elevated Magani's status in the eyes of the people and also in Magani's own mind. As the pastor is walking home, he reflects on the church service that he is planning for this week. They are welcoming new members into the church. They want the church to make the new members feel at home, and they also want the new members to feel like they now belong to a special family of God. In short, the pastor muses, "We want the new members to feel like Magani—one of us!"

The pastor calls the church elders together and discusses his thoughts with them.

"I observed how Magani's status changed today," the pastor says. "The ritual provided a meaningful transition for him and the entire village. I suggest that we contextualize this ritual for Christian meaning in our own church this week. I think that we should start to do this by . . . "

Reflection and Discussion

1. Where should the pastor start the contextualization process?
2. Which elements of the Kaninkon ritual should be accepted? Which elements should be modified? Which elements should be rejected?
3. How would you emphasize faith and guard against magic in the ritual?
4. Explain the biblical stories that you would emphasize, as well as the symbols and how they would be used.
5. How would you increase liminality in order to promote *communitas*?

7

Stories Portray It, Not Just Say It

God Presents Salvation in Story Form

Teaching in Story Form

After a hard week of farming, the church members gradually made their way to the church in the Yoruba village in Nigeria. Timothy, the local pastor, had been faithfully sowing seeds of the gospel and plowing the ground of resistance for three years. Trained in Western education models, he could not understand why the young believers in the church did not seem to grasp his teaching and grow as disciples.

This week, though, he decided to try an experiment with something new that he learned from a Chronological Bible Storytelling workshop. Instead of an abstract teaching, he picked a topic that was an important part of the Yoruba worldview—the creation of the spirit beings. Slowly and deliberately, he told the Yoruba creation myth. He then carefully told the Bible story of creation, asking someone in the group to retell the story, which they did. Then he led them in a discussion of the Bible story and its interaction with the Yoruba myth, leading to direct application.

Shocked, Timothy realized they understood the Bible story and could apply this to their lives. Even more surprising was the desire of these farmers to hear more. Overjoyed, Timothy exclaimed, "The people were very eager to hear more of the stories. . . . I have come to understand that the people are more open to ask questions with this method, unlike when I was using the [denominational] Sunday School book."

He realized some important aspects that affected the discipleship of his church members. Timothy recalls, "I also discovered as I asked them questions and listened to their questions that they were still holding on to their previous teachings of worshipping angels. To them the angels are from heaven and can reach God better, so we can pass through them to God. This session has further taught me that they have not understood my topical sermons. It now gives me

SIDEBAR 7.1

Finding Important Stories for Discipleship

There are many places to find important stories for discipleship, including local myths, folktales, proverbs, historical narratives, personal stories, and stories of others. Richard Morgan recommends identifying personal stories by constructing a "spiritual autobiography," which requires remembering the following foundational principles:

1. Every life is a unique, invaluable story.
2. God speaks to us in our stories.
3. Connecting our stories with God's Story is the work of the Spirit.
4. Painful memories can be healed through stories.

5. Remembering our stories creates community and the future.
6. Faith stories are the legacy we leave.
7. Stories create meaning . . . at any age. (2002, 17)

Reflection and Discussion

1. What stories from your own life immediately come to mind? How have they shaped your faith journey?
2. Have you experienced healing from painful stories and comfort from pleasant stories?
3. How could discipleship occur through carefully and intentionally caring for our personal stories?

the opportunity to explain to them things on this issue which I do not normally preach on." (Lovejoy and Claydon 2005)

Timothy is now addressing excluded middle issues that are not normally discussed in church. Because he looked at the cultural perspective concerning how the spirit world affects the material world, and then engaged this with the biblical story, transformation is now taking place. Perhaps one important way to transform a worldview is to transform the underlying myths through the biblical stories.

Timothy's case reminds us of the power of stories to shape worldviews. While his previous efforts at discipleship using propositional, abstract teaching failed, the stories communicated and connected with the farmers. Brent Curtis and John Eldredge note,

The deepest convictions of our heart are formed by stories and reside there in the images and emotions of story. . . . Life is not a list of propositions; it is a series of dramatic scenes. Story is the language of the heart. Our souls speak not in the naked facts of mathematics or the abstract proportions of systematic theology; they speak the images and emotions of story. (1997, 38–39)

When we engage biblical stories with local stories, excluded middle issues of culture are addressed. This contextualization leads to the transformation of worldviews, which is the goal of intercultural discipleship.

The underlying myths of the people help to shape the worldview of a culture (as discussed in chap. 4). These myths form the underlying "operating system" that is unseen but always present in the background, affecting the people's perception of reality. If intercultural disciplers do not address

> **To change a people group's worldview requires the hearing and/or seeing of different stories.**
>
> Tom Steffen (1996, 32)

the worldview issues of disciples, their spiritual growth will be stunted by syncretism or split-level Christianity.

People do not easily change their worldview, though. To begin the process of transforming a worldview, we need to utilize cultural forms that exist in culture and infuse them with Christian meaning. Stories are a powerful cultural form to transform worldviews, as N. T. Wright reveals:

> Stories are, actually, peculiarly good at modifying or subverting other stories and their worldviews. Where head-on attack would certainly fail, [a story] hides the wisdom of the serpent behind the innocence of the dove, gaining entrance and favour which can then be used to change assumptions which the hearer would otherwise keep hidden away for safety. (1992, 40)

Since stories help to shape a worldview, cross-cultural disciplers appropriate the power of stories to reshape and re-form a Christian worldview. When biblical stories are engaged with indigenous stories, the contextualization of existing cultural stories and myths occurs.

In this chapter, we will further explore the use of stories for discipleship, utilizing three major steps in the process:

1. learning and interiorizing biblical stories
2. studying indigenous stories
3. engaging biblical stories with indigenous stories for contextualization

This threefold process leverages the power of stories to help shape worldviews.

Learning and Interiorizing Biblical Stories

The growing disciple needs to learn the biblical stories. While this is obvious, the less obvious question is, which of the Bible stories are most important to learn initially? In order to find stories that address the worldview issues of the

Chronological Bible Storytelling

New Tribes Mission (NTM) missionaries Mark and Gloria Zook worked among the Mouk people of Papua New Guinea in the 1970s. They found a tremendous response to the gospel when it was told chronologically from the beginning in Genesis to the end. As a result, they pioneered chronological biblical teaching in the 1980s. Trevor McIlwain published this chronological Bible teaching approach, which other NTM missionaries used with tribal people in the Philippines. In the late 1980s and 1990s, Jim Slack and J. O. Terry, serving with the International Mission Board of the Southern Baptist Convention in the Philippines, revised and adapted this approach for oral learners. Today, there are many other approaches and activities that biblical storytellers are using in various contexts. For example, picture books and recorded stories are available in various languages from the Global Recordings Network/ Gospel Recordings, at http://globalrecordings .net/en/. For a further history of chronological biblical storytelling and the orality movement, see http://www.orality.net.

The official website for Chronological Bible Storytelling is http://www.orality strategies.org. This site contains a number of helpful articles, downloads, sample story sets, and so on. A free downloadable manual for storytelling is available at https://orality .imb.org/resources/?id=130.

Reflection and Discussion

1. What is the difference between a story told using an approach suited for print learners versus one for oral learners? What changes should be made?

2. How is an understanding of the Old Testament essential for grasping the significance of the gospel? Why do disciplers often omit the Old Testament and focus largely on the New Testament?

3. How can chronological biblical storytelling be incorporated into discipleship approaches in various cultures?

disciple, understanding the local culture and worldview issues is paramount. This undertaking is not an assembly-line approach; rather, the story set that is initially presented to the disciple is tailored to fit the worldview questions in that particular culture.

The Lausanne working group (Lovejoy and Claydon 2005) recommended a chronological Bible storytelling approach, beginning in Genesis and progressing chronologically. The early stories in Genesis address many of the common worldview issues that cultures typically ask (e.g., Who are we? How did we get here? What went wrong? How can we correct it?). The Genesis stories are often important starting places to provide alternate answers to these types of worldview questions.

Varying societies will have different worldview issues, though, and the biblical stories that are chosen to address these issues will vary accordingly. For example, for the Builsa people, the story of Balaam in Numbers 22–24 is very relevant. The fear of curses and witchcraft is a real one. This biblical story portrays the power and protection of God over his people, even when powerful curses are meant to harm them.

Storytelling in Northern Ghana

In northern Ghana, SIM missionary Dugan Lange taught me how to use picture books and stories recorded in the local language to present chronological biblical stories. He suggested that I select stones to represent the various biblical characters and place them on the ground in chronological order in order to discuss these biblical stories each week, as described below.

In the Builsa culture, we chose biblical stories that portrayed the lives of the early ancestors, starting with God's creation of Adam. Initially, I laid down a stone that was broken into three parts to represent Naawen (God), who created all things in the beginning. The significance of the one stone broken in three parts was not revealed until later. After laying down this stone, I then placed another stone next to it to represent Adam.

Since the Builsa offer sacrifices to the ancestors as part of their traditional religion, I asked, "Who offered the first sacrifice and why?" No one knew how this familiar practice started, but they were curious to learn more. Adam and Eve's story of sin and God's killing of the animal (thereby creating animal

> All storytellers must keep a steady gaze on their inner worlds of memory, perception, and imagination . . . in order to transport others through the media of sound, language, and imagery.
>
> Fred Craddock (adapted from Craddock 2001, 1)

hides to cover them) reveal God as the initiator of sacrifices. It also reveals that the reason for sacrifices is to atone for sin. Furthermore, the story hints at God's promise to send a sacrifice that would cover sin once and for all. In addition to using stones, we accompanied the storytelling with picture books for people to "read" and cassette tapes for them to enjoy later.

Progressively, I told stories of the ancestors and laid rocks down in a line to represent each ancestor in the story. The rocks were important mnemonic devices, but the Builsa also place rocks on top of the burial mounds of their recently departed ancestors. This symbolic connection to the recent ancestors and those of long ago did not go unnoticed.

Each week, a different Bible story was told that provided an alternative answer to the Builsa's worldview questions. As the stories progressed, I eventually talked about the prophets who were anticipating the arrival of the one

The Art of Storytelling

Professional storyteller John Walsh has observed that everybody has a storytelling style. Improving your own individual style requires practice and helpful advice from listeners. In his workshops and book, *The Art of Storytelling: Easy Steps to Presenting an Unforgettable Story*, Walsh (2003) offers the following tips for presenting good stories:

1. Choose a short story (three minutes) that you know well and can visualize clearly, as if you were at the scene now.
2. Know the story well enough to tell it, but do not memorize it word for word.
3. Round 1: Find a partner who will be a good listener (i.e., someone who can focus on the story, *appear* interested, provide appropriate feedback, and laugh at the proper times). Tell the story to your partner without referring to written notes. If you forget something, just push through it anyway.
4. Ask the listener, "What part of that story had the most energy, or where did it grab you or hook you the most?"
5. Round 2: Reshape the story, beginning at the spot that your expert (listener) felt had the most energy.

Find another partner and retell the story, using this new beginning location. The point of this exercise is to determine the initial hook to grab your listeners such that they want to hear the rest of the story.

6. Ask the listener, "Did the ending finish the story well?" Ask for his or her suggestions for how to end it properly. Once the conflict of the story is solved, the story should end quickly. One of the biggest errors of beginning storytellers is that the story plot ends but the storyteller doesn't. Find a good ending and memorize this. Now that you have identified the two most memorable parts of the story (the beginning and the end), you are ready for round 3.
7. Round 3: Since you likely have been telling the story from the first-person perspective, adopt another perspective to tell the story. For example, tell it from the perspective of someone else in the story. It could even be the perspective of something else (e.g., a bird, a fireplace, the car). Find another partner and retell the story using this new perspective.
8. After you have told the story, have the listener ask questions as if he

who was to be the ultimate, final sacrifice. When God's perfect time finally arrived, God sent his own son, named Jesus. At this point, I walked back to the first rock, which was broken into three pieces. Picking up one of the pieces, I then carried it to the end of the line and told them, "God finally kept his promise and sent the perfect sacrifice for all humans. This sacrifice was his own son." This put the arrival and background of Jesus into a context that made sense for the Builsa people. Working through the Old Testament stories first had made the importance of Jesus's arrival and eventual death/

or she were a reporter at the scene, such as: What was the color of her shoes? What did the room smell like? How was her hair arranged? How big/tall was he? You should respond to these questions. If you do not know the answer, use your imagination and simply make it up.

9. Round 4: Find another partner. Decide which details from the previous round really help people to picture the story well. Also, decide which perspective to tell the story from (i.e., first person initially used or the perspective used in the last round). Then retell the story using the appropriate descriptions that portray the scene instead of simply talking about the scene.

10. Ask the listener, "Did you follow the main point of the story? What is the main point?" Listen to his or her feedback to see whether changes need to be made in the beginning, the ending, details, and perspectives so that the listener gets the main point.

11. Round 5: Boomershine describes the "Lion Hunt" game, in which people follow the actions and sounds of the storyteller (1988, 29–30). Find a new partner, and this time, using the "Lion Hunt" technique, incorporate some audience participation and enthusiasm. For example, include sounds, motions, voice fluctuation, facial expression, repeatable phrases, and pauses. You are limited only by your imagination.

12. Ask the listener, "Which of the audience participation aspects are helpful? Which are distracting? Can you suggest more appropriate audience participation aspects?" Incorporate his or her suggestions into the last round.

13. Final round: Return to your original partner and retell the story.

14. Ask the listener, "How did the story improve? Have I left out any important aspects that would make the story memorable and impactful?"

15. You should now be ready to tell that story in "public," since your team of "experts" has helped you improve in the art of storytelling.

Reflection and Discussion

1. Why do storytellers often start where the story's energy is focused instead of at the chronological beginning?

2. Which round was the most helpful to you? Which was the least helpful?

3. Why is it so important to have six rounds of private storytelling before telling the story in public?

resurrection understandable. Eventually, the stories continued to the end of Revelation.

Interiorizing Bible Stories

It takes more than simply hearing stories for the stories to change a person's worldview, though. Thomas Boomershine posits that the stories must be "interiorized." He notes, "The first step in the journey is to get the story off the page or out of the air and inside yourself" (1988, 23). This means that the stories must be visualized, remembered, and experienced by disciples such that they become part of their interior lives. The goal is for disciples to "live in the story" so that this story now "lives in them" as part of their own story. The ancestors such as Adam, Noah, and Abraham now become disciples' ancestors. These stories are important because they now shape who disciples are and where they are going. They formulate how disciples arrived at the state they are in, and the hope of God to make it better. These worldview answers become integrated into the lives of disciples as the biblical stories are interiorized.

For disciples to interiorize Bible stories in their lives, Boomershine recommends the following process:

1. Learn the story. The best way to learn the story is to listen to it being told well. If this is not possible, then you will need to read/hear the story several times. Listen for the story content and structure so that it can be remembered. Look for important words that thread their way through the story, or vivid images that make the story come alive. It will take several sittings to memorize the basic story line. One memory approach is to focus on one story for the week.

   On the first day, read/hear the story three times. Then meditate on the story as you become one character in the story. Try to live in the story through the eyes of this character. On the second day, read/hear the story three times again. This time meditate on the story as you become a different character in the story. You will now live in the story through the eyes of a different character. Repeat this approach for several days. The goal is to vividly see the story lived out from multiple perspectives. In the prodigal son story (Luke 15:11–32), for example, you could view the same story differently through the eyes of the prodigal, the father, the older brother, the servant, and even the pigs.

2. Listen to the story. This means digging into the initial background, context, and other details of the story. Connect this story to other biblical stories that you know. For those with access to biblical study tools, this is the place for biblical exegesis.

3. Connect the story to your life. This will be discussed shortly, but Boomershine wants the disciple to "bring the distinctiveness of his or her experience to the telling of the story. . . . This distinctiveness emerges naturally as the story is internalized" (1988, 36). These connections arise from personal or communal experiences.

4. Tell the story. Practice telling the story in front of others. As Boomershine recognizes, "people become the stories they love to tell" (1988, 19). Make the telling of the story a performance of oral art (see sidebar 7.3).

Once the Bible stories are interiorized, the discipler is then able to draw on these stories to begin challenging the people's existing worldview assumptions. For these existing worldview assumptions to change, though, the discipler will have to expose them or bring them to the surface, as Hiebert describes: "One way to transform worldviews is to 'surface them'—to consciously examine the deep, unexamined assumptions we have and thereby make explicit what is implicit" (2008, 319). This requires an additional step so that Bible stories do not simply occupy another layer on the existing indigenous worldview.

Studying Indigenous Stories

Studying a society's indigenous stories brings to the surface existing worldview assumptions. These stories include myths, historical accounts, and personal accounts the people value. If this step is omitted, intercultural disciplers will miss the opportunity to address excluded middle issues in culture. These intimate issues often do not emerge without some prodding. The close relationships between disciples and intercultural disciplers play a key role, since the indigenous people may not articulate these stories unless asked.

Bible storytellers may shy away from this important step, since it requires time and effort. By carefully considering the indigenous culture's stories, however, they touch the very point at which worldview assumptions are identified, as the following Builsa storytelling event portrays.

Men's Side of the Story

Immanuel, surrounded by a large audience, sat down and recited a story that every Builsa man knows yet loves to hear again.

"A young man got married. He trusted his wife and felt that she loved him tremendously. Shortly after the wedding, his father warned him, 'Son, do not tell all of your secrets to your new wife. She may seem nice now, but, on the day of conflict, she will use your secrets to destroy you.'

"The young man protested and insisted that his father was wrong. Surely, his wife was different."

The ladies in the room wore nervous smiles on their faces. They knew where the story was heading, just like the men did.

Immanuel continued, "The father asked his son to do a simple test. 'Take this egg and give it to your new wife,' the father advised his son. 'Tell her that your power source is in this egg—it is your *tiim* (spiritual power source). As long as this egg is safe, then your power will be safe. If the egg breaks, however, then your life will end. Tell your wife that you trust her and you want her to keep the egg in a safe place.' The son obeyed his father's advice.

143

Biblical Insights from Indigenous Stories

Del Tarr (1994) notes that indigenous stories from other cultures can provide insights into biblical passages that are overlooked in one's own culture. In particular, he notes how the more agrarian and less technological/industrialized cultures in West Africa are much closer to the Old Testament cultures; to illustrate this point, he describes West African parables that provide insight into biblical passages that are hard to understand in Western contexts. While Western theological education and discipling approaches have undoubtedly affected majority world nations, Tarr points out that the majority world cultures also have something to offer.

For example, Psalm 126:5–6 is often difficult for Western cultures to interpret:

> Those who sow in tears
>   will reap with songs of joy.
> Those who go out weeping,
>   carrying seed to sow,
> will return with songs of joy,
>   carrying sheaves with them.

What American farmer sows in tears? They are usually quite hopeful sitting on their tractors during the planting season. Tarr portrays a different scene on the edge of the Sahara in Burkina Faso, West Africa:

> Harvest time is a joyous time on the savannah in West Africa, because food is in abundance. . . . There is much dancing far into the night as the African in his traditional ceremonies gives thanks to the "creator" and "sustainer." . . . The staple crop all across the savannah is millet, and from this a meal is ground to make mush which is eaten twice a day during the months of plenty (October, November, December).
>
> April and May are the saddest months of the year. Many families are running

out of food. It is not unusual to hear, in the hush of an African dusk, small babies and young children crying from real, physical hunger, as well as from discouraging prospects that the day's one meal will satisfy the gnawing pains in their tummies.

> When the first rains come and the hard cracked ground begins to soften, the whole family goes to the field in their weakened condition. . . . The father will take down that leather sack [filled with millet seeds saved for sowing], and with tears in his eyes, literally throw away and bury the very commodity that the bodies of every member of his household desperately need. He weeps because he is sorry for the delay between planting and harvest. Oh, if one only dared to eat it. In spite of that sorrow, he plants it—he invests it in Mother Nature. He has faith in the harvest! He weeps now; he believes he can dance and sing later. (Tarr 1994, 21–24)

Reflection and Discussion

1. What insight does this story provide for understanding Psalm 126:5–6?
2. Tarr concludes with the words from bush preachers: "If we haven't wept over the things that we hold most dear, then we have probably never 'sown in tears'" (1994, 24). How can this story be applied for discipling related to the stewardship of time, talent, and treasure?
3. Can you think of other biblical stories/passages that could apply to this topic for discipleship, such as the story of the widow's mite (Mark 12:41–44) and Jesus's words about the kernel of wheat that must fall to the ground and die (John 12:24)?

"After a year or so of marriage, the husband and wife got into a quarrel. They were angry and shouting at each other. The wife ran into her room and pulled out the egg for the man to see.

"'You think you are so strong. I am going to drop this egg and humble you right now,' the wife said.

"'No, please do not do that—I will die if you do!' begged the husband.

"Ignoring his plea, the wife slammed the egg on the ground where it smashed to pieces. They each waited for the young man to die.

"Now the father entered the room. He heard the whole discussion and arrived just after the egg exploded into a million pieces across the floor.

"The father advised the son, 'You see, that is why our elders have said, "Ba kan de tiim ale nipowa" (They do not eat medicine with the wife, Builsa proverb). On the day of conflict, she will destroy you if she can. That egg was not really your *tiim*. I just pretended this to be your *tiim* to make the point—do not show her your real *tiim* or you will regret it.'"

The room erupted with laughter. Even some of the young women seemed to enjoy and affirm certain aspects of the story.

One of the older women, though, slowly lifted her body off of the wooden bench and rose to her feet. "I have another story to tell that explains that first one," she exclaimed in a loud voice for all to hear. (Moon 2009a, 120–24)

Before continuing with the next indigenous story, let's pause and consider how the first story reveals some important worldview assumptions. I had been living in the Builsa area for several years prior to hearing this story, and these important areas of discipleship had never surfaced or been addressed prior. I had been faithfully using the chronological Bible storytelling approach described above, but I did not know that this excluded middle issue existed. I was shocked to hear the degree of mistrust and suspicion that existed between husbands and wives. Husbands fear that their wives will gossip, run to another man, or leave them and go back home to their parents. Some husbands are even convinced that their wives may use spiritual power to hurt or destroy them. This story and accompanying proverb provided undeniable evidence, as far as they were concerned, of this underlying worldview assumption. If this excluded middle issue were not addressed, the discipleship of Builsa families would be greatly hindered.

Women's Side of the Story

Let's probe a little further and expose these worldview assumptions. The older woman has a story to tell from the female perspective.

Slowly, the old woman lifted her frail body from the wooden bench. Standing on her own two feet, she suddenly came alive and responded with emotion, "Some ladies are like this and some are not, just like there are some good men and some bad ones. Do not let the bad ladies convince you that all ladies are the same. 'Waung yeng ale soa ate ba a wi ayen wiima' (Because of one monkey they say [all are] monkeys.) Let me prove to you that ladies are different."

The more she spoke, the more energized her old body became. Speaking with the vigor and conviction of a woman twenty years younger, she continued, "A man had three wives. One day, the youngest wife said to him, 'I am more beautiful than the other wives, and I love you more than the others. Please send the other wives away.'

"The husband replied, 'Let me think about this.'

"After he thought awhile, he decided to test the three wives.

"That night, he stood outside the door of the youngest wife and disguised his voice. 'Knock, knock. I am DEATH. Should I come in or should I go to your husband?'

"The youngest wife quickly replied, 'I am still young and beautiful, while my husband is older. I still have a long life to live. Please do not come in here—go to my husband instead.'

"The husband went to the second wife. 'Knock, knock. I am DEATH. Should I come in or should I go to your husband?'

"She hesitated a little, but then replied, 'I am still young and have a lot left to do. Please do not enter—go to my husband instead.'

"The husband finally arrived at the door of the oldest wife. 'Knock, knock. I am DEATH. Should I come in or should I go to your husband?'

"The older woman did not hesitate. 'You should enter and take me. That way, my husband will live; he will then be around to take care of the children.'"

The women in the room erupted in applause for the storyteller! She proved the point—not all women are the same.

As the noise settled down, Pastor David acquiesced. "Ma, you are correct. Ladies are not all the same. It is true that some ladies run to another man when there is a conflict and some will gossip about our secrets. On the other hand, some ladies stay with their husbands even if they have only one child or even during a conflict."

A young woman added, "Some men will sit and discuss their problems with you, while others will not discuss anything with you—they just discuss things with their male friends."

An older woman replied, "Some men bring other wives in the house. If they are fed up with the first wife, then they will not take good care of her. This drives her away." (adapted from Moon 2009a, 120–24)

We will return to this indigenous storytelling session shortly. At this point, notice how several important worldview assumptions surfaced that are rarely, if ever, discussed in the church. If these excluded middle issues are not identified and addressed, the discipleship process will stall. Men are afraid that the wives will gossip, or will run to another man, or will leave and go home to their parents. Women also have legitimate fears. They worry that the husbands will bring home another wife and neglect them, will not discuss intimate things with them, and will keep secrets from them. These issues can breed mistrust, disunity, fighting, and separation. They are important discipleship issues.

Contextualization: Engaging Biblical Stories with Indigenous Stories

Once we have identified the discipleship issues found in the indigenous story, the last step is to engage these indigenous stories with biblical stories. Once again, we will use the principles of contextualization discussed in the last chapter. The four-step process of critical contextualization will also be used for the indigenous stories, similar to the way rituals were contextualized in the last chapter. In practice, the following steps do not have to be conducted in the exact order shown below. The Builsa stories recounted above will be used as examples.

1. *Phenomenological study*: Learn the indigenous stories, including the cultural stories (as described above), myths, historical stories, and personal stories. Similar to a reporter's account, record the stories along with the interactions, as described above. It is important to keep the original context in mind. The goal is to accurately describe the story and context so that the excluded middle issues become apparent and are clearly understood. In these stories, the mistrust between husbands and wives is identified.

2. *Ontological critique*: Identify the important root issues in the story. Since "cultural stories indicate what is important in culture" (S. Johnston 2009), listen carefully for the excluded middle issues that emerge. In addition to the stories, the Builsa proverbs contained in them affirmed the validity of these worldview assumptions. In these stories, several root issues produce the mistrust identified. For the men, these issues include the fear of gossip/betrayal, unfaithfulness, and desertion. For the women, these issues include the fear of the husband adding another wife, neglect, and lack of close communication.

3. *Critical evaluation*: Once the root issues are identified in the stories, the Bible now becomes the interpreter of culture to accept, modify, or reject aspects of the indigenous worldview. Observe how the Builsa critically evaluated the stories immediately after the stories were told.

Before discussing the last step of missiological transformation, we turn back to the storytelling session.

Pastor David chimed in first, "Naawen Wani (God's Word) says that a husband and wife should become one (Eph. 5). By keeping secrets from each other, we are not allowing our marriages to be what Naawen wants them to be. Instead of becoming one, we are remaining two. This root of the proverb Naawen Wani rejects."

One of the older women added, "Yes, we want to become one with our husbands, but they need to sit and talk with us so that they do not hide things from us. Doesn't Naawen Wani say that the husband should love the wife as he loves himself?"

Pastor Kofi jumped in. "At times, we are afraid to reveal all of our secrets, since we fear that they will be told to others. Do you remember how Delilah told Samson's secrets? She promised to keep the secrets, but she repeatedly passed them on to his enemies. In the end, it destroyed him."

"I think that is why our wives are told in Naawen Wani (1 Tim. 3:11) that they not become gossips, but they should have self-control and speak the truth," added Pastor David. "If this occurred in the marriage, then it would be easier for the husbands to reveal secrets and not look for other women either."

A big round of applause arose spontaneously, since everyone knew that this was the way things should be.

Immanuel now asked, "Are there any aspects of this story about not eating *tiim* with the wife that Naawen Wani affirms as *magsi*?"

There was a short silence as the people were reflecting on the proverb and Naawen Wani.

Finally, Pastor David shared, "Going back to Delilah's case, she was a nonbeliever. Samson was warned not to be one with a nonbeliever, but he did anyway. We are also warned in Naawen Wani not to marry nonbelievers. Samson shows us the consequences of rejecting this advice and marrying a nonbeliever."

The pastors all shook their heads in agreement. This was a problem for the church, even for young male pastors who are not married. Samson provides a good concrete example for them all.

The holistic, integrated approach to story—tell the story, sing the story, dance the story, drum the story, and dramatize the story—has allowed the story to be owned by the local people. It enters into the collective memory of an entire community; it becomes a permanent part of the lives of the people . . . to follow a God-given cycle of evangelism and discipleship.

Jim and Carla Bowman (2013, 231)

The missionary had been pondering this story ever since he heard it. He now added, "There are times when I am counseling someone from the church. The issues are sensitive, and I do not want my wife to know others' problems; otherwise, she will think negatively about this person and it will hurt her relationship with them. People also trust me not to tell their problems to others. I think that this part of the story that Naawen Wani would say is *magsi* here."

Pastor David's face lit up. "I agree. If I tell my wife how others treated me in the church ministry, then it often bothers her more than me. She carries it for a long time, and it does not help her or the situation. I think that some of these secrets of others in the church should not be told to our wives."

Pastor Kofi agreed that this made good sense. He knew that God's work was hard at times, and people do not always treat pastors kindly. This proverb and story serve as a good reminder about using wisdom concerning when to reveal hardships with one's wife. Sometimes it is better for her sake that a husband not reveal the negative side of others who have mistreated him. That is helpful wisdom to prayerfully consider for ministry.

As the storytelling session ended, everyone agreed that they learned a lot, and they were eager to do this again. They had just scratched the surface of some critical worldview assumptions that needed to be addressed. (adapted from Moon 2009a, 120–24)

Let's now consider the last step in critical contextualization, missiological transformation.

Missiological Transformation

In the final step, worldview transformation occurs. Once the indigenous worldview assumptions have surfaced, they can be challenged by the biblical stories. The intercultural discipler can play a critical role in helping the issues to surface. There are many possible ways for disciples to be transformed. For example, their transformation could result in further marriage counseling, biblical training on godly families, or rituals of trust. One transformation occurred as I observed a Builsa wedding. The wedding vows, composed by the Builsa man and woman, were shared in front of the packed church as follows.

The groom Joseph, repeating after the pastor, proclaims in a loud voice so that even those crowded outside the windows can hear,

"I promise not to beat her."

"I promise to keep her even if she does not give birth."

"I promise to keep her even if she becomes blind."

While these vows may sound strange to foreign ears, they reflect the concerns and issues in the local culture. Wife beating is a concern in the village. Also, a wife is expected to provide a child in the first two years of marriage. If this does not occur, then the groom's father exerts pressure to find another wife. Furthermore, Joseph is living in an "oncho zone," named after the disease onchocerciasis, or "river blindness." While drug treatment and spraying have mitigated the disease in recent years, several blind people in the village are walking testimonies to the devastating effects of the small fly that brings this disease. Since blindness limits the ability of a woman to carry out her daily farming and chores, some men have sent their wives away as blindness sets in.

One man told me that it is like playing the lottery—you keep picking a wife until you get lucky!

The bride Ajua now repeats after the pastor:

"I promise to stay with him even if he becomes poor and cannot buy me new clothes."

"I promise not to go after other men to sleep with them." (adapted from Moon 2012c, 74)

These wedding vows reveal that the indigenous worldview assumptions are being transformed to reflect biblical faithfulness and cultural relevance, one wedding at a time. While many disciplers simply pass on the Bible stories and then assume that the disciples will be transformed by them, intercultural disciplers go a bit further to reach the worldview level of the disciples. Galen Burkholder has observed, "For too long we have assumed that discipleship

---

The stories people tell have a way of taking care of them. If stories come to you, care for them. And learn to give them away where they are needed. *Sometimes a person needs a story more than food to stay alive.*

Barry Lopez (1998; emphasis mine)

---

happens when we fill people's minds with biblical truth and knowledge" (2011, 484). The engagement of indigenous stories with biblical stories provides room for the Holy Spirit to transform disciples.

Where to Locate Other Indigenous Stories

Proverbs

Many indigenous stories that are useful for discipleship derive from indigenous proverbs. The Builsa story recounted above about the egg is the summation of a Builsa proverb. Proverbs are such a rich source for identifying worldview assumptions for discipleship that their usefulness will be discussed further in the next chapter.

Folktales

Traditional stories or folktales are often told to pass on important cultural values. For example, the American story of George Washington chopping down the cherry tree is a common folktale. A wonderful resource for African stories can be found at http://afriprov.org/resources/storiesdatabase.html.

Personal Stories

Common personal stories of struggle are also helpful for identifying excluded middle issues for discipleship. Auli Vahakangas collected the stories of Christian couples coping with childlessness in Tanzania. After collecting the stories, she then uncovered the root issues influencing the mind-set of the disciples. She notes, "The shame of childlessness is closely linked to the shame of not producing new members for the clan, and therefore, not following the African view of immortality" (2009, 154). Culturally, a man's goal is to become an elder who is remembered after he is dead. This is achieved by producing male children who offer sacrifices to him when he is no longer alive. When these worldview assumptions were critically evaluated with Scripture, the following transformation occurred for these disciples:

> Only through a correct understanding of the Christian concept of resurrection can the identity crisis, shame, and coping problems of childless couples be solved. Through salvation by the cross a person can be seen as complete in the eyes of God, and understanding this will enable a childless person to restore his/her identity. On the cross God himself suffered and was weak. The theology of the cross helps a childless couple or a childless spouse to tolerate their problem. The Christian faith, which enables a childless couple or a childless spouse to trust in Christian immortality through salvation in Christ, was found to be an important part of the coping process in Kilimanjaro. (Vahakangas 2009, 160–61)

These indigenous stories identify excluded middle issues that are important for discipleship.

Historical Narratives

The history of indigenous people often provides evidence of God's prevenient grace, even in their darkest hours. The Builsa people of northern Ghana remember the stories from the time when Muslim slave raiders came into their villages to capture them. In 1994 I met with the paramount chief of the Builsa, Ayieta Azantilow IV, and his elders to discuss these events. The slave raiders were from the Zambarama people group in the region of Niger. The names of these raiders are still remembered by the Builsa—Babatu and Samori are the most famous. Babatu was reportedly on a jihad into the Builsa homeland and the surrounding territories. Azantilow was born in 1901 (only five years after the final slave raid); his father had participated in the final battle against the Zambarima slave raiders and passed these stories on to him. Although the last slave raid was estimated to have occurred in 1896, these battles are still an important part of Builsa identity.

One story describes how the slave raiders were approaching on horseback (Moon 2009b). An *acham* (sheanut tree) warned the Builsa ahead of time. This helped them to prepare well and defeat the enemy. The Builsa also climbed up on the rocks to find protection from the raiders. The slave raiders' horses could not maintain good footing on the rocks; therefore, the rocks helped to rescue the Builsa again.

Several Builsa church leaders reflected on this story and asked the question, "Is there any evidence of God's presence during this time?" In discussion with the Builsa church leaders, they considered, "Who created the sheanut tree? Only God could make this tree talk. Who created the mountains that we could run to for safety?" Are these things not evidence of God's prevenient grace during the darkest days of their history?

Builsa church leader George Atemboa (1998, 29) notes how God provided the rock in the desert during the Israelites' time of need so that Moses could strike this rock and find water (Exod. 17:1–7; Num. 20:1–13). First Corinthians 10:3–5 explains that this rock was Christ, even though the Israelites were not aware of it at the time. Atemboa surmises, "In the same way, we see that Jesus Christ was the spiritual rock which helped our fathers to defeat Babatu and his raiders" (1998, 29). In Scripture, God often reminds the Jews of times when God used creation to rescue and protect them, whether it was a river to flood the Egyptians, a donkey to talk with Balaam, or hail to beat back invaders. Could the above Builsa story also be a good starting point to explain God's prevenient grace?

Atemboa concludes,

> If not for God's timely intervention, the slave raiders could have forced the Builsa to become Muslims. In many other areas, Babatu forced people to become Muslims or be killed. As it stands today, very few Builsa are Muslim but many are now open to receive the good news of Jesus Christ. I see this as Jesus' intervention in Builsa history. (1998, 29)

This historical narrative is an important discipleship opportunity for Builsa believers. Each year the Builsa commemorate their freedom from Babatu and the slave raiders during the Fiok festival.

Stories from Others

Elizabeth Barnes (1995) describes discipleship as the "interlacing" of biblical stories with other contemporary stories. Drawing stories from contemporary movies and books, she describes the process of contextualization:

> The Bible's authority resides in its power to interlace with our diverse stories in ways that challenge our errors, correct our distortions, and transform and complete our unfinished narratives as stories of love, justice, and peace. . . . Worship and discipleship function as connecting links between the biblical stories and our other narratives. (1995, 15)

She artfully interlaces biblical narratives and contemporary stories in movies and books to show how the stories of Israel, Jesus, and the church become our stories as well. Stories from movies will be discussed further in chapter 11.

Further examples of indigenous stories for intercultural discipling are offered by Joseph Healey and Donald Sybertz (2000), who describe the collection and use of stories and other oral literature from the Sukuma Research Committee in East Africa. They advocate collecting and then contextualizing these stories in a hermeneutical community to address ultimate realities in the indigenous cultures.

Summary

In this chapter, we discussed the important role of stories for intercultural discipleship. Stories help to shape our identities (McIntyre 1981). Some postmoderns go so far as to say that we even construct ourselves by storytelling (Holstein and Gubrium 2000). For intercultural discipleship, we emphasized the following points:

1. Worldviews are constructed by underlying myths (sacred stories). As a result, people are resistant to changing their worldview. Alternate stories become a potent means to challenge the existing worldviews such that discipleship takes place.

2. The first step is for the disciple to learn the biblical stories that relate to his or her own worldview. For a story to become interiorized, the disciple should learn the story well by memory, listen to it in its original context, connect it to his or her own life, and then tell it to others.

3. The next step is to study indigenous stories in the disciple's culture. These stories include indigenous myths, folktales, historical narratives, personal stories, and the stories of others. Look for the excluded middle issues that surface through the stories.

4. The third step is to engage the relevant biblical stories with the indigenous stories. Once the discipler has identified the worldview assumptions from the indigenous stories, he or she can then use the biblical stories to challenge these assumptions. The goal is to reshape the underlying system of myths, resulting in a transformed worldview. The process of critical contextualization is once again applied to these stories for intercultural discipleship.

Now that we have applied the intercultural discipleship approach to contextual rituals and stories, we are ready to move on to other important areas of culture. We will next turn our attention to indigenous proverbs, which

153

are closely linked with stories. We will try to understand the meaning and value of proverbs such as "Pukawgi a laa ka tuik po" (The widow laughs at the pounding spot).

Activity for Discipling

1. Ask your disciple to tell you an important story that he or she has heard or experienced. This could be a recent event or one from the past, even the person's childhood. It could be a folktale, a myth, a historical narrative, a personal story, or someone else's story. It could be what Mike Breen and Steve Cockram call a *kairos* moment, "when the eternal God breaks into your circumstances with an event that gathers some loose ends of your life and knots them together in his hands" (2011, Kindle location 707). Constructing a "spiritual autobiography" as described by Richard Morgan (2002) may also be a way to gather meaningful stories for discipleship. Listen carefully to the story. Then try to help the disciple identify excluded middle issues and possibly underlying root concerns. Finally, apply the critical contextualization process described above.

2. Try the process of interiorizing a biblical story of your choosing, and follow Boomershine's approach described above. Did you learn or feel something new from the various perspectives? What insights did you gain? Can you connect this with other stories in your life?

3. Gather family and friends for a "storytelling night." This could be in a home, a coffee shop, a chapel, a classroom, or some similar location. We conducted "Storytelling Night" events at some local coffee shops. The store owners advertised the event on their signs and offered to provide free coffee to whoever told a story. These events were very enjoyable and often resulted in conversations with strangers that helped to point them Christ-ward.

Baby and the Lion Cub

Reprinted from Motty *(2013, 250–55).*

Bauta Motty relates the following folk tale from the Kaninkon people of Nigeria, which he recommends for use in intercultural discipling.

One day, a pregnant woman went into the bush to gather firewood. While there, her time came and she was not able to return to the house. She found a cave in the rock and gave birth to a little boy. That evening, a lioness came to the entrance of the cave and gave birth to a son. The frightened woman saw the lioness, but the lioness did not know that the woman was there. Her first thought was to cry out, and maybe she could thus frighten the lioness away. But on further thought she decided to patiently wait and see what would happen. She watched for her chance; when the mother lion went away for food, she would rush out and get food, and then rush back to her little one.

Many days went by, and the babies grew. One day when the mothers were away, the little cub went into the cave and found the little boy, and they played together. When the little lion knew that it was about time for the mother to return, he went back to his nest and pretended to be fast asleep. Day after day, they had happy times together such that the lion club learned the language of the little boy.

One day, the little cub said, "My friend, I surely like you. You are sweeter to me than my own mother. Tell your mother to be very careful, because my mother is very mean. I fear that the day they meet, my mother will kill and eat your mother."

The little boy appreciated his little friend ever so much, but he was always in fear for his mother's life. One evening, as he loved her, he told his mother about the danger and the warning. She was always very careful, but the sad day came when the lioness caught her and brought part of her mangled body home to her cub. The little cub seemed very sick and would not touch it because he was so sad. He could not think of anything but the sorrows of his little friend. His anger toward his mother was deep and bitter.

When his mother went out again, he ran to his little friend and said, "My friend, a great loss has come to us. My mother has killed your mother. But now it is finished. I beg of you, tie your heart, and do not let it become bitter toward me, please. About your food, I will see after that. When I have food, you will have food, and when I have no food, only then will you be without food. You shall have your share of everything. I vow that when I am grown, I will kill my mother because she has done this wicked deed. Then the two of us can live in peace."

Months went by, and never did the cub forget his friend. Whenever the lioness would bring home meat, the cub would always put back part of it. After several long years had gone by, the young lion felt that he was strong enough and big enough to kill his mother, and save his friend. That very day he killed her and freed his friend.

"Now we are free to walk where we will, and I am young and strong and able to catch plenty of food for both of us," exclaimed the lion.

Then one day they came near a village and the boy heard other boys talking about being circumcised. He wanted to be circumcised too, but he had no father to help him, so he was sad.

"What is wrong?" said the lion. "Why do you have nothing to say?"

"I hear that all the boys are being circumcised. If I had a father, he would help me, and I could be circumcised, too," sobbed the boy.

"Dry your tears, and do not let anything like this disturb you again, for I am able to take the place of your father," urged the lion. "You tell me what you want, and I will get it for you."

The boy suggested that he needed money with which to buy food during the time of the circumcision.

Immediately, the lion went off. Before he had gone far, he met a man on the way to market, from whom he got plenty of money. When the boy had his money, he went to be circumcised.

When asked where he would get food, he replied, "God will give me food."

Usually, he would buy food with the money that his friend the lion gave him. At times, he would meet his friend out away from the village and receive meat from him.

Years went by, and one day the young man saw a young woman he loved.

"If I could only have had a father like other young men," he sighed.

The lion was quick to recognize the young man's mood and urged that he could be a real father to him.

"Well, I want a wife, and I need a father to help me," he said.

"All right," said the lion, "select your wife, and I will help you take her."

"I have selected my wife. She is the daughter of the chief. Many men have asked to take her, but her father will not give her up."

The strong lion stretched himself up and boasted, "I can get her for you easily. You go into the village. I will watch the chief's farm. When she goes to plant, I will catch her. Then the whole village will come out to take her away from me, but I will not give her up. You be brave and come after her. Even though I try to catch you, do not be afraid."

The young man was delighted. He said, "I will go into the village at once."

And away went the lion for the farm. That afternoon, when the villagers were beginning to come from their farms, there was a cry from the river, "Lion! Lion!"

The whole village rushed out to frighten away the lion, but, to their dismay, he had caught the daughter of the chief, and he was not afraid of the noise and the dogs. The young braves were afraid to try to rescue the daughter of the chief. The chief saw that she was lost, and he shouted, "Whoever rescues her shall have her for his wife. I will also give him half of my kingdom."

When the men heard this, they made desperate attempts to rescue her, but the fear of the lion kept them back.

With a rush, this young man went for the lion, shouting, "I will rescue her."

When he was about to strike the lion a blow, the lion dropped her and ran away in the tall grass.

She became his wife.

He received a part of the father's kingdom.

They lived happily with their friend the lion, ever after.

Reflection and Discussion

1. In Motty's approach, indigenous discipleship is related to socialization. How could this folktale be used as a parable for socialization in the Kaninkon church community?

2. What biblical passages/stories could engage this indigenous story to promote contextualization? What aspects of the indigenous story could be affirmed? Modified? Rejected?

Proverbs Are Worth
a Thousand Words

Proverbs are the horses of speech; if communication is lost, we use proverbs to find it.

—Yoruba proverb (Lindfors 1973)

When a Man Loves a Woman

"'When a man is in love, he doesn't count how long and steep the road is to his fiancée's house.' This is a Meru proverb from my hometown," announces Peter proudly. Smiling from ear to ear, he continues, "I learned this proverb at a young age. It helped me when I was courting my wife, and it helps me now in my walk with Jesus."

The satisfaction written on his face clearly reveals that this proverb taps into something deep in his life. Peter had discussed theology with the other African church leaders before, but this time it is different. In his mind, he is in another world, conveying thoughts and feelings from his own culture that are not contained in doctrinal statements.

Without needing any prompting, Peter, looking like a wise sage, eagerly presses on. "When I was courting my own fiancée, it was a long walk to visit her. To make it worse, rumors circulated about lions roaming the area. Some people tried to convince me not to make this long and dangerous walk. I refused to listen. In my heart, this path was not long or dangerous at all. My love for her compelled me to go. I did not even consider *not* taking the journey—I simply went!"

Each of the African church leaders gathered around him is drawn into this vivid picture being painted. They are all from exogamous clans, so they cannot marry someone inside their clan. The nodding of heads up and down indicates that they all have experienced the same difficulty.

Peter is not finished yet, though. "God is in love with his fiancée too. His fiancée is the church. Because of this intense love for his bride-to-be, Jesus did not count how long or steep the road was from heaven to earth. He knew the suffering of the cross and the rejection by his own people that awaited him on that road. Yet, he did not consider the option of staying home, since his love compelled him. Jesus did not just speak his love for us. He showed us his love by coming to earth to visit the home of his fiancée—the church."

Smiles give birth to laughter. This is the way these African church leaders understand and communicate theology. One church leader adds, "You are right. We often display love through actions instead of words. We show love instead of just speak words of love. The tangible expression is more meaningful than words that can easily be spoken but not sincerely felt."

Peter, excited and speaking with full vibrancy now, knows that his friend is following his thought pattern. "Yes. When a friend is sick, we visit them to show them that we care. When there is a funeral, we visit and greet the family to express our sympathies. In the same way, to show a young girl that we love

---

Gwom gwomda ne a pagedo—Bi a yam soaba yoalen wegese. (Words are spoken with peelings/shells—let the wise person come to shuck them.)

Mossi proverb (in Tarr 1994, 11)

---

her, we will walk the long distance to her house and visit her and her family. That is how we 'show' love instead of 'speak' love. God also shows his love through actions. Romans 5:8 explains, 'But God demonstrates his own love for us in this: While we were still sinners, Christ died for us.'"

Growing up in the Meru culture, Peter was taught that God was very distant, cold, and uninterested in the daily affairs of humans. This proverb, though, paints a brighter picture of a God who loves and anticipates seeing his fiancée. This compelling love knows no bounds—God is willing to travel any steep or long road for his bride (Eph. 5:25). This picture captures the heart of God.

It sank deep into Peter's heart as well.

Excited about this theological understanding, he exclaims, "I can't wait to return to Kenya soon for an evangelistic ministry. I will use this proverb to express Christianity in a way that is African and Christian. This would surely be 'sweet talk' in the Meru culture."

The summer months pass.

After returning home, Peter writes back to his pastor friends at seminary to share how over six hundred people came to Christ over the summer.

He explains, "I used many proverbs at home, and the people became very excited when I told them the proverbs. The young people were taught in the past to leave the old things behind, but the messages were very foreign. Now, they see me as a wise man, and I speak wisdom in a way they can understand." (adapted from Moon 2009a, 118–19)

When proverbs are used as vehicles to convey the intimate love of God, the Christian message is not regarded as foreign. It is African. It is wisdom from Africa and from God. It is good news in Africa, and it is worth the long, steep walk!

Alternate Reasoning Patterns

In many cultures, proverbs provide a reliable pattern for reasoning. Be it solving complicated problems, resolving disputes, or understanding new concepts, the person who can state the most appropriate and relevant proverb will likely settle the matter. The proverb is an extended metaphor to help people conceptualize difficult matters.

Intercultural disciplers look for indigenous reasoning patterns to communicate and transform people. When proverbs are the main method of reasoning in the culture, indigenous proverbs are ideally suited to communicate the gospel in ways that make sense. As a Nigerian pastor told me, "If one does not speak in proverbs, he will not carry people with him for long—they will walk for a short way only and then leave him. If he speaks in proverbs, however, the people will not be able to close their ears!"

In Western culture, proverbs are often dismissed in favor of written logic patterns and syllogisms, such as: if a = b, and b = c, then a = c. Many oral cultures, however, do not value this type of logic. Paul Hiebert states, "Proverbs, parables, and sayings are not supplementary to logical argument. They are the substance of thought itself, the storehouses of wisdom" (2008, 116). For worldview transformation to occur, intercultural disciplers must identify the indigenous reasoning patterns and use these for discipleship.

Buli Speech Patterns[1]

In the Buli language, there are three main speech patterns, as shown in table 8.1. As one moves further down the list, the communication becomes more indirect and obscure. While some cultures may value conversation that is very direct and simple, for the Builsa people this type of communication indicates that the matter is not very weighty. If theology is expressed in these terms alone, it is not considered mature conversation. For mature conversation, the lower communication methods (in table 8.1) are used so that people know it is a weighty matter that must be listened to. Expressing and reasoning through theology in these indirect and obscure patterns results in a deeper level of communication.

1. This section is adapted from Moon (2009a, 12–13).

TABLE 8.1		
Direct versus Indirect Buli Speech Patterns		
Buli term	English translation	Meaning
Biik-pieli	White/clear speech	Direct, clear, and simple
Biik-wiani	Obscure speech	Somewhat indirect/obscure
Biik-sobili	Black/dark speech	Very indirect/obscure

Biik-pieli is used to speak very clearly and simply. This type of speech is used by a child or someone speaking to a child. An example is the proverb "Ba kan dak yauk a sak biiga" (They do not point to the elephant and show the child). This means that some things are so obvious that they do not need lengthy explanations.

Biik-wiani is used to speak in a way that obscures the meaning so that some of the listeners will not understand it (even though they may understand every individual word spoken). This speech pattern can be used when adults do not want children to understand what is being discussed or to insult another person. An example is the proverb "Fi dan sak bulorik dueni deka, ku chum le faari fi ma" (If you teach an ugly man how to marry women, in the future he will marry your mother). When people understand and use this proverb appropriately, it indicates that they understand the Builsa people and their culture (see the use of this proverb later in this chapter). This elevates the speaker from being a child who uses *biik-pieli* to being a skilled adult who aptly uses *biik-wiani* in the appropriate context. In explaining the usage of *biik-wiani*, one Builsa explained that Jesus spoke this way. He spoke so that his enemies could not trap him, yet those who were truly interested could come back and learn more.

Biik-sobili is used by the elderly to convey ancient wisdom. Often archaic words are used that most Builsa do not normally employ or understand in everyday speech. An example is the proverb "Ba kan kali dai yeng a nak peesa a sue yui ya" (They do not sit in one day and harvest Fra-Fra potatoes to fill a leather bag). The leather bag referred to is rarely used anymore and is not a part of routine vocabulary; hence, it obscures the meaning. A Builsa explained to me the usage of *biik-sobili* in this way: "If a boy wants to learn *biik-sobili*, he must sit with his father and ask him [the meaning]. If a child does not sit with his father, then the child will not know *biik-sobili*."

While the above characterizations are not exhaustive, they portray the value of using proverbs to reason with others, using obscure, indirect reasoning. Proverbs create oral art. The listeners enjoy the images of the proverbs and then reason through the metaphors involved. When theology is discussed using indigenous proverbs, these "proverbs are a vital and important mode of communicating and key to penetrating the worldview of Africans" (Pobee 1996).

Indigenous Regard for Proverbs

An indication of the high regard that some cultures have for proverbs is the prevalence and regular usage of proverbs in these cultures. Writing about the Igbo language, Maazi Chijioke Asogwa notes, "[I was] able collect up to two hundred proverbs from a single person in one sitting. We have also been able to collect up to one thousand in several sittings from one person" (2002, 49). Similarly, many of the Builsa were able and willing to share many proverbs with me. One night a group of youth shared seventy-three proverbs with me in an hour and a half with no sign of letting up.

Clearly, proverbs have an emic value that those outside the culture do not always appreciate. Intercultural disciplers look for emic reasoning patterns to transform worldviews. When they overlook indigenous reasoning patterns, Christianity appears foreign and irrelevant, which leads to split-level Christianity.

Once the proverbs are valued and used to express Christianity, the heartfelt, intimate issues of culture can be exposed and transformed by the gospel. This leads to intercultural discipling that uses indigenous reasoning, as the following story demonstrates.

"This proverb encourages me to do the right thing," shares Kofi. "During difficult times, it has helped me many times. Our elders say, 'Pukawgi a laa ka tuik po' (A widow laughs at the spot where she pounds millet)."

SIDEBAR 8.1

The Value of Proverbs

Consider the following indigenous proverbs, which highlight the emic value of proverbs:

- A conversation without proverbs is like stew without salt. Oromo proverb.
- Proverbs are the palm oil with which words are eaten. Nigerian proverb (Achebe 1959, 7).
- Proverbs are the horses of speech; if communication is lost, we use proverbs to find it. Yoruba proverb (Lindfors 1973).

Reflection and Discussion

1. Why are proverbs held in such high esteem in some cultures but not in others?
2. Consider the above metaphors used to describe proverbs. How are proverbs like salt, palm oil, and horses? What is being expressed by these open-ended metaphors?
3. What metaphors could be used to describe intercultural discipling that contextualizes proverbs?

For additional African proverbs, including an "African Proverb of the Month," see http://www.afriprov.org.

Joe, a missionary from another culture, is puzzled at first. How could this proverb inspire Kofi so deeply? It is so short; perhaps that is why he is able to recall it so readily. Joe knows that millet is a major crop for the Builsa, and he sees women at the *tuik* (mortar/pestle for pounding) each day pounding millet seeds into millet flour to make *saab* (staple food). Joe understands the words but not the meaning.

Kofi can see that Joe is puzzled. Kofi enjoys this proverb, and he relishes the opportunity to explain it to Joe. "When a husband dies, the oldest son is responsible to look after his mother, who is now a widow," Kofi explains. "The son now has a very delicate problem to work out. How does he show love to his mother and take care of her in his house without making his wife jealous by feeling that she is not cared for as well as before?"

Joe has not considered this before. Relationships are crucial in this culture, since the people's very survival depends on harmonious relationships. The man has to find a way to give the appropriate amount of food, time, affection, and so on to both his mother and his wife, who share the same house; otherwise, critical relationships will be damaged.

Kofi picks a millet stalk from a house that has a full head of white millet on the outside. Joe can see that the millet seeds grow on the outside and that they can easily be removed from the husk and roasted or ground into flour. Kofi continues, "This millet is called *zaapiulik* or *gmankarik*. The man gives this millet to his wife, and she is happy since she knows that she can make a good meal out of this for the family."

Kofi picks up another millet stalk that does not look like millet to Joe. Joe can't see the millet seeds, since they grow inside the husk. Kofi continues, "At the same time, he gives *zaabuluk* to his mother." *Zaabuluk* is millet that has to be pounded first to remove the husk, and then it can be pounded again into flour. At first glance, it looks as if there is not much millet in the *zaabuluk*.

Kofi is smiling widely now. Joe knows the punch line is close, so he hangs in with Kofi's long explanation.

Kofi adds, "When the man first gave the *zaabuluk* to his mother in the sight of his wife, the wife felt like she had gotten the better part of the bargain. The wife's millet looked much fuller and she thought, 'My husband still loves me since he gave me the better millet!' When the widowed mother finally took her *zaabuluk* to the *tuik* and pounded it, she realized that she had a larger bowl of winnowed millet than the wife. At the *tuik*, she laughed and laughed since she knew that she had raised a loving and wise son. Not only did her son still love her by giving her the larger amount of millet, but he also was wise enough to let both women feel that they were loved the most!"

Joe laughs along with Kofi. The man in the story has skillfully negotiated two very important relationships, and he has found a way to show love and concern to both without either one getting mad or jealous. In the end, the widow laughs since she has received the greater amount of millet to bless her amid her suffering. Joe enjoys the story but still isn't sure of how this encourages Kofi's faith.

Kofi concludes, "This has encouraged me for a long time now. When I first followed Jesus, some people ridiculed me and did me harm. They were trying

The Way of Righteousness

A radio broadcast, *The Way of Righteousness*, was developed for Muslims in the Wolof language in Senegal, West Africa (https://www.twr360.org/programs/view/id,49701/action,pdf/lang,1). This chronological Bible-story approach incorporates Wolof proverbs to help explain biblical concepts. The following is an excerpt from lesson one:

You may have heard the African proverb that says: "Slowly, slowly one catches a monkey in the forest" or "A water pail will find the person who waits diligently at the well." God tells us in His Word that He "rewards those who *earnestly* seek him" (Heb. 11:6). . . . Sometimes we encounter those who fight against God's Book, saying, "No one can trust it! It is full of errors. It has been changed!" However, the one who fights with the Word of Truth is fighting with God Him- self. Another African proverb says, "An egg should not wrestle with a rock!" The Word of God is the Rock, and man

is the egg! Man cannot change the true Word of God—but the true Word of God can change man! God is great, and is able to protect His Eternal Word. That is what the Lord Himself said in the book known as the *Injil* [the gospel record is called the *Injil* in the Qur'an, Arabic for the "good news" or the "gos- pel"]: "Heaven and earth will pass away, but my words will never pass away!" (Matt. 24:35).

Reflection and Discussion

1. If your mother tongue were Wolof and you recognized these proverbs in this radio program, how might the proverbs affect your regard for this message?
2. How does the reasoning expressed in proverbs differ from direct, linear, propositional approaches?
3. How might this influence your ap- proach to discipleship among Wolof speakers?

to push me away, and I felt like a widow who was rejected. In the middle of the persecution, this proverb reminded me that I will one day laugh again. Others may mean harm to me, but Naawen will work it out for good in the end. Today, I am laughing with joy since Naawen has helped me. Naawen has become my millet for me. People used insults and difficulties to discourage me, but Naawen used those very difficulties to encourage me. He turned their insults into good. I have seen Naawen bless me, and now I am laughing at the *tuik*!"

Joe claps with joy for Kofi. On the inside, his heart claps for Jesus. It is a wonderful testimony of what Jesus can do for a believer in the midst of trials and difficulties. Joe knows that many young believers face trials from their families, especially when they reject the traditional sacrifices to the ancestors. These difficult excluded-level issues test their faith and resolve to the limit. Joe thanks God that this proverb has helped Kofi hold onto the promise in 1 Peter 5:10, "And the God of all grace, who called you to his eternal glory in Christ, after you have suffered a little while, will himself restore you and make you strong, firm and steadfast." One day, the widow will again laugh under the *tuik*. (adapted from Moon 2009a, 129–31)

The short proverb greatly aids Kofi's discipleship. The suffering he experienced is a significant excluded middle issue. He struggled to find God's presence amid these difficulties. If there were no satisfactory Christian response, then he would likely go to another source for answers, resulting in split-level Christianity.

For intercultural disciplers, the intimate issue of suffering is not a secondary one. Kofi needed a Christian response in order to maintain his Christ-centered faith. Using indigenous reasoning patterns through proverbs strengthened his faith. More than abstract doctrinal discussions of suffering, the indigenous proverb sank deeply into his soul. The metaphors involving the widow, millet, and her suffering provided mental images that he was able to connect with and draw strength from. These images then connected Kofi to his faith in God. While this reasoning pattern seems strange to the Western missionary Joe, Kofi is very much at home with it. By providing reason to his faith, this proverb facilitated his discipleship in a way that was fully Builsa and fully Christian.

Proverbs Express Christianity in Local Clothing

In addition to providing indigenous reasoning, indigenous proverbs aid discipleship by expressing Christianity in local clothing. Proverbs use local terms and expressions that make Christianity feel "at home." As one Builsa explained to me, "I know that God's word [the Bible] is not just words from the white man, but it is God's word for the Builsa, since our own proverbs confirm it."

When foreign terms and concepts are used for discipleship, the discipleship process is stilted. It often feels just a bit out of place. An African proverb

> The proverbs and sayings of the Oromo [in Ethiopia] show that the Holy Spirit sowed the seeds of the gospel in the culture of these people long before they ever heard Jesus' words.
>
> George Cotter (1989, 17)

describes it this way: "Borrowed pants: if they are not tight at the ankle, they are loose at the thigh." When a pair of pants is tailored to fit an individual, it feels just right for that person. When someone else borrows those pants, however, their measurements are different, and the pants will not fit exactly. Either the ankle will be too tight or the thigh will be too loose. Similarly, imported theological concepts/terms often feel out of place. The disciple feels inhibited, since the theology is shaped by terms that are not cut from the local cloth. Christianity then feels like a foreign gospel. Proverbs shape contextual discipleship by expressing theology in indigenous terms and concepts.

Contextualization of Proverbs

When these indigenous terms and concepts are engaged with Scripture, contextual discipleship results. In previous chapters, the critical contextualization process was demonstrated with rituals and stories. Proverbs can also serve this purpose. The following steps are used to contextualize proverbs for discipleship. While the steps do not have to be taken in the exact order shown, the information provided at each step facilitates contextualization.

1. *Phenomenological study*: State the proverb and describe the possible meanings. Also describe the context in which the proverb is used, including its history and the circumstances to which it applies.
2. *Ontological critique*: Discover the root issues in culture that the proverb addresses. What concerns are addressed by the proverb and why?

SIDEBAR 8.3

Sukuma Research Committee in Tanzania

The Sukuma Research Committee was formed to collect and interpret the oral literature (particularly proverbs) of the Sukuma people, the largest ethnic group in Tanzania. The purpose of this group is to help construct a local Christian African narrative theology. The group advocates a seven-step process:

1. Collect and transcribe the original proverb.
2. Note the context of the proverb, including the history, meaning(s), and use of the proverb.
3. Identify a theme of the proverb to facilitate Christian interpretation.
4. Group other similar proverbs together to confirm/nuance the meaning.
5. Find biblical parallels and connections.
6. Choose a Christian teaching on the theme of the proverb.
7. Provide concrete suggestions for using the proverb in religious teaching.

Adapted from Healey and Sybertz (2000)

Reflection and Discussion

1. Compare/contrast this process to the four-step critical contextualization process recommended by Hiebert (phenomenological study, ontological critique, critical evaluation, missiological transformation). What differences/similarities are most striking?
2. Who should take the lead role in each step? What are the roles of both insiders and outsiders in this process?
3. How can intercultural disciplers use this process to identify and then transform worldviews?

Of the possible meanings identified, which ones are most likely? What common themes are addressed by proverbs similar to this one? Often we can understand the meaning of a proverb by comparing it to another proverb.

3. *Critical evaluation*: Engage the root issues with Scripture. Often Scripture will confirm the wisdom in the proverbs. There are also times when Scripture will modify or reject some of the cultural values portrayed in the proverb. See my extensive exploration of how this works in an African setting (Moon 2009a).

4. *Missiological transformation*: Help growing disciples apply the proverb in a way that keeps them kingdom centered amid their own culture.

Chicken Theology

The following event portrays the steps listed above. Twelve Builsa pastors gathered to discuss their indigenous proverbs and how these proverbs interact with Scripture. This is an important part of discipleship, since the indigenous proverbs express Christianity in indigenous terms and concepts.

Laughter and excitement pour forth like perspiration under the hot African sun. Finding refuge under the cover of a shade tree, the pastors gather with excitement.

Kofi opens with his favorite proverb, one that had helped his own faith in Yezu: "*Nurubiik a labri ka kpiak kawpta po*" (A human being hides in the feathers of a chicken). Joe is totally puzzled, while the Builsa seem to enjoy reflecting on this proverb. On Joe's request, the church leaders explain the background of the proverb.

In the life of the Builsa people, fowls are used to hide shame or problems. If someone comes upon a problem requiring money, they can always sell some of the fowls at market and then use the money to solve the problem. In this way, they hide behind the chicken's feathers so that the shame of the problem does not reach them. The fowl is also commonly used in situations requiring sacrifice to the ancestors or earth shrines for problems such as sickness, infertility, drought, and famine. The fowl is sacrificed to the ancestors or earth shrine to solve the problem and cover the shame. In this way, Builsas feel safe or protected as long as there are fowls around the house; hence, they feel they can "hide inside the feathers of the fowl."

Joe is catching on slowly. "So the chicken is an essential part of the Builsa culture. It is used to solve problems so that the chicken receives the brunt of the problem and it will not reach us. If we have chickens around our homes, then we feel safe from dangers that may come. Is that right?"

"Yes, Joe, chickens help us to feel safe and protected. They are sacrificed or sold for us. They take our problems upon them, and we hide safely in their feathers. They also help us initiate friendships," responds Kofi. "If I want to start a friendship with someone, I offer him a chicken for us to share a meal together, or I offer him a chicken to take home."

Kofi continues, "Now that I am a *Kristobiik* [Christian], I feel that Yezu is the chicken that I hide under. When problems come, I can run to Yezu in prayer and ask him to cover my shame and protect me. He will bear the full impact of the problem that has come upon me, and I can safely rest in his feathers."

Immanuel adds, "When we rest in the feathers of Yezu, we no longer need to have a *jiuk*, *bagi*, or any other black medicine to protect us. The feathers of Yezu will cover us—our relationship with him assures us that he will cover us with his wings. Naawen Wani says that Naawen will 'cover you with his feathers and under his wings you will find refuge; his faithfulness will be your shield and rampart'" (Ps. 91:4).

Joe is stunned. He remembers reading this verse in seminary while studying in the West. The imagery of "hiding under the wings of God" was strange to his ears, and it was difficult for him to gain the meaning of the metaphor back then. Now the meaning is starting to dawn on him. The perspective of the Builsa culture brings out a richer meaning of this Scripture passage. It deals with protection from harm, shame, and difficulties. It also implies a close relationship with God, who is willing to receive the brunt of our difficulties as we hide under God's protection. "What a wonderful metaphor," Joe thinks to himself, "and it took another cultural perspective for me to gain this insight." Little does Joe know that the best is yet to come.

Immanuel adds, "This proverb has touched me deeply, and it helps me to understand the heart of Yezu." The earnestness in his voice reveals that this is a deep matter of discipleship for him.

Joe is eager to hear more.

"When I hear this proverb and read Matthew 23:37, I can feel Yezu's heart and desire for us Builsa people," continues Immanuel. "Yezu says, 'How often I have longed to gather your children together, as a hen gathers her chicks under

---

For many non-literate people, the wisdom of the people is embedded in proverbs. . . . For Africans these are vistas into ultimate reality.

John Pobee (1989, 86)

---

her wings.' That is Yezu's desire for us—to protect us, cover our shame, receive the brunt of our difficulties. That is a closer friend than I have ever known!"

Kofi's eyes light up. "Are you sure that is in Naawen Wani—let me see that."

He reads slowly in Buli how Yezu wanted to "pawbi ni meena a tara ase kpiak ale pawbi ka bisa dii la." This literally means to "wrap you all up like a fowl wraps up her children (under her wings)." Since fowls are a daily part of the life experience of the Builsa, the picture of a hen wrapping up her chicks under her wings in order to protect them from hawks and other dangers is a

Values in American Proverbs

Stan Nussbaum took a unique approach to help visitors to the United States understand American values by analyzing 234 American proverbs and common sayings in American culture (2005). Based on the values portrayed in the proverbs, he extracted the ten most common values and called them the "Ten Commandments of American Culture," summarized here:

1. You can't argue with success (be a success).
2. Live and let live (be tolerant).
3. Time flies when you're having fun (have lots of fun).
4. Shop till you drop.
5. Just do it.
6. You are only young once (do whatever you can while you have the chance).
7. Enough is enough (stand up for your rights).
8. Rules are made to be broken (think for yourself).

9. Time is money (don't waste time).
10. God helps those who help themselves (work hard).

Reflection and Discussion

1. Meet with some Americans and ask them whether these values seem to be accurate.
2. How do proverbs tend to balance one another such that one proverb will correct the excesses of another proverb? Compare this to the two "counterproverbs" in Proverbs 26:4–5.
3. If proverbs are maxims that are valid for particular contexts instead of truths that are applicable everywhere, how does one know which proverb to apply in a particular situation at a particular time? (Hint: Where does the book of Proverbs say that wisdom and knowledge come from, as in Prov. 1:7?)

very vivid and concrete picture in Kofi's mind. Kofi sits back and smiles as he reflects on this picture of Yezu and what it means to him.

David then adds an application from the book of Ruth. "Do you remember how Ruth was a widow? Like our widows here in Buluk, she had little hope for the future. When she placed herself under Naawen's feathers, Naawen covered her shame and brought about a wonderful blessing. Listen to the praise she received from Boaz in Ruth 2:12: 'May you be richly rewarded by the LORD, the God of Israel, *under whose wings you have come to take refuge*'" (emphasis mine).

It is Joe's turn to be surprised. "Are you sure that is in the Bible? Let me read that."

Joe had read the book of Ruth several times before, but he never noticed the imagery of "hiding under the wings of God." He can now feel Ruth's desperation of widowhood, and he also understands the imagery of taking refuge under God's wings. Joe is learning new things from Scripture that he had previously overlooked.

For the next month, they chew on these thoughts. This proverb raises other connections to Scripture. Can this proverb give additional understanding of the significance of the cherubim's wings covering the ark of the covenant in the tabernacle (Exod. 25:17–22) and God's words "There, above the cover between the two cherubim that are over the ark of the covenant law, I will meet with you" (Exod. 25:22)? This imagery is repeated in Solomon's temple (1 Kings 8:6–11), where "The cherubim spread their wings over the place of the ark" (1 Kings 8:7). Again, Joe wonders whether it might explain some of the imagery behind God carrying the Israelites on eagles' wings when bringing them out of Egypt (Exod. 19:4), as well as shed some light on difficult passages in Ezekiel 10 and elsewhere. (adapted from Moon 2009a, 111–13)

In the above example, the indigenous proverb engages Scripture such that indigenous expressions of Christianity result. This proverb shapes Christianity in terms and concepts that are uniquely Builsa. Chicken theology is a handcrafted theology that helps articulate a Builsa Christian worldview.

Many proverbs are useful for expressing Christianity in culture. Often the values of indigenous proverbs are accepted into disciples' new Christian worldview. The proverbs, then, are effective communicators of Christianity. Once again, the mother-tongue Scripture interprets aspects of the proverb to affirm.

Scripture will also modify or reject aspects of proverbs at times. Critical contextualization helps to identify these aspects for discipleship. To portray the critical contextualization process with proverbs, once again we turn to the Builsa pastors who gathered to engage their proverbs with Scripture. This time, there are values in proverbs that Scripture modifies or rejects, thereby creating a ripe moment for intercultural discipleship.

The discussion leader presents the proverb "Fi dan sak bulorik dueni deka, ku chum le faari fi ma" (If you teach an ugly man how to court women, in the future he will marry your mother). The entire room explodes with laughter. The imagery is painfully funny.

"I don't think that we should discuss that proverb. It is not good, and it will not help our discussion," responds Pastor David. The look of concern written on his face lets us know that there is a lot in that proverb that he can say, but he would rather not bring it out in the open.

Several others nod their heads in agreement. Pastor Kofi adds, "Sometimes, these proverbs are used to insult certain people. They can also be used to hide things from some people, since the meaning is not clear. We should be careful not to use proverbs like this. In addition, there are some proverbs that use language that would be embarrassing to use in church!"

Sensing how the group is uncomfortable discussing this proverb, the discussion leader points out, "Yes, it is true that we need to be careful how, when, and with whom we use proverbs. On the other hand, this proverb exists in our culture for a reason. It points out some issue or problem that is a part of how we Builsa think and live. Look at that tree over there. What do you see?"

"I see big limbs and some baobob fruit on the ends of the limbs," answers Immanuel.

"I see the leaves and birds resting in there," replies another.

The discussion leader continues, "Good. That huge tree, leaves, fruits, and birds are all the things that you can see. The tree only stands strong, though, because of the roots that you do not see. If there were no roots, the tree would not be there. The tree is there because of the roots. In the same way, this proverb is there because of some roots in our culture. We should not dismiss it too quickly. Let us take the time to understand the proverb well so that we can understand the roots in our culture that are allowing this tree to stand."

"I see what you are saying. You are right that there are some roots in our culture that we do not like to talk about. How do we uncover these roots so that we can see them?" Pastor Kofi asks.

"We need to dig down to the roots by asking some questions. This is hard work, just like it is hard to dig up the roots of the baobob tree. Let's ask questions like:

"'Who says this proverb and to whom?'

"'When does this proverb come into conversation? What happens just before it that brings this proverb forth?'

"'Where is this proverb spoken—in the market, at a funeral, in the house, at the chief's court?'

"'Why do they say this proverb?'"

Immanuel can't stand it any longer, and he has to jump in to answer some of the questions. "I'll tell you who says this proverb. You say this to a person when you help him, but then the person turns around and does something harmful to you. I had a friend who called me to come and help him on the farm. I agreed and helped him all day. Later, I called him to come and farm for me, but he never showed up. I struggled hard to get the farming done. I did good to him, but he repaid me with unkindness; therefore, I used this proverb to describe how he treated me."

Pastor Kofi adds, "I had a similar experience. The elders say, 'Fi dan pa poning a poni nuru zuk, wa chum le pa takaribaling a poni fi zuk' (If you take a pair of scissors and cut someone's hair, in the future he will take a piece of broken pot and cut your hair). A friend of mine was out of food one year, and I helped the family by giving them some food. Another year, my crop did not do well, and I asked that friend for help. He totally forgot about the past help that I had given him, and he refused my request for help."

"Why does that happen?" the discussion leader asks the group.

"I think that it is greed," replies one pastor.

"That is a root in our culture, isn't it? Does Naawen Wani talk about this?" asks the discussion leader.

"Yes. Galatians 5 says that greed is from the heart of people. This proverb reveals our sinful nature. Naawen warns us that those who practice greed will not see Naawen's kingdom. Greed can destroy our community and our church," replies Immanuel.

Sweet Talk

While learning the local language through cultural immersion, I often observed the Builsa people engaging in lively, entertaining, and seemingly effective forms of communication. They were using traditional proverbs, which made the conversation "sweet," meaning pleasant to listen to and easier to digest or understand. I wondered, "Could this be an effective vehicle for intercultural discipleship in a way that was sweet to the listeners' ears and also sweet to their hearts?" After ten years of exploring this question, I suggest three reasons that intercultural disciplers in predominantly oral cultures should actively incorporate the use of traditional proverbs:

1. Proverbs open ears to hear the gospel that may otherwise be closed.
2. Proverbs clear away the fog in theological understanding.
3. Proverbs root the gospel in vernacular soil such that it feels "at home."

Adapted from Moon (2004, 162)

Reflection and Discussion

1. How may these three observations assist intercultural disciplers in the contextualization process?
2. What are some of the difficulties in learning and using local proverbs?
3. How can we overcome these difficulties in order to realize the benefit of "sweet talk" for intercultural discipling? Consider the role of learning in community, visiting elders, expressing appreciation for local proverbs, concrete-relational versus abstract-propositional reasoning, and role models/apprenticeship.

"True, this proverb is telling us to not have mercy on others since they may return evil to us. If I have mercy on an ugly man and help him, he may cause problems for me by marrying my mother. How would my father like that?" replies Pastor Kofi. Laughter bursts forth like a thunderclap! The entire room is animated and full of life.

Pastor David adds, "In Scripture, we see that Naawen had mercy on us; therefore, we should show mercy to others. You never know how Naawen can use that person. Think about the conversion of Saul. Naawen turned him around to be a blessing to the church."

"I think that this proverb is used because someone has been offended or mistreated. As a result, he wants to get back at that person. As we are discussing it here, I remember that Naawen Wani tells us not to repay evil for evil. We should repay evil with good," Immanuel adds.

The discussion leader pulls it together for them. "We are discussing some roots in our culture that Scripture rejects. We should not withhold mercy from others; rather, we need to show mercy as Naawen has done for us. Remember what Yezu has done for us—then act that way to others. Another root that we discussed was greed. We need to warn our people about greed, since it can destroy our church and community. This may help church members understand why it is important to bring their tithe to church. We also talked about how to deal with those who mistreat us. Does that ever happen in the church? How should we respond as church leaders? Instead of rejecting those who persecute us, we should repay evil with good."

"But wait. . . . If I try to not be greedy and give all my food to others and help everyone, then I may not have enough for my family to eat," responds Immanuel. (adapted from Moon 2009a, 93–95)

Let's pause the conversation for just a minute to learn how these Africans are using indigenous proverbs for discipleship. Instead of appealing to abstract systematic theology, they are learning from the concrete-relational images embedded in the proverbs. These images are entertaining, like "sweet talk," and they are also memorable. More important, they open the ears of the Builsa to learn new truth.

Also, note how one proverb becomes a stepping-stone to nuance and explain another proverb. While the meaning of the first proverb may not be totally clear, the other proverbs are used to explain the first one. This type of reasoning is highly valued in oral cultures, and thus it can clear away the fog in theological understanding.

In addition to providing quick understanding, the use of proverbs roots the gospel in the local soil such that it feels at home and not like a foreign import. This is an important factor if the local people are to be transformed by the gospel.

Thus it makes sense that intercultural disciplers employ proverbs for discipleship related to excluded middle issues. Let's now return to the conversation:

Pastor Kofi has a pensive look. "Mmm. This is not easy to follow. The person that offends you may be very troublesome. There may be a reason that this person is this way, and he needs to feel the consequences of his actions. The elders say, 'Fi dan nya diok a bo nyiamu po a cheng, fa yieri; fi dan nya nuru a bo nyiamu po a cheng, basi' (If you see wood floating by in the water, you pull it out; if you see a person floating by in the water, leave him)." Nervous smiles cross every face as the listeners enjoy the vivid imagery of the proverb.

"Can you explain that one to us?" asks the discussion leader.

"Well . . . a story goes like this. A man made a promise to the river shrine that he would bring an animal sacrifice to the river if it helped him to get wealthy. Later on, the man got wealthy, but he did not fulfill his promise to the river shrine by bringing the sacrifice. One day, while he was near the river, it pulled him into the water to pay the debt. A bystander saw him floating by, calling for help. If the bystander pulled the man out of the water, the debt to the river would still not be paid back. The man who owed the debt would then push the bystander who rescued him into the river to pay back the debt that he owed. The bystander meant to do a good thing by rescuing the man, but he would be repaid with evil. It would have been better if the rescuer let the man float by. If it was a piece of wood, however, he could use it in his house, and it would not push him in the water; therefore, he should pull the wood out of the water. Do you understand now?"

The fog is slowly beginning to clear. It touches some deep feelings in the process. Each of the pastors can think of other instances where they had intended good for someone, but it turned out that they were not appreciated, and the person turned against the pastor.

Pastor David notes, "This proverb talks about how to deal with difficult people. It implies that we should be careful concerning who we help and how we do it. Naawen Wani also warns us to be careful with people. We should not throw our pearls to swine. We should be wise as serpents but harmless as doves. We know that we should not repay evil with evil, but we should also be careful and wise how we help people."

The discussion leader adds, "Yes, I think that is one root that we can accept. When I think about Yezu, though, he did not leave us in the water. We were like that man who was drowning in the water. Because of our sins, we were going to die. Yezu saw us floating in the river, and he pulled us out of the water. What did people do to him? They pushed him in the water so that he would die for us! He *knew* that people were going to push him in the water by sending him to the cross; yet he still pulled us out of the river."

A somber hush falls over the room like the settling of dew in the early morning. "I never thought about that before. He knew that people would hurt him for his good deeds, yet he did it anyway. That is powerful love, isn't it?" speaks Immanuel.

"It sure is," responds Pastor Kofi. "It was not easy for Yezu to reach in the water and grab us, particularly since he knew that we would push him in. Yet, he obeyed Naawen—that is why we see Naawen's blessings today. We can help others see Naawen's blessings today in Buluk by following what Yezu did."

"I have to be honest, though. Sometimes, a small misunderstanding happens in the church, and the church members get angry with me," one pastor confides. "They forget all the good that I have done and remember only the thing that made them angry. As a result, they start talking about getting a new pastor. I heard a proverb in Tamale the other day that said, 'If you only consider the smoke, you will put out the fire.' They forget the benefit of the fire and think only about the irritation of the smoke; therefore, they want to get rid of the pastor and put out the fire."

The mood in the room now changes. Each pastor can identify with this struggle. It is not easy being a pastor. The pastors struggle to care for the people because they love Naawen. There is no salary from the mission, and they receive just a small collection from the church. They are often rejected by other Builsa because of their faith. When church members complain, it is very discouraging, and the pastors, at times, consider quitting. They try to do good and help the ugly man learn how to marry, but this kindness is occasionally returned by complaints against the pastor—it feels as if an ugly man has just married the pastor's mother!

This creates a long discussion about how to deal with misunderstandings in the church. They all agree that leaders can expect problems to come at times even though the leader has not done wrong, citing the example of Moses. They then discuss Matthew 18 to deal quickly with misunderstandings so that they do not grow into big problems. If not addressed quickly, gossip will destroy the pastor's reputation, which will put out the fire.

After this long discussion, the discussion leader asks, "We all know how it feels to be misunderstood and to have our good intentions repaid with evil. Do you think that missionaries sometimes feel this way?"

There is a long pause. The pastors remember how they complained about the missionaries at times. They talked about them behind their backs. Pastor David finally breaks the silence. "I had never thought of that before. We all know that they make mistakes at times that become like smoke in our eyes. When that happens, we forget all the good that they have done for us, and we think about putting out the fire. It would be better for us to discuss the problem with them so that we can manage the smoke and still enjoy the fire."

Pastor Kofi adds, "This is true. I do not think that any of the missionaries have meant to do us harm. They have done many good things to help us. Their intentions were good, but they have made mistakes, since they did not understand our culture and they were also human beings with their own weaknesses. When we complain and gossip about them instead of discussing the root issues with them, they may feel as if the ugly man has married their mother."

"I can now understand how they feel at times, since I have felt this way too," adds Pastor David. The pastors are all very reflective as they recall their recent interactions with the missionaries. They each have a new sense of understanding that they had not considered before.

The discussion leader concludes, "You all have identified roots in the proverb that Naawen Wani affirms. We need to understand that leadership will include some misunderstanding along the way. We should not be surprised when it happens. 'Gingeling ale nyinga dom chaab alege ba bo ale chaab' (The tongue and teeth bite each other, but they live together). How we respond is critical. Matthew 18 tells us how to quickly discuss the root issues so that the misunderstanding does not grow into a big ugly situation. This is better than talking behind the backs of others and gossiping since 'Bumborim ale wang yeri' (Gossip will scatter a house). We also discussed how we need to use wisdom regarding whom we help and how we do it. We should feed and take care of our own households first; otherwise, we will be worse than unbelievers. We should not give all our food away such that our own households are starving. We should use wisdom before we jump in the water too quickly. You have all done well to discuss the root issues and use Naawen Wani to teach us those that are *magsi* (suitable) and those that are not *magsi*." (adapted from Moon 2009a, 95–98)

The above conversation is presented at length for several reasons. Note how the reasoning process depends on one proverb to describe another. Like stepping-stones placed in a river, proverbs are dependable maxims to guide the reasoning process.

As in the other chapters, note the importance of a hermeneutical community. Intercultural discipleship relies on the community, not the individual alone, to transform people. It starts with a proverb that someone identifies in the culture. This proverb identifies important issues that reside in the culture.

> **Proverbs are a mirror on which a community can look at itself and a stage on which it exposes itself to others. They describe its values, aspirations, preoccupations, and the particular angles from which it sees and appreciates realities and behavior.**
>
> Patrick A. Kalilombe (1969, 3)

Then the hermeneutical community uses the critical contextualization steps to identify aspects of the proverb to affirm, modify, or reject.

For the disciple, this discipleship process is full of discovery and learning. In the process of discipleship, intercultural disciplers also discover aspects of Scripture and their own culture that they may have overlooked before. In addition, they discover aspects of the host culture that are not quickly revealed in other contexts. This process becomes like a window into the soul of another culture.

Cultural Mirror for Insiders

For insiders, this process becomes a mirror into the soul of their own culture. While they may not want to admit that certain aspects of their culture exist, the proverbs bubble these issues to the surface. Note the reticence of the Builsa to discuss certain proverbs. This indicates that some excluded middle issues have not yet been addressed in the church. This is ripe material for discipleship. As the proverbs are addressed, these excluded middle issues can be exposed, providing opportunities to transform the worldview.

At times, excluded middle issues persist in culture, even though they are harmful. While rarely discussed openly, they tend to reside in deep symbols, as described by Edward Farley:

> As instruments of corrupted power, deep symbols can mirror the society's stratification of privilege. All actual societies privilege some members over others: citizens over slaves, gentry over plain folk, males over females, majorities over minorities. And no society in history has ever been able to keep these arrangements from affecting its deep symbols. Thus, the deep symbols can be

Resources for Intercultural Discipleship with Proverbs

There are several resources that encourage the contextualization of indigenous proverbs for intercultural discipleship, based on their application in various countries; see, for example, Stan Nussbaum in Africa and the United States (1996, 1998), Joseph Healey and Donald Sybertz in Tanzania (2000), Janice Raymond in Mongolia (2012), and me in Ghana (Moon 2009a). The most comprehensive effort is the African Proverbs Project, a three-year project designed for the "collection, publication and study of African proverbs with particular attention to their relationship to Christian mission, their role in modern Africa and their significance for a number of academic disciplines" (see http://www.gmi.org/about-us/what-we-do/project-portfolio/research-projects/the-wisdom-of-african-proverbs and http://www.afriprov.org).

so framed as to advance the privileged members and suppress the voice of the unprivileged. They still may function as deep values and ideals, but in those ideals lurk racism, the disenfranchising of women, the maintenance of social policies that favor an existing social elite. For these reasons, the religious community must never pretend that its own deep symbols float above history in a world of ideal meanings. It must never maintain a passive, uncritical relation to its deep symbols. (1996, 8)

As a case in point, Mineke Schipper (1985, 23–27) maintains that proverbs and other literary genres, such as myths, are used by the dominant power group to maintain the status quo. She observes that most proverbs are attributed to men and are used by men to maintain power over women. This is an important critique and demonstrates why proverbs must be critically evaluated instead of passively accepted.

Issues that may arise in the proverbs are prejudices against women or other vulnerable groups. These deep-seated issues are often not exposed or addressed in discipleship. A careful phenomenological study as part of the critical contextualization process, however, will uncover these underlying attitudes in culture. While the cultural insiders may not want to discuss these issues, they are "forced" to acknowledge their presence, since they are exposed by their own proverbs. This provides a powerful opportunity for intercultural discipleship.

Summary

For many societies, indigenous proverbs provide an alternate reasoning process. Instead of shaping thought in systematic, abstract, and analytical categories,

177

these societies base their reasoning on the use of proverbs. For intercultural disciplers, proverbs can be used for discipleship in several ways:

1. Proverbs tap into the deep aspects of language that are used to convey weighty matters. This type of speech is used to create oral art, and it is highly valued in many oral societies.

2. As a result of using indigenous reasoning patterns through proverbs, excluded middle issues arise. Once these issues are exposed, they can be addressed to help disciples maintain a kingdom-centered life.

3. Proverbs express Christianity in local clothing. In addition to the internal reasoning process, proverbs help in outward communication so that Christianity is not a "foreign gospel."

4. The critical contextualization process facilitates the proper use of proverbs for discipleship. Often proverbs can help insiders understand and express Scripture. These proverbs can be used with very little, if any, modification. Other proverbs, however, will have aspects that need to be modified or rejected by Scripture.

5. For insiders, indigenous proverbs become a mirror into the worldview of their culture. Issues such as prejudice against other ethnic groups and women bubble to the surface. Once these issues are exposed, they can then be addressed.

6. For the outside discipler, proverbs become a window into the worldview of the host culture. Indigenous proverbs can reveal hidden aspects of culture and explain hidden aspects of Scripture.

In the next chapter, we will explore more of the oral arts for discipleship. In particular, the time-tested value of music will be discussed as well as the more recently recognized arts of dance and drama.

Activity for Discipling

1. Collect proverbs in the host culture. Begin by listening to the conversations of elders and notice when they interject proverbs. Try to record the proverb, including the context, to whom it was addressed, and its possible meanings. If possible, identify proverbs that address the excluded middle issue of your discipling group.

2. Search for proverbs in literacy primers, stories, dictionaries, and proverb collections. Also observe the conclusion of a conflict or a big decision and listen for proverbs that are used to settle the issue.

3. Gather a hermeneutical community. Try the four-step critical contextualization process described in chapter 6.
4. Learn a few proverbs in the host culture. Learn how to use them in the proper context.

Look for major themes that emerge in the indigenous proverbs. Compare these themes with those from the proverbs in your passport culture. For example, consider the top ten values that Nussbaum identified in American proverbs in sidebar 8.4, which provides a good resource for comparison. Intercultural disciplers can learn a great deal about their birth culture and host culture through this comparative process.

The Heart Guides the Legs

Adapted from Moon (2009b, 126–27).

After being away for a while, one day I return to see Jaffa. Knowing my interest in proverbs, Jaffa says with a smile, "I knew that you would return to see me. We have a proverb in Hausa that says, 'What the heart loves, there the legs will go.'"

As Jaffa sees me pondering the meaning, he nudges my understanding. "Look at your legs. Where are they?"

I look down to my legs as he gently prods. "What does that say about your heart?"

"Ahh," I reply, "since my heart was here with you, you knew that my feet would find a way back to see you."

Jaffa breaks into a broad smile with the satisfaction that he has once again taught me another piece of the worldview and thinking pattern of his people. "You see," Jaffa reiterates, "what the heart loves, there the legs will go!"

We clasp hands and walk together. As I ponder further the meaning of this proverb, I respond, "It is true, as you say, that the legs must follow where the heart is. Do you think God's heart is close to us?"

It is now Jaffa's turn to ponder a bit more deeply.

I continue, "Since God created you and me, don't you think that God's heart is close to his creation? God loves people and wants to be with them—his heart is already with us. Don't you think that God would have to find a way for his feet to follow where his heart already is?"

Jaffa stops as he processes this thought amid the meaning of the Hausa proverb. "Do you mean that God wanted to move among the people?"

I am pleasantly surprised by his choice of words, since Jesus is perhaps best described as Immanuel, meaning "God among us."

"Yes," I affirm, "that is why Jesus came to earth. God's heart pulled so strongly that his feet had to come among us. Jesus was the feet of God!"

Jaffa now seriously ponders the meaning and implications of what has been discussed. I and many others have spoken to him before about faith in Jesus. As a Muslim, he agrees that Jesus was a good person, but he does not understand why Jesus was necessary. Why would God want to come to earth anyway? Jaffa feels that God created everything and is now far removed from daily events. He understands God as the ultimate judge, but he has not considered before how God's heart may be touched by the people he created. It is a new thought to him, but it makes perfect sense using the logic and time-tested wisdom of the Hausa proverb.

While all of Jaffa's questions are not answered that day, he is beginning to understand the ways and purposes of God in terms and concepts that he can understand. After all, this explanation of Jesus affirms something that he already held to be true in his own worldview. It describes the meaning of Jesus in terms and metaphors that are uniquely Hausa and also fully Christian. Previously, Christianity was presented to Jaffa in ways that were foreign, using literate points, analysis, comparisons, and so on. Thanks to the use of Hausa metaphors and concepts contained in Jaffa's own proverbs, Jesus's coming to earth starts to make sense and is congruent with some of the deeply held core values of Jaffa's culture.

"There is a God whose heart pulls so strong that his feet must come to be with us," Jaffa thinks out loud. "That is good news. I would like to know more about this."

Reflection and Discussion

1. How did I, the outsider, learn this proverb and meaning?
2. Compare/contrast the reasoning process using proverbs to the reasoning process using points, principles, and definitions.
3. Why does Jaffa respond so readily to this "sweet talk," particularly since this addresses a deeply held obstacle in Islam?

181

Music, Dance, and Drama—We Become What We Hum

Gami a gok ka di nyam sungsung. (A leper dances in the midst of his relatives.)
—Builsa proverb

Hospital Dedication in South Dakota

The Native American elder, a full-feathered headdress covering his hair, strikes a match to light the sage, tightly bundled in his hand. The smoke freely explores all the directions and permeates the air with a pungent odor. Moving from the center of the circle, he slowly makes his way to the perimeter, gently carrying the burning sage. Passing along the circumference, he invites us to brush the smoke over our bodies.

Gathered outside the building, the employees are participating in the dedication ceremony of their newly constructed hospital in Sioux Falls, South Dakota. A local Native American elder, making his way around the circle, is officiating at the ceremony at the request of the Anglo-American staff. After completing the circle, the elder announces, "We are going to have a prayer in the four directions. Everyone face this way." We all face east.

Pom. Pom. Pom. Like the steady pounding of my heart, the drummer pounds the round drum he is clutching in his hand. Another Lakota, dressed in a red shirt, sings a prayer song in Lakota, as his wife accompanies him. The elder announces that this song is their prayer.

Not understanding a word that is sung, the observers all watch the elder. When he turns south, we all turn that direction. The song mixes with the sage to cleanse the air. We turn to the west, then to the north.

The elder walks clockwise around the circle, shaking hands and welcoming people to the dedication ceremony. He explains that there will be some special dancing for the ceremony.

Pom. Pom. Pom. The drum once again pumps the air like blood pumping through my veins. A young dancer enters the center of the circle, wearing his dancing regalia. Eagle feathers extend from his headdress up to the sky. Beautiful beadwork covers his moccasins from his toes up to his knees. The dancer glides inside the circle. The beaded breastplate moves up and down as the shaker in his hand keeps time with the beat.

"This is a traditional dance that we learned from the Omaha," the elder explains. As the dancer slowly makes his way around the inside of the circle, I notice that a plumage of feathers flows down his back. Gradually, the drum fades away as the dancer exits the circle.

"This next dancer will do an original Lakota grass dance," the elder announces as another dancer appears. Leaping in wide movements, this dancer moves through the circle as if he were navigating through high grass on the plains. Long, thin, flowing fabric strips of yellow and green follow his every movement.

"Some of our dances tell a story. A dance may describe how we won a particular battle or how we hunted buffaloes," the elder explains. His next words explain why my heartbeat is keeping time with the drum. "The drum is like your mother's heartbeat when you were inside the womb."

It sure feels like it.

"Our next dance is the 'sneak up.' We used this to approach in a war party," he explains, his teeth flashing as a wry smile crosses his face. The person next to me gives me a look that says, "I think he is joking." Just when I think the ceremony is over, the elder announces one last surprise to the bystanders.

"Our last dance is a circle dance. All are welcome to come join the circle and hold hands," he invites us. I slowly move forward and join hands with those next to me. The drum beats again. Swaying to the beat gently, up and down, back and forth, the elder demonstrates the proper movements. The guests, with tentative looks scrawled across their faces, move clockwise around the circle. Once the circle makes a complete revolution, the drum stops.

"That is the end of our dedication ceremony. I hope you enjoyed it," the elder concludes.

A bit bewildered, the hospital workers slowly disperse. These observers were expecting a formal spoken prayer, perhaps a reading from a book. Or maybe a speech, since that is what Anglo-Americans usually receive at a dedication ceremony. Little did they know that the dances were the prayers, spoken elegantly the whole time they were gathered.

This event highlights the need for intercultural disciplers to consider other genres for discipleship. Since music, dance, and drama are prevalent genres in oral cultures, their discipleship potential will be explored as oral literature in this chapter.

Oral Art

We are searching for discipleship patterns residing in cultures that speak deeply to heart issues. Our assumption is that God has placed in societies unique forms that express the glory of God. Instead of destroying culture, the gospel starts with these cultural genres and transforms them into a Christian worldview. When used for discipleship, these genres encourage disciples to maintain their kingdom centeredness within the culture where God has placed them. Once intercultural disciplers find these cultural genres, they nurture and contextualize them for discipleship.

Oral arts provide cultural genres that both speak deeply to heart issues

---

Everything important has its own song and dance.

African proverb (in Chiang 2010, 122)

---

and provide a distinct cultural identity. The international evangelical leaders at the Lausanne conference have noted,

> Indigenous arts are expressive, intrinsic communication forms that are integrated within and across the structures of society where they define and sustain cultural norms and values. We must come to see that becoming acquainted with the artistic expressions of diverse cultures is as important as attending language school in preparation for mission work. The arts provide a window to the language of the heart. (Claydon 2004b, 33)

The arts connect people deeply to their own culture, as a type of heart language. For example, a particular dance is unique to a particular people group. Both observers and participants are moved by this cultural expression. The arts also communicate in a creative, sensory, and intuitive manner that can "move us, engage us, and help us to see with fresh eyes" (Claydon 2004b, 8). When these genres are appropriated for discipleship, this nurtures cultural identity and deep heart transformation.

In this chapter I discuss three oral arts: dance, music, and drama. While these arts have often been neglected in formal discipleship efforts, intercultural disciplers recognize them as powerful genres for shaping contextual disciples with a Christian worldview. The great potential of these oral arts for intercultural discipleship can set your feet to dancing!

Dance

Most people agree on the importance of prayer for discipleship. What is not always as readily understood, however, is that prayer can be expressed differently in various cultures. This is exemplified in the opening story. "Our dancers are a prayer made visible!" reads an advertisement (National Native American Cooperative 2011) for a Native American powwow. Native American

Ethnodoxology

The oral arts have tremendous potential for discipleship; unfortunately, this has often been overlooked. Ethnodoxologist Robin Harris explains, "It never occurred to most early mission workers that, just as they needed to learn new, complex, and 'strange-sounding' languages in order to communicate with local people, so also did they need to study and understand local music and other artistic systems like dance and drama as well as visual and verbal arts like proverbs, poetry, and storytelling. Instead many workers simply brought their Bible in one hand and their hymnbook in the other" (2013, 85).

So what is ethnodoxology all about? Harris explains, "In the late 1990s worship leader and missionary Dave Hall coined the term 'ethnodoxology' . . . as 'the study of the worship of God among diverse cultures.' He stressed a broad understanding of worship beyond the Sunday morning corporate gathering to emphasize 'first and foremost a life to be lived, and secondarily as an event in which to participate'" (2013, 86).

To engage the arts in intercultural discipleship, Brian Schrag has noted three broad approaches:

1. *Bring It—Teach It:* Intercultural disciplers bring arts from their own faith community and then teach them to another community. While this can lead to unity among diverse faith communities, it overlooks the gifting and cultural uniqueness of local artists and local art forms.

2. *Build New Bridges:* Intercultural disciplers from one faith community find artists from another community in order to work together for collaborative efforts. Schrag notes that this is often done in response to traumatic events.

3. *Find It—Encourage It:* Intercultural disciplers search and find local artists and encourage them to create in the local art forms that they know the best. Schrag observes, "This approach usually requires longer-term relationships with people, and above all, a commitment to learn" (2014, 6).

Reflection and Discussion

1. Why do you think that intercultural disciplers have often overlooked indigenous music, dance, and drama in the past? How does this affect the discipleship process?

2. How may ethnodoxology reveal a larger portrait of God's glory to help intercultural disciplers overcome the danger of ethnocentrism?

3. Describe when/where each of the three approaches may be appropriate for discipleship. Which one do you recommend for worldview transformation?

4. In addition to symbols, rituals, proverbs, stories, music, dance, and drama, what other oral arts may be explored by intercultural disciplers in various cultures?

Christian leader Richard Twiss has discussed how Natives are "dancing their prayers" (Twiss 2002), and he demonstrates this each year at a powwow conducted by Wiconi International (for more information and video, including

The Second Great Awakening

Revival burst out among the African American slave population during the Second Great Awakening in the United States (early nineteenth century), with dance and music having a clear influence. Patrick Allitt notes:

> Many slaves were converted during the Second Great Awakening and became preachers in their own right, some with their masters' support and approval; others, covertly. Reading bans in the slave code made theirs a largely oral tradition. . . . The emotionalism of the Second Great Awakening was compatible with the emotionalism of African dance and musical traditions. . . . Historians debate the extent of African influence on African-American Christianity. The influence seems clear in music, chanting, and dance. (2001, 47–48)

Reflection and Discussion

1. While some may question the value of dance for discipleship, what does the above example suggest?
2. What would have been the likely results had dance been excluded or prohibited in the context above?

Native American dancing, see http://www.wiconi.com). At an international gathering, Twiss describes the power of this Native practice:

> On more than one occasion we were deeply touched and wept openly when the Holy Spirit visited us as different nations offered their traditional songs and dances of praise in honor of Jesus Christ. For some of the delegations, even after decades of serving the Lord, this was the first time they had felt free to use their tribal songs and dances for worship. This was especially true of the Native American, Saami and Australian Aboriginal delegations. (2000, 195–96)

For Native Americans, dancing is often deeply connected to spirituality. John Hascall notes, "The drum, dance, and song are central to our worship" (1996, 181). After observing and then participating in a crown dance, Juanita Little describes her experience: "When the dances began at sunset the songs were so beautiful, so prayerful. I had never seen the Crown Dance performed in such a prayerful manner. I can't explain. It was very moving and a very spiritual experience for me" (1996, 212). To understand how dance communicates spiritual depth, we need to look at the variety of dances from an emic perspective.

Dances Communicate Various Messages

While outsiders may not understand the spiritual significance of dances due to their etic perspective, insiders differentiate dances and the messages they communicate. Like a heart language, these dances communicate deeply to both the local participants and observers. Kateri Mitchell describes a few of the different Native American dances and what they express:

> We continue to express gratitude for life in the steady beat of the drum and the oneness of heart as we sing our chants during our solemn religious ceremonies and rituals or during intertribal social gatherings. For instance, our Round Dances symbolize the joy and love of being in union with our Creator and with

---

We have a 70 percent rule—if you find yourself comfortable more than 70 percent of the time, then something is wrong, because that means your culture is dominating the community!

David M. Bailey (2013, 445)

> one another and gratitude for the many gifts shared throughout the cycle of life. So too, our Honor Dances acknowledge the giftedness of our people and, in particular, our women who are respected as the life-givers for the tribute. Also, many of our dances are in recognition of God's creatures and are so named to show our respect for animals and birds. For example, beauty, power, and strength are shown in the Eagle Dances. Some of our dances tell a story about the life expeditions and events of our people, such as in the Canoe Dance, which is a journey; and, then, that eventful time of life—mating as expressed in the Partridge Dance. (1996, 173)

Her emic perspective provides cultural depth and meaning that are easily overlooked and unappreciated by outsiders. These dances also maintain her cultural identity as a Native American. Christian disciples can appropriate these dances to identify themselves as both Native American and Christian, instead of having to choose one or the other.

Cultural Identity

Many Africans also value dancing and retaining their cultural identity through dance. This connection to culture and family is so deep that even "a leper dances in the midst of his relatives." This has important implications for people to identify themselves in the Christian family, as described in the following account.

The *Gwandara-wara* (Hausa for "a people who prefer to dance") of Nigeria for centuries resisted both Muslim and Christian conversion, finding repugnant the legalistic strictures they perceived in both religions because they preferred to dance! They relented, however, about thirty years ago, and embraced Christianity when African missionaries of the Evangelical Missionary Society (an agency of the Evangelical Church of West Africa) decided to dance the gospel to them. Through rhythm and movement, applying the art language of the heart of these people, they further instructed them in some detail regarding doctrine, especially creation and redemption. (Gasque 2007, 28)

Clearly, dance is an important cultural genre that is connected to spirituality in many cultures. If this deep cultural area is not engaged with the gospel, split-level Christianity will result, as dancing is done everywhere but the church. To help us understand how deeply dance is woven into the fabric of some cultures, a college dance professor in Ghana explains:

In Africa the performing arts are not just for the stage. They are part of the life of the people—a language that is seen in everyday activity. It is therefore sad that Christianity has not explored using much of the arts as they already exist in Africa. Songs that came with the faith are foreign. Our many traditional musical instruments were all rejected. So even though our people embraced the Christian faith, it is still seen today as a European religion. This is why it is necessary to initiate moves that will lead to the Christians in Africa incorporating their

SIDEBAR 9.3

Do They Have Sin?

Roberta King describes one potential result when intercultural disciplers overlook the value of dance, as she describes an African worship experience:

As the drumming continues, rattles and bells enter in, and singing starts. Often in a call-and-response style, the singing includes vibrato and improvised harmony. The congregation rises and moves energetically in celebration of their new life in Christ.

One newly arrived missionary joined in the celebration of song and dance. Others sat motionless, uncomfortable with the non-Western form of worship and unaware of the statement they were making through their refusal to participate.

The service ended and the believers surrounded the dancing visitor with expressions of welcome and thanks for worshiping with them. Then they asked, "Why don't the others worship with us? Do they have sin in their lives?"

Apparently among these Africans only those who have sin in their lives find it difficult to enter into worship and dance. (2013, 184)

Reflection and Discussion

1. What does participation (and non-participation) in worshipful dance communicate in some cultures?
2. How can this awareness influence intercultural disciplers?

dances, drumming, and singing into the expression of their faith for upcoming generations to see Christianity as their own. (Claydon 2004b, 33)

Since cultural identity is so deeply tied to dance, the exclusion of dance from the church inhibits contextualization. For intercultural disciplers, this is a missed opportunity at best and a deep disservice to indigenous disciples at worst. A better approach is to utilize critical contextualization to determine how to contextualize cultural dances for Christian discipleship.

Contextualization of Dance

In order to guard against the extremes of split-level Christianity and syncretism, critical contextualization with a hermeneutical community engages the Scripture with dance. How can this be done?

In 1996, Reverend Little, a Filipino pastor, proclaimed, "The Church must be the sanctuary of the arts of song and dance, not the cemetery" (Twiss 2000, 198). The evangelical church leaders at the 2004 Lausanne conference (Claydon 2004b, 33) noted some exciting developments in the Philippines in the last decade. Although the mainline Filipino church has not fully embraced these cultural expressions, experimentation with the contextualization of dance gives hope to intercultural disciplers, as described below.

An artistic group known as Kaloob has embarked on a mission to "decolonize" Christianity in the areas of theology, liturgy, music, dance, and other formal expressions. They propagate the use of indigenous music and musical instruments, dances, rituals, and costume tradition in worship and celebration.

Our method includes painstaking research on existing indigenous folk dance and musical traditions. Researched materials are analyzed and filtered through scripture to decide which art forms, or parts of such art forms, may or may not be used in Christian worship and practice. Forms or symbols whose meanings do not offend biblical principles are considered "redeemable." These art forms are then formally offered to the Lord by way of a performance we call a "prayformance." Instruction and propagation follows, in which we teach these renewed music and dance forms that are then interpreted by leaders for use in local church worship and other events.

In the past ten years, more than 100 distinct dances and rituals and their accompanying music have been "redeemed" and are now used by believers. Kaloob has also steadily risen to become one of the country's top five folk dance companies, and in the last few years we have been featured by the Cultural Centre of the Philippines in its annual Festival of the Arts. More notable is the change that has taken place in the Philippine Christian church. For example, our home church, which features a rich tapestry of indigenous music and dances, has grown from a congregation of 200 in 1994 to more than 7,000 today. Many Filipino Christians no longer demonize their cultural and artistic heritage, but

189

Starting Point for Indigenous Oral Arts

In order to identify the local oral arts and begin the contextualization process, Brian Schrag recommends a five-step process:

1. Learn to know a community and its arts.
2. Identify ways particular artistic genres can meet particular community kingdom goals.
3. Spark creativity in these genres by local practitioners.
4. Encourage community members to improve the new creations.
5. Integrate and celebrate the new works and plan for continuing creativity (2014, 7).

Once these oral arts are identified and encouraged, the process of contextualization can begin.

Reflection and Discussion

1. Compare/contrast Schrag's five steps to the first step in the critical contextualization process (phenomenological study).
2. How does Schrag's approach provide a starting point for intercultural discipleship? What else would you recommend?
3. What are the roles of the emic and etic perspectives? How do they balance each other?

aspire to share that same, albeit redeemed artistic heritage to the world and for the further enrichment of the Body of Christ. (Claydon 2004b, 33)

A contextual approach to indigenous dancing directs disciples to maintain a Christ-centered life, using culturally available genre. As Cloud-Chief Eagle, a Dakota traditional hoop dancer, described, "When I dance, I do it as unto the Lord. I never think of dancing as performing. It's more like worship and celebrations to me" (Twiss 2000, 210). As a result, she maintains her identity as both a Native American and a Christian. That is something to sing about!

Music

Music is closely related to dance. Both music and dance were integrated in most of the African church services that I participated in. This is also true

---

When we sing, we pray twice.

Augustine (in *The Feast* 2011)

---

of any celebratory African event that we attended. In practice, songs rarely exist alone; they are mixed with other oral arts, as Julie Taylor explains:

"They [songs] are intertwined with language, poetry, narrative, and riddles, accompanied by movement and instruments, found within dramas and stories, and partnered by visual arts such as masks, body ornamentation, costumes, and illustrations" (2012, 39). Music, then, is a potent genre for intercultural disciplers, since music is so tightly embedded in the cultural fabric, ready to shape worldviews. Taylor concludes, "It is through arts that such scriptural truths are connected to lives in memorable, motivating ways" (ibid.).

Power Encounter

Many of the observations made above concerning the use of dance for intercultural discipleship also apply to music. Music is a prayer form for disciples to express themselves to God, as described in the opening story of this chapter. Roberta King takes this a step further and notes that music can be a prayer shaped in the form of a power encounter for the Senufo people:

> People often sing as a means of power encounter, where they order Satan out of their lives. They sing "Satan get away from us," and inform him that they now belong to Jesus. In addition to this, the songs call for a change of allegiance: "Abandon Satan, the Devil," and make a plea to "offer yourselves to Jesus." Songs are a means of spiritual exchange among the Senufo. (2009, 156)

More than simply prayers of praise, these songs are intended to be prayers of a spiritual power encounter. For intercultural disciplers, music is an important genre to address excluded middle issues. My following personal account describes how the Builsa song discussed in chapter 3 was used to address spiritual powers:

> Greeted with warm smiles and eager faces, we enter the church building. These are new believers in Jesus, and they are eager to learn more. While they want to learn more about the way of Jesus described in the Bible, the first request, which comes from the women, involves song.
> "Can you teach us some songs?" they beg us.
> Peter understands the importance of songs for discipleship. He grabs the *gungong* (talking drum) under his arm and starts to pound out a beat.
> Swaying to the beat, he strains his lungs to the limit as he belts out the lyrics,

> > Wa chawgsi mu, Wa chawgsi mu, Wa chawgsi mu.
> > Wa chawgsi mu, Wa sum jam chawgsi.
> > Wa chawgɔi mu, Satana yaa de mu,
> > Wa chawgsi mu, Wa sum jam chawgsi.

> > He [Jesus] wraps me tightly. He wraps me tightly. He wraps me tightly.
> > He wraps me tightly. He really does wrap me tightly.
> > He wraps me tightly, even though Satan wants to destroy me,
> > He wraps me tightly. He really does wrap me tightly.

Like a match dropped on dry tinder, the song catches on immediately, and everyone sings out. In an instant, all rise to their feet and dance toward the center. As the dancers form a circle, their feet move to the beat, and the song is sung over and over . . . for five minutes.

I look over at Peter. The flashing of his teeth and steady pounding of the drum testify that this song has found a welcome home in his heart. The words have been steadily pounded into his heart as well. He is sure to remember this song for months to come.

The song affirms that Jesus wraps Christians tightly in his arms to protect them. Even though Satan tries to destroy them or cause harm, they do not have to fear, since Jesus wraps them tightly in his arms. This song can be sung when the disciple fears spiritual forces.

Months later, I am in the house when I first hear the eerie noise outside.

"Waaa-hooo. Waaa-hooo." The shout is faint in the distance.

Gradually, the noise is carried by closer voices.

"WAAA-HOOO. WAAA-HOOO." The vigorous shouting is from my neighbors' house.

When the millet crop is about ten feet high, the Builsa sometimes fear the presence of a *sakpak* (witch) in the millet field. It is believed that yelling will drive the witch to another location; otherwise, the witch will stay around your home and bring problems in the home.

Fear. Panic. Both emotions arrive like an unexpected guest.

I start to pray. The song I learned a few months before comes to mind. As I sing this song, my faith is strengthened.

Gradually, the shouting subsides. . . . So do my fear and panic.

In their place is a stronger faith, empowered by a song used for spiritual warfare.

Since this theology is contained in the memorable form of a song, disciples can quickly draw on it for spiritual encounters, thereby addressing critical excluded middle concerns.

Mnemonic Device

When looking for culturally available genres for discipleship, music is attractive, since songs are shaped in readily memorizable patterns. Catherine Ellis

> **One can gauge the strength of an organization by the strength of the original musical culture it produces.**
>
> Jonathan Pieslak (in Lindsey 2015)

notes, "Music in non-literate societies often functions as a mnemonic device and in this and other ways, replaces literature as the repository of important information" (1985, 17). For many oral cultures, music is the main carrier of theology. This is called "lyric theology" (Hiebert 1985, 162), since these oral cultures are able to remember and communicate their theology through the lyrics of the songs. Long into the night, the songs can be sung from memory, one after another (Luke and Carman 1968; Lovejoy and Claydon 2005). It has been said that "we become what we hum," that is, the theology that shapes us is stored in the songs that we sing and can recall. Christian songs composed in the indigenous music style can thus carry theology for growing disciples to remember and reflect on for spiritual growth.

Communicates Spiritual Truth

Music, then, is an important genre for communicating spiritual truth. C. Peter Wagner (1987, 91–92) describes the power of music to speak spiritual truth among the Tiv people in Nigeria. Missionaries preached to the Tiv for twenty-five years with very few responding by faith in Jesus. Indigenous music, though, effected a change:

> Some young Christians set the gospel story to musical chants, the indigenous medium of communication. Almost immediately the gospel began to spread like wildfire and soon a quarter million Tivs were worshipping Jesus. . . . Prior to this the gospel had been "proclaimed," but it had not been heard! The communication strategy had not spoken to the heart of the people. (Lovejoy and Claydon 2005, 15)

Music communicates at a different level from mere words alone. In this sense, music functions like a symbol. In particular, music exhibits the polarization property of symbols (described in chap. 4), whereby they connect a deep sensory experience with a deep ideology. As a result, music stirs the heart to make people want to do what they should do. This is extremely important for intercultural disciplers who are looking for indigenous genres that speak the heart language of the people to address their worldview.

Heart Language

By speaking a heart language (similar to the description of dance above), music connects the disciple to God at a deep level. This is particularly important during times when the disciple is stressed or in great need. After years of ministry, one American pastor observed,

> When I would talk with folks, especially when they had gone through difficult times in their lives, and they were looking for ways that their faith as a Christian could anchor their life, give them a place to stand, and orient them to keep on

going and go forward, what they would draw from would be a hymn . . . and now contemporary songs. We absorb [songs] into our being, and they form our lives and orient them to God. We recall them often unconsciously at times in our lives when we need them the most. (*The Music* 2011)

These difficult times are often the excluded middle issues for disciples. Music can address the heartfelt issues, as the music provides a rich source to draw from. Theology, contained in indigenous songs, is easier to draw on than other sources, since the songs provide theology in cultural containers that are easy to remember.

Identity

Music also provides a sense of social identity in culture. This is invaluable for intercultural disciplers, as traditional music forms identify the disciple with the

SIDEBAR 9.5

Stages of Contextual Music Development

James Krabill (2014) notes the following six stages of music development that frequently occurred in sub-Saharan African faith communities:

1. *Importation:* Hymn tunes, texts, and rhythms all originate with the Western missionary.
2. *Adaptation:* Imported hymn tunes or texts are in some way "Africanized" by rendering them more suitable or intelligible to worshipers in a given setting, for example, by incorporating drums/rattles and translating words into local language.
3. *Alteration:* Some part of the missionary's hymn (tune, text, or rhythm) is replaced or otherwise significantly modified by an indigenous form.
4. *Imitation:* Tunes, texts, and rhythms are locally composed or performed, but in a style that is inspired by or replicates in some way a Western musical genre.

5. *Indigenization:* Tunes, texts, and rhythms are locally produced in indigenous musical forms and styles. This results in "singing and dancing the indigenous 'heart music' of the culture" (Krabill 2013, 149).
6. *Internationalization:* Tunes, texts, and rhythms from the global faith family beyond both the West and the local context become incorporated into the life and worship of the church. This stage is the newest and often unexplored territory for the church of the twenty-first century.

Reflection and Discussion

1. Based on your intercultural experiences, can you provide examples of each of these categories?
2. Which stage is the most common? Why?
3. How does music development affect intercultural discipling?

local church and the universal church beyond. Ingrid Byerly notes, "Music can be used to retrieve identity ('mirror'), express identity ('mediator'), or preserve identity ('prophet'). It is music's powerful role as a mediator between social and personal identity through its ability to express emotions which makes it such a significant social practice in Christian mission" (cited in Pass 2007, 250).

The retrieval, expression, and preservation of identity is evident in Richard Twiss's (2000) description of the Native American, Saami, and Australian Aboriginal delegations expressing their faith through their traditional songs and dances, quoted earlier in the chapter. The music facilitated their identity as fully Christian and fully Native in a powerful and emotional manner.

Contextualization of Songs

Wendy Atkins (2012) provides a good example of the contextualization of songs among the Zande people in the Central African Republic. She applies the critical contextualization process to transform the worldview of the Zande people. This process should look familiar.

Thirty-four Zande gathered to form a hermeneutical community. They were encouraged to "explore the use of traditional song styles, to determine how traditional song genres could be adapted for use in the church, and to mirror the rhythmic and tonal aspects of Pazande in the rhythmic structure and the melodies of the newly-composed songs" (Atkins 2012, 40). Atkins describes the process:

> To determine their current worldview and how it affected their faith, the students were taken through a brainstorming process in which they answered the following questions:
>
> - What problems are you dealing with as a Christian in the society in which you live?
> - What do any of these problems have in common? (The larger list developed in response to Question #1 was divided into groups based on commonalities.)
> - What is the root problem of each group of problems?
> - What scriptures give you a response to each of these root problems?
>
> Students identified problems such as a lack of commitment by choir members, criticism of choir leaders, and choirs dissolving after regional choir festivals as main deterrents to the development of church choirs. These "surface" problems were discussed and found to be a result of jealousy. Through group discussion, it was determined that jealousy affected much of Zande society, not just musicians. (2012, 40–41)

The hermeneutical community identified jealousy as an important issue in Zande culture. Jim Harries, a long-term missionary in Kenya, postulates that one of the root causes of witchcraft is envy (2012). Addressing the issue of jealousy, then, will address one of the root social causes of witchcraft. Leveraging the power of song to communicate spiritual truth in the Azande heart language creates a power encounter that addresses the excluded middle issue of witchcraft. This discipleship process can transform the worldview of Azande believers.

Once the issue of jealousy was identified, the group searched Scripture to discover what it teaches about the subject. Songs were then composed in the contemporary music style using the familiar call and response. The songs were then introduced into the church.

Other issues were addressed in additional songs. Atkins concludes,

> We have seen people moved toward deeper commitment to Christ as culturally-relevant, scripture-based songs have been composed. Entire churches have been challenged to confront syncretistic practices in their villages as appropriate songs have been taught during Sunday morning church services. The edification of believers is taking place among the Azande as these new songs are shared. (2012, 42)

As excluded middle issues are addressed through the culturally available genre of music, the Azande worldview is slowly changing. This is an important discipleship approach.

King used a similar approach with songs to address deep-level issues among widows who survived the Rwandan genocide. She formed New Song Fellowships in order to identify and address the issues resulting from the deep trauma. Biblical texts focusing on a Christian's identity in Christ were set to songs. This work "created a new level of reconciliation and consolation between Hutus and Tutsis who participated. This was reinforced each time the women sang this particular song throughout the workshop. The hope of the gospel was embedded into their worldviews" (King 2006, 73).

Music has great potential to transform worldviews, thereby forming disciples who are centered on the kingdom. Intercultural disciplers can utilize this genre, particularly since it is so readily available and enjoyable.

Drama

The last oral genre to be discussed in this chapter is drama. In many cultures, drama is intertwined with other oral arts, particularly dance, music, and storytelling. Drama is also closely associated with spirituality as rituals are enacted in many cultures.

SIDEBAR 9.6

Arts and Trauma Healing

Harriet Hill describes excluded middle issues that can result from violence and conflict:

> When people are overwhelmed with intense fear, helplessness, and horror in the face or threat of death, they are traumatized. Trauma manifests itself by symptoms such as
>
> 1. intrusive thoughts in which people reexperience the event;
> 2. avoidance of things associated with the event, along with detached, numb emotions; and
> 3. hyperarousal.
>
> For traumatized people to find healing, they need to express their pain. They need a safe place to express it, where they will not be attacked physically or verbally.
> Both internal and external forces work against this expression of pain. Since pain hurts, denial can sometimes seem like a better option. The church is often complicit in this denial, teaching Christians that they should express praise and joy in all circumstances. (2013, 177)

Hill recommends that people use their art forms to address and express their pain, as the Bible illustrates through the use of laments (e.g., Psalms, Lamentations). She notes,

> In Africa almost every culture has a lament tradition: certain melodies, cer-
> tain kinds of poetry, certain dances and postures. Often these lament traditions have been condemned as heathen and off-limits for Christians. When African Christians understand the structure of lament Psalms in the Bible, it only takes a bit of encouragement for them to use their own lament traditions to express their pain to God. In thirty minutes of centering prayer and listening to the cry of their hearts, laments are expressed.
> Sometimes these laments are expressed in prose, but more often words alone do not suffice; they must be sung and danced. Sometimes these laments are expressed by individuals, but more often they are performed by a group. The piercing cry of a Niaboua pastor grieving the death of his sister still rings in my ears. . . . When pain is expressed, healing often follows. (2013, 177)

Reflection and Discussion

1. Why do you think that there are more lament psalms than any other category in the book of Psalms (Hill 2013, 177)? When people are not encouraged to express their pain in the church, what other options do they have?
2. While deep traumas and hurts require time and counsel, how can indigenous forms of lament be incorporated into other oral genres that have been discussed already (symbol, ritual, proverb, story) for discipleship?

Historical Connection to Spirituality

Some scholars trace the very beginning of drama to religious rituals. For example, the Abydos Passion Play (ca. 2500 BC) enacted the death and resurrection of the Egyptian god Osiris (Senkbeil 2007, 102). In addition, the classical Greek theater (ca. fifth century BC) was one of the dominant forms to express Greek mythology. Peter Meineck notes, "The Greek theatre had its origins in the cult worship of Dionysus and was influenced by the performance of Dithyrambic poetry in honor of the gods" (2005, 48). Even today, Indian theater has a religious underpinning, especially when compared to Western theater (Rowe 2006, 17).

Thomas Boogaart postulates that many Old Testament narratives were originally enacted as dramas for the Israelites prior to their recording in Scripture. He summarizes, "In short, [Old Testament] narratives as they have come down to us are scripts of Israelite plays" (2008, 41). Jeff Barker (2011) takes this a step further and argues that the scriptural narratives cannot be fully understood apart from their dramatization. Simply reading a text does not provide the details about facial expressions and responses that drama provides. I observed Barker's acting group perform a short play about Elisha providing for the widow with jars of oil, from 2 Kings 4:1–7. Watching details such as the faces of the young children as they were being carried away as slaves and the resulting despair of the widow brought this story closer to me personally. In a short reading, these details are not noticed. For intercultural disciplers, dramatization is another powerful genre to help disciples internalize Scripture so that they live and participate in the story of God.

Drama Encourages Participation

People participate in a drama in a different way than they simply read a message. I once heard Jeff Barker, drama professor at Northwestern College, say, "Drama takes the Word of God and stands it on its feet." This participation with Scripture allows for the Holy Spirit to sink the message deeper for discipleship. In some cultures, audience participation is greatly expanded. In Kenya, there is a form called *sigana* that "seamlessly weaves together acting, narration, music, and other expressive techniques, in the form of call and response, chants, role-play, banter and communal dilemma resolution. . . . Active participation of the audience is encouraged, as the line between performers and audience is eradicated" (Rowe 2006, 18–19). Audience participation is taken one step further in the technique called participatory educational theater (PET). Here the audience provides input into the actual construction of the drama at key stages. Development organizations have used this drama form to change health care habits, raise awareness about gender issues and AIDs, improve human rights, and resolve conflicts (Rowe 2006, 21). This method can also be applied for discipleship to help the church address excluded middle issues.

Participatory Educational Theater

PET was developed by Augusto Boal, who borrowed the pedagogical ideas of Paulo Freire and applied them to drama. Julisa Rowe quotes Zakes Mda's description of the method:

> Boal has developed a method in two parts, both of which are designed to transform spectators into actors. The two stages are known as *simultaneous dramaturgy* and *forum theatre*. In *simultaneous dramaturgy*, catalysts perform a short scene suggested by a local person, halt the action at a crisis point, and ask the audience to offer solutions. The actors become like puppets, and perform the actions strictly on the spectators' orders. The "best" solution is arrived at by trial, error, discussion, then audience consensus. . . .
>
> In *forum theatre*, actors and spectators converge. The participants tell a story with some social problem, then improvise, rehearse, and present it to the rest of the group as a skit. The audience members are asked if they agree with the solution. Any spectator is invited to replace any actor and lead the action in the direction that seems most appropriate to him or her. (Rowe 2006, 22)

Both forms have great potential for contextualization. Once a cultural issue is identified, the church group can dramatize a short scene in front of the hermeneutical community. The spectators then provide input that can be dramatized. For intercultural disciplers, this genre can be an important tool for addressing excluded middle issues that already reside in the culture.

Drama Is Culture Specific

Each culture has its own unwritten rules concerning what makes good drama. A drama that works well in one context may not do well elsewhere unless it is adapted to the cultural conventions, as the following story from a missionary that hosted a mime team in Mexico illustrates.

> They came to a church to present a mime on the life of Christ. They were dressed in standard mime outfit, all black with white painted faces. The church people looked at them and walked out. They were horrified that this group would bring a representation of the Day of the Dead into their church! In Mexico, the Day of the Dead is celebrated outside the church by painting faces white and portraying the spirits. By not understanding the cultural nuances of makeup and color, the well-intentioned mime team greatly offended the people they were trying to serve. (Rowe 2006, 8–9)

In addition to optical differences, those who study ethnodrama point out that there are eleven other signal systems that make drama unique in each culture (Rowe 2006). To avoid miscommunication, these differences need to be understood and incorporated into cross-cultural drama.

For example, there are great temporal differences in drama across cultures. While some oral cultures are accustomed to dramas that last all night or even over a seven-night period (Rowe 2006, 10), many Western audiences can tolerate only a maximum of two hours at a time. Olfactory differences are also prominent. In Indian folk theater, smell is used a great deal, especially the smell of incense or offerings to the gods (ibid.). Another difference is the acting style. In American acting, actors are taught to not overact; rather, they are to be natural and express natural emotions that are believable and

---

After viewing a classical kuchipudi dance drama with a biblical message an Indian Brahmin declared, "We thought the Bible was a foreign book, but today I see the smells and sounds of my culture. Those who tell of Bhagavata (God) are Bhagavatars—storytellers of God."

Julisa Rowe (2013, 61)

---

realistic. In India, however, this type of acting often seems too flat. Indians prefer emotions to be expressed broadly so that all can see it and participate. When Westerners observe Indian actors, however, this style appears overly melodramatic (ibid.).

Intercultural disciplers thus need to understand the cultural forms, meanings, and worldview and incorporate them into the drama. If not, miscommunication can easily result. Eugene Nida notes, "Dramatic representations have sometimes failed, but generally this seems to have been due to too much coaching and too much rigidity imposed by missionary instructors" (1975, 196). Dramas must be incarnated in the specific culture by the cultural insiders.

Incarnation, Community, Presence

Dale Savidge notes that theater is such a powerful genre because it "is a way to incarnate our stories, to live with one another in community, and to experience the presence of our fellows and of God" (Johnson and Savidge 2009, 50). These three theological categories (incarnation, community, and presence) are uniquely engaged in drama, making this a potent art form for intercultural disciplers. When local actors flesh out real-life issues in a local community, people feel connected to one another and to God. The audience is present with the actors such that they feel that the issues being addressed are the concerns of the audience, as well as of the actors. My following personal account of a drama enacted by Builsa church youth illustrates this method's effectiveness.

Crammed on wooden benches, arranged in a circle outside the church building, the youth cannot wait for the drama to start. Wide smiles and expressions of joy remind me of children on Christmas morning waiting to open their presents. As the sun sets, more people gather, adding to the chattering of voices that drowns out the nighttime sounds in the village.

Once the announcer walks into the center of the circle, a reverent hush replaces the chatter like a light switch going from "on" to "off."

"Tonight, we have prepared a drama for you about a young man and his wife who are facing a problem. They are not able to have a baby. See what happens to them," he proclaims.

Quickly, the young father enters the circle and sits on the bench, dressed in his white button-down shirt, pressed pants, and shined leather shoes. The young wife, dressed in a glowing gold dress, joins him on the bench and sits close to him with a wide smile on her face. The spectators roar with laughter as they tilt their heads back and point to their friends acting like adults.

The young father offers words of encouragement to his wife. Her despondent look betrays her disappointment, yet the comfort of her husband eases the pain . . . for a while. He slips away and disappears from the circle.

Out of nowhere, the young wife's mother enters the circle. Seeing her daughter dejected, she inquires about the reason.

Upon learning that the problem is infertility, the mother rises. "I know just what to do. I will take you to the *bano* (soothsayer) right now, and we will find out the cause!"

The audience roars in amazement. They know that this is what adults traditionally do to solve an issue like this one. Suddenly, carrying a calabash, some bones, and other objects, the *bano* appears. Shirtless and wearing a calabash on his head, he stands in front of the mother and the young wife.

Like an exploding firecracker, the audience erupts in laughter. As the *bano* rolls the bones and other objects on the ground, the spectators are doubled over in laughter. They do not know that the situation is about to become even more explosive!

Suddenly, the church pastor appears, carrying a Buli Bible. Realizing what is going on, he advises the wife to leave at once. She freezes—stuck in the middle of the pastor, her mother, and the *bano*.

During the discussion, the young husband finally appears. He listens to all parties: the mother-in-law, the *bano*, the pastor, and his wife. The eyes of the audience are riveted on the husband. Stuck in the middle of these four important and powerful relationships, he must decide what to do. Even more important, the spectators are relating to the dilemma and asking themselves, "How would I respond?"

Eventually, the husband asks the pastor to pray for them, resulting in a dramatic encounter with the *bano*, which causes the spectators to rise to their feet. The drama ends with the young couple seated on the bench, contented and smiling as the pastor instructs them about how to depend on Jesus, finally praying with them, in Jesus's name.

As I watched this performance, I realized that these young disciples were contextualizing the gospel for their own life questions and concerns. Through the drama, they incarnated a very real excluded middle issue in the church. This drama team formed a community that articulated a response to this very real and present Builsa concern that was scripturally faithful and culturally relevant. The spectators were very involved in the characters' dilemma and even felt as if the issue of childlessness were their own problem during the drama. The dramatization facilitated contextualization.

Contextualization

Intercultural disciplers can leverage the power of drama to enact contextualization. Instead of merely talking about issues, the dramatization forces action to be taken. Drama, though, is not always easy to interpret. Peter Senkbeil notes how drama differs from other oral communication forms:

> Interpreting a play involves ambiguities that are typically absent from interpreting a speech or a sermon. Unlike a parable that typically has one key point of comparison, a play may admit multiple (sometimes conflicting) interpretations. Theater tells moving stories, creates powerful images and depicts intense conflicts, but it is not always well suited to conveying large amounts of information in a clear and unambiguous manner. (2007, 103)

For intercultural disciplers, care must be taken to construct the drama so that it communicates effectively. Rowe recommends the following questions for ethnodramatology analysis:

1. What is the environment of the culture and how does it affect the performance and staging of drama?
2. What is the history of the culture? What is the history of drama in the culture? How do they correspond?
3. What is the prevailing economic structure of the culture? How do economics affect life in the culture? How do they affect drama (what can be performed and why, who can attend, who can perform, etc.)?
4. What is the social structure of the culture? How does society affect drama (who can perform, who can attend, what is the role of the audience, etc.)?
5. What is the culture's ideology? How does this affect what drama can be performed?
6. How are the twelve signal systems manifested in culture [verbal, written, numeric, pictorial, artifactual, audio, kinesic, optical, tactile, special, temporal, olfactory]? How are they manifested in drama performance?
7. What are the behavior patterns of the culture? How are these reflected in the drama?
8. Are there different categories of drama in the culture? What are their functions and place in the culture? (2006, 11–12)

Once the above process for the phenomenological analysis of drama in culture is completed, contextualization can proceed with ontological critique, critical evaluation, and missiological transformation. An alternate approach is to use participatory educational theater, as described previously, for disciples to discuss excluded middle issues among members of a hermeneutical community.

I have observed that many of the Builsa are natural actors. When a young Builsa church went to evangelize a nearby village using a dramatization of the prodigal son, I was pleasantly surprised to see how readily they were able to assume roles and dramatize the story. It very naturally fit the oral preference of the Builsa people. An older man assumed the role of the father, a younger disciple assumed the role of the son, and several young children assumed the role of the pigs! During the performance, the spectators were electrified, since they could observe this story contextualized in their own culture. By the end, several had made decisions to follow Jesus, and no one was bored or disinterested. In addition, the young disciples were strengthened in their faith as they made a very powerful and natural presentation of the gospel.

When given the opportunity at church services, all-night prayer meetings, Easter/Christmas gatherings, funerals, and such, the Builsa presented wonderful dramatizations of Scripture. For example, I observed the immediate and positive response of the enactment of the parable of the talents and the story of Balaam (Num. 22–24).

Summary

When intercultural disciplers are looking for genres already present in culture, the oral arts are fertile soil. Unfortunately, "perhaps in the area of esthetic culture more than in any other area of life, Christian missions have, usually unintentionally, stifled indigenous practices" (Nida 1975, 195). This is unfortunate, since the very discipleship methods that God has placed in culture are too easily overlooked, and we then wonder why discipleship is not producing the desired results. A Builsa proverb warns, "Ba kan de korum a mini Biiga" (They do not consume culture and leave nothing behind for the children). Dance, music, and drama are powerful genres that have been left behind in many cultures to disciple the children. In this chapter, we discussed the following points for using these art forms in intercultural discipleship:

1. Dance, music, and drama often speak a deeper heart language than other forms of communication. Like symbols, they help disciples want to do what they should do. This emotive aspect motivates disciples to change.

2. Dance, music, and drama instill a deep cultural identity such that disciples can retain their cultural identity along with their Christian identity.

3. Dance, music, and drama are ripe genres for contextualization, leading to intercultural discipleship.

4. Dances and songs are forms of prayer in many cultures that foster spiritual growth for disciples.

5. Songs can be used as a prayer form for power encounters. This practice addresses an important excluded middle issue in power-oriented cultures.

6. Songs are a potent mnemonic device to communicate spiritual truth. Disciples often rely on such songs during times of trial or suffering.

7. Drama encourages participation, thereby engaging the audience in deeper reflection. Participatory educational theater goes further and involves the audience in the resolution of the drama. This process can facilitate contextualization of excluded middle issues in culture.

8. Drama has the unique potential to simultaneously engage the theological concepts of incarnation, community, and presence. This makes drama a potent genre for connecting with spirituality, as the roots of drama/theater demonstrate.

Activity for Discipling

1. Concerning the excluded middle issue that you have been working on in earlier chapters, consider how dance, music, or drama may play an important role for intercultural discipleship. Try the contextualization approaches described above.

2. Identify those who are gifted artisans in the host culture. Then encourage/empower them to create music, drama, or dance to address excluded middle issues for discipleship.

3. Ask your disciple(s) to identify the songs, dances, and dramas that have been most helpful in their discipleship. Particularly listen for those that deal with excluded middle issues, spiritual warfare, healing of trauma, and the like. Discuss why these oral arts were so helpful to them.

4. In which stage of music development (per Krabill's typology) would you place your own worship experience? How could this be deepened and enriched?

Story, Song, Dance in Togo

Reprinted from Bowman and Bowman (2014, 33).

Harmattan winds have hovered over desert Africa for a week, picking up Saharan sands and filling the sky of the Paga Na village with a brown haze. In this sand-gray dusk, the hushed, unnatural silence of the windswept, sub-Saharan village is spellbinding and disconcerting. Only a subtle breeze invades the soundless, palm-lined footpaths and the swept earth patios. But the silence of this southern Togolese village is about to end; the storyteller is coming!

And into the quiet hamlet the clear, resonant voice of his recitation will emerge, startling and powerful, heralded by drums. And when the departing flamingo sun finally sets, shirtless men leave their game of *adi* (mancala), the baguette sellers disburse, the tailors close up their makeshift stand, cranky bicycles are abandoned hastily, and yawning children resting on outdoor cots under coconut trees are wrestled from sleep. As the pulse of the drums intensifies and the storyteller takes his place on the low, carved bench, the village is mobilized and excitement permeates the air. The elders arrive in regal togas made of the wild, leaping colors of African cloth. Antoine, the animated storyteller–church planter exchanges rituals, formalized greetings with his audience. The fetish priestess, clothed in white and waving her horse-hair amulet, acknowledges Antoine with penetrating eyes that speak of a past immersed in *juju* and prayer to the fetish. Night falls, the burning log crackles. They are ready for the story.

The listeners are electrified as the biblical story of creation begins: "In the beginning God created the heavens and the earth." The poetic, melodious pattern of the story flows from Antoine's lips. When he reaches the repeating phrase "and God saw that it was good," he sings a song in call-and-response style. The song was written by Antoine's friend Timothée, a believer gifted in music with a vision to reach out to his people. This song is designed to reinforce the story; the words of the song are: "In the beginning God created heaven and earth. It was empty, and darkness was over the surface of the deep." The call and response is choreographed by the composer in a traditional style that glorifies God the Creator. As the villagers quickly memorize the song response and join Antoine, their voices become a chorus of blissful harmony.

Then dancing intercepts the story. The headman dances as well, thus placing his approval on the story and the event. The drum language continues. Amidst the steaming equatorial heat sitting stiffly in the air, the pulsating rhythm of the drum reaches to the stars and sounds deep into the tropical night. The storytelling and singing continue in this way. As the fire dims, the story ends. There is not one villager who wishes to leave that place. The story in this setting has connected them to the Word and to their history. It has involved and inspired them as they interact with the story through song and dance.

Reflection and Discussion

1. What is communicated by the dance? What role does the music play in the storytelling event?

2. How do various genres combine to produce a more powerful experience of oral art?

3. What would it take to replicate this approach for intercultural discipleship in numerous villages?

Holistic Discipleship
Connects Word and Deed

When the elephants fight, the grass suffers.

—African proverb

Who Will Be Next?

A simple sip of water. Little did anyone know that this source of life and refreshment would leave fathers without sons and mothers sobbing next to their daughters' empty beds. Standing alone in a field, a father looks at his son's plow, lying still against a millet stalk. There is dryness in the father's throat, from both grief and thirst. Overwhelmed, the father falls to the ground. This village knows cholera well, like an unwelcomed relative that shows up at your doorstep, unannounced, destroys your home, and leaves without warning.

During the wet season, heavy rains flood the traditional wells in this Builsa village. Debris from the field flows into the well, turning this water hole into a breeding ground for disease. As unsuspecting villagers drank the water, they quickly began falling ill. In the span of a few days, sixteen people died. As the sun rises on the dawn of the most recent death, wails can be heard from the huts around the village, piercing wails that hurt my soul and make me pull my children close to me.

It doesn't take long for news to spread to the surrounding villages. Relatives and friends make the long walk to grieve alongside the families. The visitors are offered water, which they readily accept. Washing their dry throats with the unseen disease, some of the visitors never make the journey back home.

Panic spreads like a dirty secret, bringing hurt and alarm to everyone it touches. The village is alive with the fearful whispers: "Who will be next? Why is this happening? Which ancestor is angry?" and "What should we do?" As a missiologist, I have been taught to anticipate these questions, but I find myself speechless and confused. What can I possibly tell them to comfort them and

This chapter is adapted from Moon (2012b).

207

ease their hurting? Do they need a nurse to dispense medication? Do they need an engineer to install a new well? How about a pastor to comfort and pray for healing, or a counselor to resolve relational hurts that are rubbed raw through the deaths? And above all, how can I show them the love of God through all this pain?

There's a backstory on the church efforts that the village is unaware of. Prior to the flooding, the local church and mission had empowered believers to construct a hand-dug well in the same village. Lined with concrete and raised above the ground, this water source protected the surrounding families from the silent killer. Not one member of these families died. Bereaved families notice that all of these other families are alive and want to know why. Even more important, can the grieving families close their well and use this new water source also? Just as quickly as the water and subsequent sickness rose, it subsides.

I visit the village church shortly after the epidemic is over, only to find an entirely different community than before. Villagers are sitting nine people to a five-person bench, standing outside the windows to hear, and pushing through the doors in order to hear the message. Once a tight community, the church family is now overflowing.

"Who knew that this sickness was coming to this village?" I ask from the front of the church.

Silence. No hands in the air. No one anticipated this tragedy, including me.

"Only God knew that this was coming. God sent a church to your village to help you dig a well that saved your lives. Who would like to know more about this God who saves your village?"

Revival. Renewal. The church grows as people come to learn more about this God who rescued them from cholera. Christianity spreads—faster than the cholera ever could have. (adapted from Moon 2012a, 123–25)

This story describes how the integration of both words and deeds is needed for discipleship. A term often used to describe this practice is "holistic discipleship," which is another important aspect of intercultural discipleship.

Intercultural Discipleship So Far

Our working definition of intercultural discipleship is "the process of worldview transformation whereby Jesus followers center their lives on the kingdom of God and obey Christ's commands in culture, utilizing culturally available genres." As disciples encounter daily issues within their culture (including a cholera epidemic), they respond in a manner that is both biblically faithful and culturally relevant in order to maintain a kingdom-centered life. This lifelong process forms mature followers of Christ who overcome the extremes of syncretism, in which culture is not critiqued and the two faith systems are thereby blended, and split-level Christianity, in which Christianity responds to merely the ultimate life issues (e.g., salvation, problem of evil) but neglects

SIDEBAR 10.1

Integral Discipleship

The Micah Network (http://www.micahnet work.org) uses the term "integral mission" to indicate that the proclamation (words) and the demonstration (deeds) of the gospel need to be integrated, since "our procla- mation has social consequences as we call people to love and repentance in all areas of life. And our social involvement has evange- listic consequences as we bear witness to the transforming grace of Jesus Christ" (2001). Instead of integrating words and deeds, dis- ciplers often highlight one at the expense of the other.

Reflection and Discussion

1. How is discipleship affected when words are emphasized and deeds neglected?
2. How is discipleship affected when deeds are emphasized and words neglected?
3. How can deeds and words be com- bined to transform worldviews for discipleship?

intimate life issues (e.g., sickness/death from cholera), which are then left to be addressed by other sources, such as traditional practices and beliefs.

So far in this book, we have discussed how to use the available cultural genres to facilitate the discipleship process, including symbols, rituals, stories, proverbs, dance, drama, and music. These genres are needed to transform worldviews, since words alone are often not enough to communicate deep values and emotions.

What Is Holistic Discipleship?

In this chapter, I take discipleship one step further to describe how deeds also communicate along with words. "Holistic" implies a concern for the totality of life instead of being limited to certain "spiritual" areas—both the ultimate and the intimate issues of life are important to God. This practice is modeled on the incarnation, whereby God demonstrated a concern for both by sending the divine Son of God to preach good news and address poverty/ justice issues (Luke 4:18–19).

"Holistic discipleship," then, transforms worldviews by integrating the words and deeds of Jesus in the development of the community such that both are crucial for Christian witness and discipleship (Hughes 2008, 8). Holistic dis- cipleship addresses issues involving economics, technology, social relationships, ideologies, and beliefs. Practically speaking, holistic discipleship addresses questions such as: "How do we transform Christians who are shaped by un- spoken cultural influences such as secularism, consumerism, individualism, or fatalism?" "Where should discipleship start for those living in poverty-stricken or flood-ravaged communities?" "How do disciples deal with the unseen spirit world?" Holistic discipleship even addresses intimate concerns such as "Can Christ save my marriage?" To describe how discipleship addresses these concerns, we must first understand how the various sectors of culture are integrated.

Functional Integration of Culture

For the purposes of understanding a local society, culture can be divided into three major sectors. In this model, each of the pie pieces represents a major sector of a culture. Darrell L. Whiteman (2001) simplifies Charles Kraft's (1996, 122–26) division as shown in figure 10.1.

Figure 10.1
Sectors of culture functionally integrated

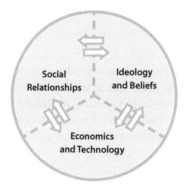

These sectors are functionally integrated such that a change in one sector will result in a change in another sector. To create a change in the ideology and belief of a maturing Christian, for example, holistic disciple-makers do not have to start in the "Ideology and Beliefs" sector. Introducing a change in other sectors will create a change in ideology and belief.

In the opening story, for instance, note how the change started in the economics/technology sector (a new well was installed). This led to a change in the social relationships sector (neighbors shared water). This ultimately resulted in a change in the ideology/belief sector (people trust in the God who sent the church to the village). For intercultural disciplers, this reminds us that each of the three sectors is important, since they all affect one another.

Disciplers must be concerned with all the sectors instead of isolating just one alone, since excluded middle issues can exist in every sector. For example, poverty can result in various excluded middle issues. Poverty, though, can be defined differently, depending on which sector is affected. While poverty is typically identified as a deficit in the economics/technology sector (e.g., lack of clothing, food, shelter), it can also exist in the other two sectors. People living in fear of witchcraft and spirit forces, for example, are poor in the ideology/belief sector. Those who are isolated from deep relationships and partnerships are poor in the social relationships sector.

For our purposes, an important question is, "What does discipleship look like when we *start* in each of the three sectors?" For example, "Where should discipleship start for those living in poverty-stricken or flood-ravaged communities?" To answer this question, let's first explore the economics/technology sector.

Economics/Technology Sector

Typically, people define poverty in this sector as a lack of things. When people lack the essential life necessities of food, clothing, or shelter, they may lose their Christ-centered focus. The intercultural discipler can start at the point of greatest need or assets. The cholera epidemic was abated in the opening story by demonstrating the deeds of Christ at a point of great need. In doing so, the disciples in this village strengthened their faith in Christ.

In actuality, the hand-dug well program introduced by the Bible Church of Africa (BCA) and SIM started with the assets of the community (before cholera was even a threat). Instead of hiring a drilling rig to drill the well while the villagers watched, the holistic disciplers looked around and asked the community to describe their assets. They noticed that men were willing to dig wells with picks and shovels. The water table was not too deep in some areas (between sixteen and forty-five feet). They also noticed that women could gather sand and children could gather stones from the farms. These were all assets that were used to help construct the curved concrete blocks to line the well. The local church was then taught how to make the concrete blocks, cure them, and then assist BCA members in the installation of the lining, cover, and protective pad.

Using the community's assets, the change in technology led to changes in the other sectors as well. This often leads to surprising discoveries, as noted in the following story.

> At the well dedication in the village of Kalijiisa, villagers come from all over dressed in their Sunday best. The sunflower yellows and electric blues of their clothing swirl around against a backdrop of a massive baobab tree. Dancing under the shade of the tree, the women keep time with the beat of the pounding drum. Children smile in delight as the music fills the air with joy. Handkerchiefs are hoisted in the air and waved about in celebration of this joyous occasion. Everyone from white-haired men to babies carried on their mothers' backs gathers around the well. Slowly, the elders come forward and announce, "We thank the church for this new well. Now, we are confident that our newly married wives will not leave us!"

I stare blankly from face to face. Confused, I ask the elders for an explanation.

They continue, "The first morning after the wedding, a young bride was asked to fetch water. She had to walk a long way to get water from a place where the water was not clean. This alarmed her so much that she quickly ran home to her father's house and did not come back again. Now that the well is close by the house and it has clean water, the new wives will be encouraged to stay."

The joy in the women's eyes brings a smile to my face and a confirmation of the wisdom in the elders' words. (adapted from Moon 2012b)

While skeptics may claim that well digging is secular work, holistic disciplers realize that there is no secular work—unless you make it that way (Myers 1990). A new well started an obvious change in the technology/economics sector. This led to a change in the social relationships sector as the relationship between husbands and wives (and the entire family) was affected. This then created a change in the ideology/belief sector as the elders recognized the positive role of the church and how the ultimate God is concerned about the intimate needs of newlyweds. Holistic discipleship helped the young men and the new brides in this village further their growth in faith as they appreciate the God who cares enough about their marriages to send a church to help.

Jobs Needed

Another area of concern for holistic disciples is the role of meaningful work. Adam was given the meaningful work of tending and watching over the garden *prior* to the fall (Gen. 2:15). This implies that work itself is not a product of sin; rather, meaningful work maintains the dignity of humans. Greg Forster concludes that since most people spend the majority of their waking hours occupied with work, this is an important discipleship area where disciplers should "ground their approach to work in an affirmation of its intrinsic goodness" (2013a, 10).

Bryant Myers (1999) notes that God created humanity to have shalom (completeness, wholeness, harmony) in four specific relationships: with God, with others, with creation, and with self. A healthy relationship with one's self is founded on the fact that humans were created in the image of God. Humans then maintain their own dignity partly through the meaningful work that God enables and gifts them for. When someone is out of work for an extended period, the resulting loss of self-respect is painfully obvious. If not addressed, the disciple's Christ-centered focus is shaken. However, "when Christians integrate their economic work with their discipleship, they not only live more fully into the calling of God in their own lives, but their potential for transformative impact on civilization becomes enormous" (Forster 2013a, 24), as my following personal account demonstrates.

The Twelve Maxims of Economic Wisdom

The Economic Wisdom Project by the Oikonomia Network (endorsed by twenty-two American evangelical theologians) discusses wisdom statements to foster discipleship in the area of economics (see http://oikonomia network.org/economic-wisdom-project).

These statements are "not absolute rules that apply to all situations, but they offer a starting point for thoughtful, biblically informed discussion of contemporary opportunities and challenges"—similar to the way proverbial wisdom is applied in context (Forster 2013b, 1). The twelve statements are:

1. We have a stewardship responsibility to flourish in our own lives, to help our neighbors flourish as fellow stewards, and to pass on a flourishing economy to future generations.
2. Economies flourish when people have integrity and trust each other.
3. In general, people flourish when they take responsibility for their own economic success by doing work that serves others and makes the world better.
4. Real economic success is about how much value you create, not how much money you make.
5. A productive economy comes from the value-creating work of free and virtuous people.
6. Economies generally flourish when policies and practices reward value creation.
7. Households, businesses, communities, and nations should support themselves by producing more than they consume.
8. A productive economy lifts people out of poverty and generally helps people flourish.
9. The most effective way to turn around poverty, economic distress, and injustice is by expanding opportunity for people to develop and deploy their God-given productive potential in communities of exchange, especially through entrepreneurship.
10. Programs aimed at economic problems need a fully rounded understanding of how people flourish.
11. Economic thinking must account for long-term effects and unintended consequences.
12. In general, economies flourish when goodwill is universal and global, but control is local and personal knowledge guides decisions.

Reflection and Discussion

1. Which of the twelve economic wisdom statements are often overlooked in discipleship?
2. What problems may result from an improper understanding of faith and economics, even if the intentions are good?
3. The Economic Wisdom Project focuses on why some people flourish instead of asking why some people are poor. How does this change in perspective affect intercultural discipleship?

213

The Oath for Compassionate Service

Robert Lupton has spent a lifetime working among the poor in various contexts worldwide. He has observed many examples of charitable intentions that had toxic results. As a result, he exhorts those who want to offer compassionate service in the economic sector to take the following oath:

1. Never do for the poor what they have (or could have) the capacity to do for themselves.
2. Limit one-way giving to emergency situations.
3. Strive to empower the poor through employment, lending, and investing, using grants sparingly to reinforce achievements.
4. Subordinate self-interests to the needs of those being served.
5. Listen closely to those you seek to help, especially to what is not being said—unspoken feelings may contain essential clues to effective service.

6. Above all, do no harm. (2011, 128)

Reflection and Discussion

1. Have you seen instances where this oath was violated? What were the effects?
2. How may this oath be contextualized for various cultural situations?
3. While the oath was intended for use among holistic development workers, how could it apply to intercultural disciplers? For example, what would it look like to "never do for the disciple what they have (or could have) the capacity to do for themselves"?

Contextual approaches to the economic/technology sector are important for intercultural disciplers. If left unaddressed, the two extremes that we have seen before will result: syncretism or split-level Christianity.

Clothes are strewn across the floor. Women trample over the discarded clothing in order to grab the nicer articles for their family. Normally cooperative and community minded, these parents are grabbing as many clothes as they can in a spirit of competition. As they stuff the best clothing into their bags, there is no time for small talk. At the end of the giveaway, the room is littered with unwanted clothing stretched across tables and spilling onto the floor.

One of the Native American elders watches this giveaway closely. Approaching the leader of the non-governmental organization, he says, "This giveaway is appealing to our lower nature. It appeals to our sense of competition. This is not good."

The leader is not surprised. After all, the entire event was not pleasant for him to watch either. However, the people were in need of the clothing, and others had donated these items with good intentions.

"Maybe this is just something we have to live with to help the people," he thinks. After a reflective pause, he asks the elder, "What do you suggest?"

"I suggest that you charge people a small fee to fill a whole bag with clothing. From the money collected, create a job for someone to check in the people,

Economic System and the Great Commandment

The economic system can be portrayed as an intricate web of relationships whereby goods and services are created and exchanged. Not only is physical capital exchanged, but social and spiritual capital are also exchanged through relational encounters in the marketplace. Disciples, then, fulfill the Great Commandment to love their neighbor by the quality of relational exchange *in* their daily work. Instead of regarding work as a secular activity and ministry as the only sacred activity, disciples can transform their work by regarding this as a holy calling just as valid as a calling to be a pastor.

Dallas Willard and Gary Black Jr. note the presence of God in the "secular" work world:

> There should be no doubt that God is as fully at work in the "business world" as he is in any other "world," including the "church world." In general, with some notable exceptions such as por-nography, gambling, or parts of the so-called entertainment industry, God is willing and able to bring about good in and through a business enterprise as easily, and in some cases perhaps more easily, than any religious or nonprofit organization. (2014, 208)

Reflection and Discussion

1. How is discipleship changed when disciples view their work as a holy calling that can produce good in order to fulfill the Great Commandment?

2. Why does work have the potential for great good and also great harm to the worker and community?

3. What steps can disciples take to fulfill the godly potential of work and avoid possible harmful consequences of work?

arrange the clothing nicely, and treat those who come as customers instead of beggars," the elder replies.

This change is announced and implemented. In a short time, the entire atmosphere is transformed from a selfish clothes-grabbing free-for-all to a shopping experience where a wise customer can get a good deal. The newly hired Native Americans are thrilled to have a job. Subsequently, they take pride in the careful and neat arrangement of the clothing in the room. They treat people as customers and listen to their wishes and desires. At the end of the day, dignity is restored to the newly hired workers and to the customers.

Economic Syncretism or Split-Level Christianity

Remember that syncretism results when two faith systems are blended together uncritically. The "prosperity gospel" is a popular example of this in the economic sector. This arises from a consumer-driven culture that blends uncritically with Christianity. As a result, disciples can be misled to expect that "God is ready, willing, and able to provide for every consumerist desire or creature comfort vaguely connected to the American Dream" (Willard and

Black 2014, 9–10). Emphasizing certain portions of Scripture while neglecting others, this blending distorts the gospel and harms the discipleship process.

In reaction to the syncretism called the "prosperity gospel," some jump to the other extreme of split-level Christianity. While syncretism does not take Scripture seriously enough, split-level Christianity usually does not consider culture seriously enough. In split-level Christianity, people disengage from culture. In economic split-level Christianity, they are "admonished to do less, have less, be less—to care less about the world of economic things" (Forster 2013a, 44). The end result of the admonition to live more simply is to disengage from the economic system. This misses the point that holding a job integrated into the economic system is an important way to fulfill the calling of God to love your neighbor as yourself. A meaningful job is a vocation and calling to serve others and maintain the worker's own dignity. The economic/technology sector in culture is a crucial area for intercultural disciplers to address.

Social Relationships Sector

In addition to the economics/technology sector, holistic discipleship addresses other sectors in culture. Considering figure 10.1, what would poverty look like if it occurred in the other two sectors of culture? Myers (1999, 88–90) describes "non-poor" poverty as the condition of those who are wealthy in the economics/technology sector but are lacking in other sectors. Steve Corbett and Brian Fikkert (2009) use the term "non-material poverty" to describe the same situation.

Poverty can also be defined by broken relationships (Myers 1999, 88–90). If a person lacks caring, trusting relationships, this leads to poverty in the social relationships sector. If poverty in this sector is not addressed, then discipleship is stunted.

After a short-term mission trip to help the poor, an American youth asked me with astonishment in her voice, "Why are those poor kids so happy with so little?" She realized that the kids she had met would never own a computer

> **The gospel of Christ knows no religion, but social; no holiness but social holiness.**
>
> John Wesley (1984, 14:321)

or an iPhone. Yet this did not diminish their happiness. As she considered her own "non-poor" poverty in the social relationships sector, she was forced to challenge the Western assumptions of secularism, consumerism, and individualism that promise happiness through the purchase of a Louis Vuitton purse, a BMW car, or an iPhone. Here is a shocking revelation: perhaps that large suburban home portrayed in *Better Homes and Gardens* can lead to isolation, loneliness, and eventually depression, thereby creating non-poor poverty in the social relationships sector.

Her cross-cultural encounter with holistic discipleship exposed non-poor poverty and created an environment for worldview transformation and kingdom focus. Other intercultural discipleship experiments have been conducted to address poverty in the social relationships sector.

Sioux Falls Seminary in Sioux Falls, South Dakota, embarked on a bold, holistic discipleship experiment in 2008. A large house, called the Summit House, was purchased in an area of the city targeted for revitalization due to high crime and low incomes. Seminary students voluntarily moved into the house in order to become servant leaders for Christ in this at-risk community. Since the neighborhood composition was 32 percent ethnic, the students learned intercultural ministry and community development through a combination of seminary courses and practical experiences in the neighborhood. They committed to spending at least five hours per week in ministry in the community combined with spiritual formation. In addition to having a significant impact in the development of this neighborhood, the students were challenged in areas that were previously neglected, thereby revealing their own non-poor poverty.

For example, many students realized that Western culture's high value of privacy leads to a poverty of community with others (social relationships sector), but they did not realize that the roots of this lie in the ideology/beliefs sector. By living and serving in a missional location, they started to understand how privacy and community are in inverse relationship to each other. Clinging to a high value of privacy (an unchallenged American value) results in a low degree of community with others (see fig. 10.2).

Figure 10.2
Trade-off between high privacy and low community

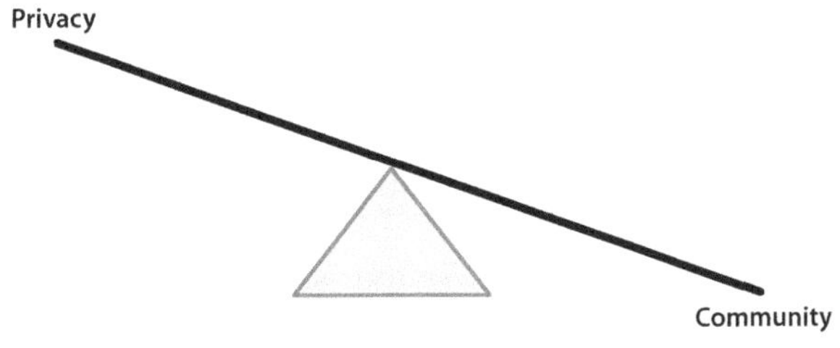

Privacy

Community

To achieve a high sense of community, privacy must be reduced. In practice, this means being available to sit with neighbors, having a meal with others, and spending less time alone and more time in "community locations." The students eventually realized that the benefit of having more emotional strength through community significantly outweighed the cost of reducing their highly cherished privacy. This shift in ideology did not occur simply by reading more books. As a result of holistic discipleship, the change in the social relationships sector exposed non-poor poverty in the ideology/beliefs sector, leading to worldview transformation.

Long-Term Community Growth Process

Holistic discipleship also reveals that discipleship is a long-term process of community growth, which may not be evident in a short-term individualistic culture clamoring for instant results. Marriage and family therapists have long recognized that a problem child usually does not exist in isolation; rather, there is a problem in the family system (Minuchin, Colapinto, and Minuchin 2007). Reflecting the wisdom of the African proverb quoted at the beginning of this chapter—"When the elephants fight, the grass suffers"— therapists focus their efforts not just on the individual but also on the whole family system. Similarly, holistic discipleship recognizes that individuals do not exist in isolation; rather, they are part of larger systems. Healthy, maturing disciples often arise from healthy, maturing communities. This requires the holistic discipler to look at the larger community-growth process that leads the community toward wholeness.

Tetsunao Yamamori (1993, 131) has noted four stages in the community development process. Each stage requires holistic disciplers to respond differently. While both words and deeds are required throughout, the proportion of each varies based on the stage in the growth process, as shown in figure 10.3. The x axis refers to the stage of community growth, and the y axis refers to the amount of ministry focus on words and deeds.

The first stage is relief, which requires immediate action to alleviate pain and prevent death during an emergency event. The second stage is recovery, which aims to restore the community to the level of development that existed prior to the emergency event. The third level is development, which aims to improve the condition of the community, such that it could withstand another emergency event if it occurred. The last stage is sustainability, which occurs when the local community has sufficient resources and connections to respond to a future emergency. At this stage, the local community is also a resource for others.

Yamamori notes that each of these four stages requires Christian development workers to respond differently. While both words and deeds are required throughout, the proportion of each varies based on the stage in the development process, as shown in figure 10.3. At the relief stage, there is a high proportion of ministry through deeds, with a smaller proportion of ministry through words. Moving further along the development process, the proportion of ministry through words increases as the ministry through deeds decreases.

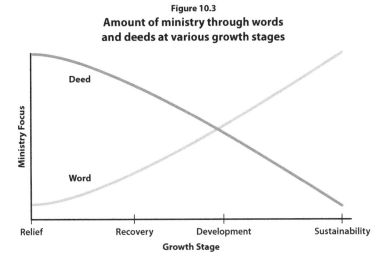

Figure 10.3
**Amount of ministry through words
and deeds at various growth stages**

For example, shortly after Hurricane Katrina, Sioux Falls Seminary students went to provide immediate relief in the affected areas. Deeds were required to address the victims' urgent physical needs and keep people alive. In the process of performing these deeds, the students used words to comfort, pray, console, and so on. Figure 10.3 anticipates that the amount of time spent on ministry through deeds would exceed ministry through words during the relief stage.

A year later, the seminary students returned to the hurricane-ravaged area. This time, however, they found the community in the second stage, recovery. At the recovery stage, many deeds were still needed—from replacing drywall to repairing roofs—to restore the community to the level of development that existed prior to the hurricane, However, the amount of time spent on ministry through words—for instance, counseling, listening to personal stories, praying—significantly increased. The proportion of time spent on deeds decreased as the time spent in ministry by words increased.

In the third stage, development, time spent on physical deeds further decreases because those ministering discuss strategies to further improve the community and prepare for a future similar event. The last stage, sustainability, occurs when the local community has the capacity to respond to future emergencies. At this stage, it is also a resource for others by sharing its experiences and lessons learned. The role of disciplers here is to minister primarily through words, with a diminishing proportion of deeds.

Short-Term Missions

Problems often occur when people go on a short-term mission and disregard the stage of community growth. For example, short-term teams go each summer to visit the Rosebud Lakota Sioux reservation in South Dakota. Confronted with the poor housing and lack of transportation and other amenities, these outsiders assume that their mission is one of relief. If their neighborhoods looked this way, it would be considered a crisis! As a result, they spend most of their time ministering by deeds (building, painting, repairing, etc.), with a minimal amount of ministry by words. While this would be appropriate in a relief situation, it is not appropriate for other stages of community growth. Many Native Americans themselves see their context as either in the recovery or the development stage. They would prefer that outsiders spend more time developing relationships through conversation (more words along with the deeds).

When bringing a team to Rosebud, we informed the local ministry leader that we were available to learn and serve. For the entire week, the people were most happy to teach us their culture, history, rituals; take us to visit families; explain how they counsel at-risk youth; and so on. They only asked us to serve with deeds for a small amount of time. As relationships are thickened with succeeding visits, this leads to more intimate and long-term engagement of the pertinent discipleship issues. Understanding the various stages of development helps identify the appropriate focus of words and deeds for holistic discipleship.

Understanding the various sectors where poverty resides alerts the intercultural discipler to be alert and address poverty in social relationships as well as the economic/technology sector. However, perhaps the greatest surprise for many Westerners who are doing intercultural discipleship may arise in the area of ideology/beliefs.

Ideology/Beliefs Sector

Many majority world societies maintain a spirit-power orientation. As discussed in chapter 1, this worldview assumes that spirit power is at the center of daily life. These societies assume that spiritual forces influence their daily activities and that humans are very weak; therefore, humans must carefully navigate through the spirit world. If the ideology/beliefs sector is not addressed, this fear of the spirit world affects all of life, which often stifles initiative, resulting in fatalism (Parris 2008). For disciples in this worldview, the categories of belief at the forefront of their thinking are very different from those of disciples with a material/scientific orientation. Larry Caldwell notes that "theological categories in many cases may be ones that the missionary (especially the Western missionary) has never dealt with before: dreams, demons, deliverances, healings, ancestor veneration, barrenness, and polygamy, to name but a few" (2005, 179). If these issues are not addressed in discipleship, the disciple is then pushed to other traditional sources for answers, which leads to split-level Christianity.

My Experience

This spirit-power orientation was not an area that I personally was prepared for when we initially became missionaries. I had to learn the hard way. After a short time in our mission location, I had severe stomach pains one night. Eventually, my wife took me to the hospital for an appendectomy. Lying in the hospital bed after the surgery, I learned a valuable lesson, as the following story describes.

> Groggy and confused, I gradually come to. A quick scan around the room alerts me that, like Dorothy and Toto, I am not in Kansas anymore. The walls are dirty, the temperature is above 100 degrees, and there is no nurse in sight. One thing I notice though—the pain in my gut is gone!
>
> I lay my head down to contemplate what is happening.
>
> Then I hear it. A voice inside me, like an internal radio, clearly speaks these simple words: "There are spiritual forces that you do not know about. Pray." That's it. Short. Simple. Direct.
>
> If I ever needed a new burst of motivation for prayer, this is it. This is a clear wake-up call for me. There are spiritual forces arrayed against the forces of God in an attempt to thwart the *missio Dei*. I do not simply need better strategy, increased education, more financing, and so on—this is a fight, and I need to be engaged in it. While I have tried to maintain a balance of Scripture reading and prayer, I have neglected intense prayer as a weapon to combat the evil forces in the Builsa area. This was not part of my seminary training.

It was new to me.

This started a journey of understanding and applying prayer for spiritual warfare. Could it be that these spiritual forces were partly responsible for the other four SIM families leaving the Builsa area after a short time? Sure, there were other reasons such as language learning, family health, and children's education, but could these spiritual forces also be at work? What could hap-

---

Life is war. That's not all it is. But it is always that.

John Piper (1993, 41)

---

pen if we engaged in serious prayer to combat these evil forces instead of pretending that they did not exist? The Bible does not say, "Ignore the devil and he will flee"; rather, James 4:7 says, "Resist the devil, and he will flee from you." Could the devil anticipate the outcome of missionaries staying in the Builsa area that would result in the Word of God reaching people and indigenous churches springing up with local leaders? Perhaps the devil knew that the gospel would take hold and transform peoples' lives such that they worshiped God.

> While all these questions were not answered that day, I gained a greater awareness of the spiritual powers that surround us. As further incidences occurred, I learned that mission is a battleground on which the kingdoms of light and darkness are in conflict. There is no neutral ground in this battle. Prayer is not simply a domestic intercom but a wartime walkie-talkie (Piper 1993, 46). But this battle was not about flesh and blood alone—my gut told me that this battle involves spiritual forces. Pray! (adapted from Moon 2012c, 19–20)

Watch and Pray

The event described above occurred early in my missionary service. It woke me up to the spiritual battles that surround us. I began to realize that this battleground is also an important area of discipleship. Jesus's words to the disciples to "watch [be alert] and pray" (Matt. 26:41) take on additional meaning. Prayer, sometimes accompanied by fasting, becomes a weapon in spiritual warfare. We must be aware, though, that this battle exists. Then we engage it.

This engagement includes prayer for individuals, homes, and communities. Instead of ignoring the excluded middle issues, where the spirit world impacts the material world, this should be engaged through the power of Christ. Often, this can be accomplished by using the discipleship tools discussed in previous chapters, particularly symbols and rituals. Marguerite Kraft notes,

> For the Thai, Christian ceremonies for baptism, for house dedication before moving in, for safety in a new car, for safety on a journey—all need to focus on God's power over the evil spirits and his protecting hand. Since ritual plays a very important part in enculturation, the church can be strengthened as group needs are met and the solidarity of the group is affirmed. (1995, 118)

To address issues such as ancestor veneration, Marguerite Kraft notes the use of intercultural discipleship methods: "In Korea the early Christians followed the missionary prohibition of ancestor worship, but now many years later some Korean pastors are seeking a functional substitute for the non-Christian ceremonies. Some have instituted memorial services (Tippett 1987, 192) to honor ancestors" (M. Kraft 1995, 123). In the past, this excluded middle area was condemned by the church, resulting in split-level Christianity. Engaging spirit-power issues gives disciples growing confidence in the power of Christ to transform them. Christ's power is displayed amid these excluded middle issues.

Marguerite Kraft describes a Navajo family whose house was struck by lightning:

According to tradition, that is a very serious evil attack, requiring one to abandon the house and build a new one. Since they were Christians, they called their pastor, who came to the home with a church group. They called on God to use his power over the evil spirits, to protect the family, and to purify and bless the house. The family moved back into the house, and the neighbors and non-Christian relatives were amazed—they had seen the power of God at work. (1995, 117)

By engaging the excluded middle with the power of Christ, using intercultural discipleship methods, this family and church maintained a kingdom-centered focus. This experience not only strengthened individuals; it also strengthened the faith of the families, churches, and communities. These excluded middle issues are important areas for discipleship.

Empowerment

To discern the proper use of objects in rituals for discipleship, Charles Kraft (1996, 149) adds one more layer on the form-meaning-worldview diagram we presented in figure 6.1. We discussed in chapter 4 how symbols have no meaning in themselves; rather, culture ascribes meaning to the outward form based on the worldview. Charles Kraft notes that there are times, however, when people may empower an object with spiritual power as they dedicate this object (see fig. 10.4). This leaves the Christian discipler the option of either destroying the object or disempowering the object and then dedicating it to God. This is the process of consecration.

Figure 10.4
Objects can be empowered with spiritual power

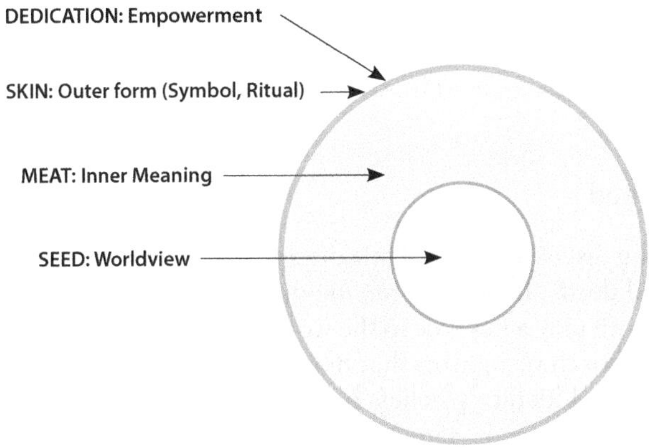

DEDICATION: Empowerment

SKIN: Outer form (Symbol, Ritual)

MEAT: Inner Meaning

SEED: Worldview

The Israelites had to wrestle with this concern. In chapter 4 we discussed how God used the tabernacle symbols and ritual process to transform their worldview from that of oppressed slaves to a holy nation of priests (Exod. 19:6). Where, though, did the gold, silver, and fabric come from to construct these elaborate symbols (ark of the covenant, lampstand, table of showbread, alter of incense, priestly garments, curtains, etc.)? Exodus 12:35–36 describes their source: "The Israelites did as Moses instructed and asked the Egyptians for articles of silver and gold and for clothing. The LORD had made the Egyptians favorably disposed toward the people, and they gave them what they asked for; so they plundered the Egyptians." Prior to this, the Egyptians had used these symbols and materials for worship; however, the Israelites were told to disempower and then dedicate them to God. Exodus 40:9 describes God's command to Moses: "Take the anointing oil and anoint the tabernacle and everything in it; consecrate it and all its furnishings, and it will be holy." Once blessed and consecrated, these forms were given spiritual meaning to shape a new worldview.

Healing

Another excluded middle area involving spirit power is the area of healing. While Westerners tend to rely on medicine for health concerns, people in spirit power–oriented cultures are drawn to spiritual sources. The 2004 Lausanne international gathering of evangelical church leaders encouraged Christians to pray for healing using symbols such as oil, laying on hands, and cloth (Claydon 2004a, 25). As discussed in chapters 4 and 5, the symbols used in rituals provide expressions of faith that invite the ultimate God to address intimate needs. This focus on faith in Christ provides an alternative to hope in magic elsewhere. Philip Jenkins notes, "Healing is the key element that has allowed Christianity to compete so successfully with its rivals outside the Christian tradition" (2011, 126). Intercultural disciplers recognize the opportunities for Jesus to reveal his power. This encourages the disciple to maintain a kingdom-focused lifestyle.

Word *and* Deed

The preceding discussion on holistic discipleship focuses on the combination of words and deeds. Instead of relying on simply one or the other, we must realize that both play a key role in the worldview transformation of disciples. A holistic approach recognizes that matters of economics/technology, social relationships, and ideology/beliefs need to be addressed, since the excluded middle issues often reside here. Ongoing debates rage about which is more important for evangelism and discipleship: words or deeds. Unfortunately, these unnecessary academic discussions provide more heat than light, resulting in stunted discipleship. As the African proverb reminds us, "When the elephants fight, the grass suffers." The emphasis on integrating word and deed is meant to correct the following common mistakes:

1. Discipleship by deed alone: This error assumes that deeds alone will communicate the gospel to people to transform their worldview. Since the gospel is not intuitive, though, people will not understand it unless it is articulated for them. Holistic discipleship must include verbal instruction.

2. Discipleship by word alone: This error assumes that words alone will communicate the gospel to people to transform their worldview. Since words are cheap and easy to speak, they are not always trustworthy. Deeds are needed to substantiate the validity of the words. Holistic discipleship must also provide opportunities to learn about God and others through deeds.

3. Give them bread first, then the word: This error assumes that we must first provide for people's physical needs to whet their appetite for spiritual ministry. Unfortunately, this is a deceitful "bait and switch" strategy. Holistic discipleship provides an alternative by doing *both*, with the proportion of each based on the stage of development.

4. Give them the word first, and then give them bread: This error assumes that people must first sit through a sermon before being fed. Unfortunately, this practice leads to ulterior motives for both the giver and the receiver. Again, the holistic discipleship alternative is to do *both*, with the proportion of each based on the stage of development.

Summary

A holistic perspective reminds us that the combination of words and deeds is crucial for intercultural discipleship. The following insights guide the discipleship process:

1. The functional integration of a culture recognizes that major sectors of culture affect one another. A change in one sector will influence a change in another. Start holistic discipleship by looking for the sector with the greatest need (poverty) or greatest asset.

2. The three sectors that comprise culture are economics/technology, social relationships, and ideology/beliefs. While poverty is usually attributed to the economics/technology sector, recognize what poverty in the other sectors looks like. Doing so alerts the intercultural discipler to where the excluded middle issues may be hidden.

3. Creating jobs and providing clean water address immediate needs, but they also affect the disciple in deeper areas. Instead of being "secular" or "unspiritual," addressing economic/technology issues often creates significant changes in social relationships and ideology/beliefs. Work is not a necessary evil; rather, it maintains dignity and provides a means to carry out the command to love one's neighbor as oneself.

4. When the economic/technology sector is not addressed by holistic discipleship, syncretism may result in the form of the "prosperity gospel." It also may result in split-level Christianity as people demonize the economic system and disengage from it.

5. Poverty in the social relationships sector results when people do not have life-giving friendships and partnerships. While people may have significant resources in the economic/technology sector, they can still be in poverty relationally, resulting in depression and loneliness.

6. Since people are connected to larger systems, holistic disciplers must look at the larger community growth stages to determine the proper focus of words and deeds. While both are always needed, the proportion varies based on the community's growth stage. Mistakes often happen when outsiders misread the growth stage of the community.

7. Poverty also exists in the ideology/beliefs sector. Many Westerners are shocked to learn of a spirit-power orientation. If this is not understood and addressed, though, discipleship is greatly stunted. Many excluded middle issues arise that need a contextualized intercultural discipleship approach. Instead of ignoring spiritual powers, disciplers must engage them with the power of Christ.

In the next chapter, we will take what we have discussed in the previous chapters and apply it to one specific context: contemporary postmodern culture. So far, we have discussed intercultural discipleship with a focus on majority world contexts and occasional references to Western culture. In the next chapter, we will focus largely on postmodern audiences in Western culture. Amid increasing globalization, intercultural discipleship is not simply needed for missionaries abroad; it is also needed in the West. Additionally, postmodernism will likely expand beyond Western cultures.

Activity for Discipling

1. Sit with your disciple and look over figure 10.1. Which sector do you see as your greatest strength? Which is your greatest poverty? Discuss the underlying issues in these sectors that contribute to your strength/

poverty. How could a change in one of the other sectors result in a change in the sectors that you selected?

2. Look at figure 10.2 with your disciple. Which side of the scale are you tending to emphasize to the detriment of the other: privacy or community? How could this be brought into better balance?

3. Consider the community in which your disciple resides. What stage has it reached in the community-development cycle in figure 10.3? What proportion of words and deeds are needed for appropriate discipleship during this stage?

For a short-term mission, discuss the stage of development that the team thinks the host community is in. Then ask the host community leaders which stage they see themselves in. Adjust your proportion of deeds and words for discipleship accordingly.

Blue Jean Selma

Adapted from Moon and Armstrong (2016).

Michael Johnson's steps quickened as he reached the famous Edmund Pettus Bridge in his hometown of Selma, Alabama. "Big Mike," as he is called due to his tremendous size and NFL career, reached out to shake President Obama's hand on this historic day. The first words to spill out of his mouth were, "We need help. We need more job training, more job opportunities. One of the big things I hear is that we don't have any jobs down here, there's nothing to do. Well, we gotta make sure that we're doing our part" (Chadiha 2016).

Selma, Alabama, has a long history of racial tensions. It was here that Martin Luther King Jr. invigorated the civil rights movement by marching across this same bridge fifty years ago. What came to be called "Bloody Sunday" was the beginning of a long overdue cry to address racial segregation back on March 7, 1965.

In addition to the need for racial reconciliation and jobs, Selma has its share of substance-abuse problems. Drug and alcohol addictions create huge problems in families and the entire community. Teens may be tempted to drop out of school, which makes them less likely to find a job later. Eventually, this can lead to criminal behavior, which can land them in prison.

Amid this litany of social concerns, there is some good news. Recently, a revival has burst forth in Selma. What started at the First Presbyterian Church in 2007 continued into a movement such that the congregation outgrew the initial church building. The Blue Jean Selma (BJS) church has since purchased an older church building downtown, where its members presently worship and do ministry.

BJS is a nondenominational family of believers committed to seeing people, the Selma community, and the world transformed through the love and power of Jesus. BJS is a very diverse family of believers. They are black, white, rich, poor, middle class, addicts, bank presidents, mentally handicapped, doctors, lawyers, blue-collar workers, unemployed, young, and old. BJS is fully integrated. About two hundred people gather each Sunday morning for authentic and meaningful worship.

BJS has no paid staff—they are all "tentmakers." Due to minimal maintenance or staff costs, almost all donations to BJS are given away and invested in outreach and in the community. A donation box is located in the back of the church, and people just put money in as the Spirit leads them.

There is no designated pastor; rather, a leadership team shepherds the church family. Different and diverse speakers from the community preach each week. The speakers have one thing in common, though: they are passionate for Jesus.

They describe their theology as "Simply Jesus. We are unified in the essentials of the Christian faith; we have liberty in the non-essentials, and we love in everything. And we want to love well!"

What is so different about BJS is that its members are just as focused on transforming the community through Jesus's love outside the walls of the church. They desire to transform the community in ways that are not traditionally recognized as "church activities."

The leadership team has recognized the various issues in the local community that need to be addressed. The team also understands that it has limited resources with which to act. The leaders of the team have decided that they must start somewhere. Now, they turn to you for advice about where to begin to do holistic discipleship in Selma. You recommend . . .

Reflection and Discussion

1. Consider the three sectors in culture and how they are functionally integrated. In which sector would you recommend that BJS start its ministry? Why would you place your limited resources in this sector? How might a change in this sector create a change in the other sectors?

2. Identify excluded middle issues in the three sectors. What role could the church play in addressing these issues for discipleship?

3. The church would like short-term interns to come and help. What role would you ask them to play? What problems may arise as a result of these outsiders living in Selma, and how would you address them ahead of time?

Read about BJS at http://bluejean selma.wixsite.com/bluejean and consider how it is addressing holistic discipleship.

Discipleship
for Postmoderns

Suom daa lang chala, fi lang yuka. (When the rabbit changes the way he runs, you change the way you throw [shoot].)

—Builsa proverb

To put into practice what we have learned in this book, in this chapter I focus on a particular group—postmoderns—and apply each of the approaches for discipleship. While this discussion is by no means exhaustive, it does explore each of the contours of discipleship among postmoderns. Since this group is partially found in the academy, I will start in a seminary classroom.

Which Grade Does David Deserve?

The shuffle of notebook paper, furrowed brows, and unsteady hands signals the arrival of the dreaded day. The paper assignment is due. David, a bright and hardworking seminary student, makes his way to the front of the room to turn in his written paper on contextual theology. As I read it over, it is unclear whether he thoroughly understands and can apply the material. Based on the grading rubric for written assignments, he earns a C grade. When making the assignments, I stated that the students should submit a written paper *or* present it orally. David misunderstood the directions and incorrectly assumed that a paper *and* an oral presentation were both necessary; therefore, he proceeds to give his oral presentation to the class.

In his oral presentation, he clearly articulates an understanding of the material, followed by an insightful discussion and creative application involving the other students. His grasp of contextual theology is probably the best in the class. When a difficult topic is discussed, David presents a metaphor to the class that perfectly fits the situation and helps many other students to get the point. The class is amazed at the accurateness and appropriateness of the metaphor. David is also amazed as he exclaims, "I have never thought of that metaphor before, and I would have never thought of it by reading and reflecting by myself. It is only during this dialogue that this came to me for the first time."

According to the oral presentation grading rubric, he earns an A grade. I later realize that he is a strong oral learner. I have to ponder, "Which grade should he get for this assignment?" When evaluated using a written preference, he earns a C. When tested according to his oral learning preference, he earns an A. It is clear that his intelligence is not the difference; rather, the difference is based on learning and assessment preferences. (adapted from Moon 2012d)

Changing Learning Preferences

David's story reflects a growing number of students in the West who have an oral learning preference. Some have termed this the "twenty-first century literacy" (NMC 2005), yet the roots go back much further. Rick Brown notes, "A general trend in history has been the progress from primary orality to some literacy with residual orality, and from then in some cases to a print-oriented culture. The modern trend is to move on to secondary orality, to a post-literate or multi-media culture" (2004, 123).

Whereas previous generations assumed that print-based learning methods were effective for discipleship, many contemporary Westerners prefer to learn through oral means. This shift in learning preference does not necessarily correspond to a shift in intelligence; rather, this preference indicates how these students learn best and have their lives most transformed. A significant cultural shift is occurring in the Western world that is changing the learning preference of disciples. Intercultural disciplers recognize that a cultural shift requires a change in discipleship methods, as the Builsa proverb reminds us: "If the rabbit changes the way he runs, then you change the way you throw [shoot]." What is the source of this cultural shift?

The Rise of Postmodernity

Many have observed this cultural shift, which has been termed "postmodernity." While not everyone agrees on the nature of this cultural change, it is a significant one that intercultural disciplers must adjust to. Prior to the rise of postmodernity, the foundations of modernity were built on objective scientific laws, abstract principles, rational reasoning, and a naive realist epistemology. Postmoderns critique these foundations and recognize the value of subjective emotions/values, cultural perspectives, concrete-relational thinking, and an instrumentalist epistemology. Paul Hiebert notes,

Postmodernity is the situation in which the world finds itself after the collapse of the Enlightenment project, which lasted from the latter part of the eighteenth century until well into the twentieth. That project, whose goal was for the world's diverse peoples to see things in the same rational way, is now questioned. What was secure, foundational, and established is now questioned. The assertion now is that our modern perception of "the way things are," rather than being knowledge based on reason and empirical evidence is instead merely a set of self-serving ideologies constructed by those in power, ideologies that marginalize those who disagree. (2008, 211)

Amid the postmodern critique, the Western church is often at a loss concerning how to disciple postmoderns in the Christian faith. Since the foundational discipleship methods relying on things such as the Four Spiritual Laws; rational, outlined systematic theology; print materials; and three-point analytical sermons are now called into question, where is the discipler to turn?

Premodern Approaches to Disciple Postmoderns

We have discussed intercultural approaches to discipleship in this book. Many of these approaches have formed over centuries amid premodern cultures. George Hunter (2011) suggests that these premodern discipleship methods are the very ones that can be used to reach postmoderns in the West today. Table 11.1 presents this connection between premodern and postmodern learning preferences. While these time periods are rough estimates, they provide a helpful characterization for understanding the shift in discipleship preferences.

TABLE 11.1		
Cultural Periods with Associated Learning Preferences		
Cultural Period	Learning Preference	Time Period (roughly)
Premodern	Primary oral	Antiquity to eighteenth century
Modern	Print	Eighteenth to twentieth century
Postmodern	Secondary oral	Twentieth century to present

Premodern Period

From the dawn of humankind until around the seventeenth or eighteenth century, disciples often preferred primary oral learning approaches. Hunter describes how the premodern Celtic Christian movement in the fourth and fifth centuries used "indigenous oratory, storytelling, poetry, music, dance, drama, etc. in God's service" (2000, 70). This should sound very familiar.

These oral methods, which we have discussed, are the keys to the discipleship of postmoderns, according to Hunter.

Modern Period

Beginning in the seventeenth or eighteenth century, the modern period was born out of the age of the Enlightenment. Previously honed oral methods of discipleship, such as symbols, rituals, stories, and proverbs, were discarded for print methods. Instead of relying on oral genres, as in the past, disciplers replaced them with systematic theology, objective principles, analytical reasoning, propositional truths, and such, since they were considered superior for discipleship. The quest for objective truth—following the lead of scientific reasoning—seemed to put a nail in the coffin for oral learning approaches . . . at least for a while.

Postmodern Period

In the late twentieth century, people became more and more disillusioned with the supposed certainty of the scientific method. They realized that there is more to discipleship than simply knowing more about God; rather, God can also be known by experience. Michael Pocock notes, "Postmodern people rely more on intuition, are more subjective in their judgments, do not trust systems and institutions, and treat most truth claims as personal or cultural" (Pocock, Van Rheenen, and McConnell 2005, 106). Discipleship in the postmodern period is returning to oral learning strategies. While premoderns were *primary* oral learners, postmoderns increasingly prefer *secondary* oral learning methods. Secondary oral learners can read and write, but they prefer to learn via oral means. Intercultural disciplers can utilize the discipleship lessons from primary oral learners that were discussed in previous chapters to disciple secondary oral learners, as shown in figure 11.1.

Figure 11.1
Primary oral methods to disciple secondary oral learners

Pre-modern	Modern	Postmodern
Primary Oral Learners	Print Learners	Secondary Oral Learners

Secondary Oral Learners

Walter Ong (1982), a seminal author on orality and literacy studies, notes that oral learners think quite differently from print learners. A primary oral learner is one who cannot read or write; rather, he or she relies on oral means to remember and utilize information. As a result, disciplers in primary oral cultures have developed elaborate mnemonic devices and procedures to aid in recall, such as storytelling, ceremonies, symbols, proverbs, songs, dances, and drama (discussed previously). Ong notes, however, that a new type of orality is occurring due to recent technological advances, such as television, radio, movies, and, more recently, computers, iPods, cell phones, tablets, and so on. Secondary oral learners are those who have the ability to read and write but prefer to learn or process information by oral rather than written means, aided by electronic audio and visual communications (Lovejoy and Claydon 2005, 63–64).

Following the trend that Ong noticed in the 1980s, Jonah Sachs has observed that contemporary learners are now accessing information through digital means to the extent that they exhibit the characteristics of oral learners. As a result, Sachs describes these secondary oral learners using the term "digitoral."

> The oral tradition that dominated human experience for all but the last few hundred years is returning with a vengeance. It's a monumental, epoch-making, totally unforeseen turn of events. . . . Our new digital culture of information sharing has so rejected the broadcast style and embraced key elements of oral traditions, that we might meaningfully call whatever's coming next the *digitoral era*. (Sachs 2012, 20, emphasis in original)

At one end of the continuum, then, are primary oral learners who cannot read or write, and at the other end of the continuum are print learners who rely entirely on print-based media. In between is a range of learning preferences. The secondary oral (or digitoral) learners fall near the middle, as they shift from a print to an oral learning preference, as shown in figure 11.2.

Figure 11.2
Shift in learning preference from print to oral

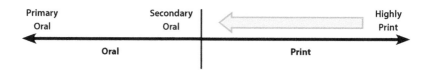

The oral versus print learning preferences were summarized in chapter 3. While there are many ways to describe the characteristics of oral learners, the mnemonic CHIMES summarizes helpful questions to consider when designing learning experiences for oral-preference disciples:

1. Communal: How can you encourage the disciples to learn from one another (by using small groups, group discussions, panels, visits, rituals, etc.)?
2. Holistic: How can you connect what disciples are learning to other areas of life so that you are adding to and critiquing what they already know?
3. Images: What images, symbols, and object lessons can be used so that words are not the only communicator of meaning?
4. Mnemonics: What formulaic devices, genres, and so on can you use to "hook" the disciples and then form memory "triggers" for later recall?
5. Experiential: How can disciples experience something, particularly events associated with real struggles of life, instead of simply learning at a distance?
6. Sensory: How can the senses be engaged to encourage deep discipleship experiences? (adapted from Moon 2016, 10)

So what does this digitoral learning process look like? Due to the ubiquity of digital means to gather information, people are changing how they receive,

> **James B. Slack defines "secondary oral learners" as "people who have become literate because of their job or schooling, but prefer to be entertained, learn and communicate by oral means."**
>
> Grant Lovejoy and David Claydon (2005, 54)

reason through, remember, and then re-create messages. This change in the learning process from print to digitoral learners is summarized in table 11.2.

TABLE 11.2		
Print versus Oral Learning Preference		
Process	Print	Oral
Receive message	Words carry meaning; therefore, the teacher carefully prepares and reads words	Mental images, symbols, gestures carry meaning; therefore, the teacher paints mental pictures and creates an experience
Reason through message	Learners take notes on main points, principles, and definitions	Learners picture themselves interacting with and participating in the metaphors or mental pictures in dialogue with others

Process	Print	Oral
Remember message	Learners review notes, written handouts	Learners review mnemonic devices (music, proverb, story, symbol, ritual, drama, dance)
Re-create message	New teacher refers to written outline or manuscript	New teacher guides a journey using a storyboard, memory palace, "chunking" information

Adapted from Moon (2016, 11).

It should be clear by now that the very intercultural discipleship approaches discussed in this book are the ones advocated for the discipleship of postmoderns. Each of these genres can be applied to the discipleship of postmoderns. Let's apply each of the genres discussed to postmodern discipleship:

Symbols

Postmoderns live in a symbol-rich environment; therefore, symbols are important components of spirituality for them (Flory and Miller 2000). Postmoderns are often not satisfied with mere hard, cold facts that talk *about* God; rather, they want to also *experience* the presence of God. Symbols provide this bridge to connect both a Christian ideology and experience so that disciples sense the ultimate God in an intimate way. Symbols can be used for discipleship in various settings at home and at work. In chapter 4, we observed the use of sage to help a man overcome his addiction to pornography. This symbol was a powerful reminder that his body is a sacred space created and cleansed by God. At the end of chapter 4, I also discussed how a candle or sage was used on Sunday to remind the family that the Sabbath is a special, sacred day. The symbol encourages family members to rise and worship at church as the symbol helps them want to do what they should do.

Symbols in the Workplace

Symbols in the workplace reinforce the reality that God blesses our work space and makes our work holy, as my following personal account illustrates:

Excitement hums through the chatter of the crowd as the Sioux Falls Psychological Services prepares to dedicate its new building. This experienced group of counselors understands the role that rituals and symbols can have in moving people toward healing. For this dedication ceremony, they selected the theme "Journey Ahead." After an introduction by the director and a Scripture reading, the counselors each present one symbol to the group that he or she feels helps to communicate the journey ahead. Counselors reach into their own life histories and present personal symbols to the others.

Several present gifts from previous clients of twenty years ago, but these gifts still hold powerful meaning for the counselors. A small bird's nest is presented, representing hope, growth, and life from small beginnings. A white cane is offered that reminds us that we heal others from our own brokenness. A cat figurine surrounded by blind mice is brought forth. A new mother unveils some baby shoes that remind her of the baby steps necessary to learn to walk. Another counselor presents a picture of a small plant growing out of a dead tree in a rock with the words, "God brings growth from the most difficult places." As each gift is offered in turn, a quiet, reverential hush blankets the room like a gentle fog settling over a valley on a cool morning. The space becomes holy as each person offers a symbol from the treasure chest of their soul.

Following the presentation of the symbols, sage is lit and the smoke released into the room by the waving of a feather. "The sage represents the cleansing of sacred spaces," it is explained, "and this space is now sacred ground." As they walk from counseling room to counseling room waving the smoke, counselors quietly pray and dedicate themselves and their offices to God. A final prayer of consecration and blessing concludes the event. Throughout the rest of the day, the smell of sage saturates the rooms, permeating into the clothing and minds of each person that this is a cleansed, dedicated, and sacred space. Months later, the white cane is still in the office waiting room, quietly reminding both counselors and clients of what is needed to continue the journey ahead.

The symbols at this work site continue to speak to the workers, reminding them of the holy nature of their work. Other symbols can be used to remind workers of the presence of the ultimate God at their work site.

Labyrinths Symbolize Life Journey

A hospital in Sioux Falls, South Dakota, recently installed a labyrinth outside the building to provide a place for people to reflect, pray, and meditate. Labyrinths are usually concentric circles mapped out on the floor that direct

---

The labyrinth has been used for centuries as a pilgrimage, a way back home. When Christian pilgrims could not get to Jerusalem, they walked the labyrinth.

Donna Schaper and Carole Ann Camp (2012, 1)

---

a person to the center. Participants take their time and stop along the way. The physical act of walking while praying in this winding path represents the journey of life. Amid the turns and surprises, God draws them close to the center of God's heart. At the center of the labyrinth is an open space where people can pause again and receive from God what they need. Finally, the journey out of the labyrinth symbolizes their preparation to reenter the world, energized by their experience with God. The labyrinth is a symbol that helps to connect the senses and ideology.

Some churches have built labyrinths into the inner floor of their building or outside in a courtyard; others have laid down a temporary "labyrinth mat" for special seasons. Sunnycrest United Methodist Church in Sioux Falls makes the labyrinth available (via a temporary "labyrinth mat") throughout the Passion Week preceding Easter. Sometimes people leave symbols (e.g., keys, Bible, oil, money) along the path for participants to stop and reflect on. Some people play soft music, light candles, or walk barefoot. In the labyrinth, the liminal environment encourages creativity and deeper bonding to Christian faith.

Symbols can also foster creativity in prayer. About twenty years ago I heard Dr. David Yonggi Cho from South Korea describe a prayer pattern based on the symbols in the tabernacle. He explained that each symbol God instructed the Israelites to construct in the wilderness (Exod. 25–30) had a New Testament fulfillment. Disciples can close their eyes and imagine stopping at each symbol as a form of prayer walking. Starting at the outer gate, disciples can enter the outer courtyard and picture Jesus meeting them at the bronze altar. Embracing Jesus, disciples can offer thanks to him. The smoke from the altar reminds disciples of the sacrifice that Jesus made on their behalf. Sequentially, disciples can stop at the various symbols, including the bronze laver, the table of showbread, the altar of incense, the menorah, and the ark of the covenant. Cho describes some of the details at http://tabernacle-prayer.com/tabernacle-prayer-basics.

Since that day I heard Dr. Cho speak, I have regularly used this prayer pattern. I have not become bored in prayer, and when my mind wanders, it is easy to bring it back to the next symbol in the tabernacle. This pattern provides creativity in prayer as I picture myself at each "station." Some days I will linger at particular stations longer than others. This prayer pattern can help postmoderns pray with creative and fresh expression, using the symbols of the tabernacle as a guide.

Rituals

Rituals utilize the power of symbols to foster discipleship. For discipleship with postmoderns, Richard Flory and Donald Miller (2000) advocate the "recovery of ritual and the visual arts as vessels for spiritual awakening and for the mediation of experience rather than the traditional rational, propositional approach of the past" (cited in J. Morgan 2011, 454–55). Rituals are often designed to maintain continuity amid transition. Using symbols as building blocks, good rituals help disciples continue their kingdom focus during transitions such as crises, growth stages, and other major life events. When a cultural ritual already exists, it can be contextualized for Christian meaning. When there is no ritual that addresses a particular excluded middle issue, a new ritual can be constructed.

Healing Rituals

During times of sickness, the disciple needs to experience the intimacy of God. A simple ritual of pouring oil, laying hands on the sick person, and praying over him or her invites the presence of the Holy Spirit to do what he wants for this person's life. A simple ritual such as this one I witnessed as a child can change a person's life.

As a boy, I visited Camp Pecometh United Methodist Men's retreat each year with my dad. On Saturday evening there was an anointing ceremony that I will never forget. One time a man came forward and asked for prayer. He explained that he was addicted to alcohol and his wife was about to leave him. He felt powerless to overcome this habit, and he did not like the person that he was becoming. With tears welling in his eyes, he begged for prayer. The men gathered around him, laid hands on him, anointed him with oil, and prayed for God to intervene in his life.

The next year I returned to Camp Pecometh. Early in the meeting, this man rose to his feet and proclaimed, "It has been one year since I last had a drop of drink! My wife is overjoyed at the man I am becoming, and I even respect myself now." Every year he would return and recount the story of God's healing in his life. I remember him testifying, "It has been ten years now since I last had a drop of drink!" As a young man, this nurtured my own discipleship as I saw the power of God to deliver this man from bondage. The ultimate God became intimate, and I was a part of it.

Other Healing Moments

Rituals are particularly helpful during moments when healing is needed. God desires to bring shalom to humanity, and we invite God to do this in our rituals. I have observed rituals conducted for women dealing with the trauma of sexual abuse. Others have constructed rituals to help a blended family come together as one. Another family constructed a ritual to help them accept the woman whom their widowed father was now about to marry. A ritual was also designed to help a military man reenter the life of his family after being away at war for a long period. In each case, the people were dealing with very sensitive issues that are hard to discuss and resolve with words alone. For communicating deep values and emotions, words alone are often not sufficient. Rituals with symbols fill that gap so that disciples can stay kingdom focused.

Coming of Age

Another ripe opportunity to focus disciples on the kingdom is the "coming of age" stage of life. When my children were near the age of thirteen, I told them that I was watching for signs of maturity in them. Once I observed these signs of maturity (e.g., looking out for others, helping around the house, signs of faith commitment), I took them away for "their weekend." My wife did this with the girls, and I did it with the boys. During the weekend they did not know where we were going and what we would do. It was a very liminal experience. For one son, we drove a motorcycle to a mountain for the weekend. For another son, we took a canoe to a remote spot. During the weekend, we made our own meals over the fire and talked about the "secrets of manhood." Listening to Dr. James Dobson's audio book (1999) *Preparing for Adolescence*, we discussed peer pressure, puberty, emotions, identity, and so on. The liminality of the weekend provided precious opportunities for deep bonding to the Christian faith and to each other. This bonding experience is particularly beneficial during the teenage years when young people are trying to find their identity.

Camps

For five years I conducted a weeklong camp for teenagers because of the tremendous discipleship potential it offered. Counselors were instructed in the three-stage ritual structure discussed in chapter 5. They were then encouraged to create liminal moments to foster *communitas*. All electronic devices (e.g., cell phones, tablets) were removed, and no schedule was posted, so the youth were totally reliant on one another and their counselor. This liminal condition nurtured deep bonding to one another and to the faith of the counselor.

The heavy use of symbols connected with the youth at a deeper level than mere words alone. For example, they were encouraged to write faith commitments on a strip of cloth, then roll it up like a tube and ask someone to tie it to their wrist. This reminded them that they needed others to help them keep their commitments. Months after camp, I observed youth still wearing the bracelets as a daily reminder of their commitments. This yearly camp for many is an annual pilgrimage to help adolescents refocus and renew their kingdom focus.

Odyssey Years

Another life phase when postmoderns are searching for identity has been termed the "odyssey years" or "emerging adulthood" (Arnett 2004). Traditionally, humans in all cultures go through the four life phases of birth, adolescence, adulthood, and old age. In postmodern culture, there are now six life phases, namely, birth, adolescence, odyssey, adulthood, active retirement, and old age. The odyssey years are the "decade of wandering that occurs between adolescence and adulthood" (Brooks 2011, 190). David Brooks notes that adulthood is often defined by four characteristics: moving away from home, getting married, starting a family, and becoming financially independent. In 1960, 70 percent of American thirty-year-olds had accomplished this, whereas fewer than 40 percent had accomplished it in 2000 (Brooks 2011, 190).

Jeffrey Arnett notes that contemporary emerging adults cite the following markers as most important for achieving adulthood status: taking responsibility for oneself, making independent decisions, and becoming financially independent (2004, 209). He further states that previous markers such as marriage and childbearing do not make the top-ten list; rather, they are further down the list. Unless these markers are crossed, a lack of identity often results in a time of wandering, as described by a student in a class post in 2012:

> Although I am married, I have found myself in a place of some confusion, out of adolescence but not quite into adulthood. It's somewhat disconcerting, as I feel the pressure to make my way into adulthood but not necessarily having all the tools to get there. I do, however, have a strong family network that has continued to guide and direct some of that transition. I have definitely seen this at work in the lives of others my age who are trying to figure out this "odyssey" portion of their lives. I think a more clearly defined ritual would definitely help this transition.

When no ritual exists, postmoderns tend to wander aimlessly, or they construct their own ritual for identity formation. Noting the rise of body tattoos among the "twenty-something" generation, Matthew Anderson observes, "The absence of meaning-making rituals within the Church has left an empty space that tattoos have admirably filled" (2012, 76). Social critic Michael Barone contends that this odyssey stage tends to make moderately impressive twenty-year-olds but very impressive thirty-year-olds (Brooks 2011, 192).

This is an important life transition that needs to be understood and addressed. Symbols in ritual are a good "fit" for this discipleship need because they help maintain continuity amid the transition of the odyssey years. When done well in a church community, ritual can shape disciples' worldview and identity as mature members of the body of Jesus Christ.

Intercultural Mission Trips

Exposure to other cultures reveals disciples' own worldview assumptions, perhaps for the first time. Hiebert states that a powerful way to transform a worldview is to "step outside our culture and look at it from the outside, and to have outsiders tell us what they perceive as our worldview" (2008, 321).

Short-term mission trips provide an excellent opportunity for this type of worldview exposure and transformation.

John Hull's doctoral research indicates that three factors are necessary for faith development on short-term mission trips: cross-cultural interaction, relevant Bible studies and discussion, and liminality (2004). Teams that have had the highest levels of these three factors saw the highest levels of faith development. Unfortunately, those that have had the lowest levels of these three factors experienced significantly lower levels of faith development.

A short-term mission trip can be conducted as a positive discipleship ritual by intentionally incorporating each of the three stages of the ritual process structure. To enhance liminality and establish learning relationships, I encourage short-termers to spend the first half of the mission trip in language learning. This often results in *communitas*, whereby participants form deeper bonds to their faith and other Christians (both in the host community and among team members).

Dedications/Cleansing

Other intimate moments when a kingdom focus is needed may include the construction or purchase of a house. Dedication ceremonies are rich opportunities to remind disciples that houses should be used for hospitality. Prior to the construction of a house, a young couple whom I worked with stood outside and prayed over the land. During the construction process, they wrote down the names of people on the subflooring (later to be covered with carpet) whom they wanted to invite to the house when it was finished. At the completion, they had a simple ceremony with their pastor and builder. They walked into each room, prayed over it, sprinkled it with water, and dedicated the house for God's use. This was a powerful discipleship moment for the family as well as the builder. A similar dedication and cleansing can be done whenever a family moves into a house. This integrates the spiritual with the secular to help disciples stay kingdom focused.

Revitalized Eucharist

Jesus gave us the rituals of baptism and the Lord's Table (Eucharist, Communion) for our discipleship. After studying emerging churches in the United Kingdom, Janine Morgan recommends that postmoderns revitalize the Eucharist by recovering dramatic creativity, as she describes it in an emerging church:

> The drama is low key, meditative rather than energetic. It begins with the "set," staging an ambient mood of transcendence and mystery through the use of candles, multi-media, and art/icons. "The whole effect, with the candles, is one of mystery, peace and transcendence that helps me tune into God." . . .

The juxtaposition of silence followed by the "techno-monastic" music track that reaches a crescendo at the breaking of the bread, and the simple *Agnus Dei* that is then sung, has deep emotional impact on participants. "It draws me in; it reminds me of when I've just walked into the service and come in from the cold, like I'm about to enter on a journey." Such sensory richness enables a meaningful experience. (2011, 453)

The rich use of symbols, drama, and music described above helps connect postmoderns to the mystery of God, thereby furthering their journey of discipleship.

Stories

Storytelling as a means to convey truth connects with postmoderns. For discipleship with postmoderns, Tommy Jones asserts, "Narrative is becoming the primary means of telling beliefs. Since propositional logic has fallen on hard times, stories carry more weight in carrying truth . . . 'abductive' reasoning. As opposed to deductive or inductive methods, when you tell a story, you 'abduct' listeners from their known worlds into another world" (2001, 27). The blossoming of storytelling in postmodern culture has a natural connection to the Bible, since the majority of the Bible is written in narrative form. As in premodern times, storytelling is an important art form for postmodern discipleship.

Learning Biblical Stories

For the stories of the Bible to become "our stories," disciples must internalize them such that they live out the truths expressed in these stories. Thomas Boomershine's approach (1988), noted in chapter 7, can be applied to postmoderns. For postmodern youth, Michael Novelli (2008) recommends a chronological presentation of the biblical stories in order to demonstrate the biblical story as a grand epic. He presents a symbol for each story, to be followed with retelling and dialogue following the storytelling. The dialogue helps disciples connect with the story so that they are shaped by the epic story of Scripture.

Movies Contain Indigenous Stories

Indigenous stories are shaped by experiences in culture. Tom Steffen (1996, 167) advocates looking for stories that emerge from moments of crisis, courage, conflict, commemoration, comedy, chastisement, charismatic events, and celebration. Postmodern stories are often shaped by the media. In particular,

Postmodern Approaches

Several approaches to postmodern discipleship have been developed based on the genres previously discussed, including the following practices:

1. Chronological Bible storytelling has found a welcome home among postmoderns, since they "are more interested in story than in doctrine" (Pocock, Van Rheenen, and McConnell 2005, 126). See http://www.biblicalstorying.com.

2. Walk Thru the Bible ministries developed an approach to describe the epic story of the Bible. "Its use of body motion, repetition, and story likewise appeal to postmoderns" (Pocock, Van Rheenen, and McConnell 2005, 126). See http://www.walkthru.org.

3. The Alpha program birthed in the United Kingdom by Nickey Gumbel "is aimed at postmodern people in post-Christendom cultures and capitalizes on the postmodern yearning for reality and the use of story and drama in settings that are relationally warm" (Pocock, Van Rheenen, and McConnell 2005, 126–27). See http://www.alpha.org.

4. Since the millennial generation is reading less and less, a new form of book has been developed recently in response to the digitoral learning preference. Called the "digi-book," it features an embedded video introduction in each chapter that summarizes the chapter. Readers can then skip to the next chapter and actually get a summary of the book contents in about thirty minutes. Once a reader dives into reading one of the chapters, a blog allows them to interact with others. In this way, they are cocreating the content as they form community based on a shared story. A free digi-book sample can be obtained by searching the iBook app on a phone or computer for the book *Orality*. See http://www.digibooks.io.

Reflection and Discussion

1. Compare these discipleship approaches to traditional approaches used in your church. What differences and similarities can you identify?

2. Why do you think these approaches have found a positive response among postmoderns?

3. How can these approaches be contextualized for your own context? What innovations would you recommend?

Robert K. Johnston notes the power of the stories contained in movies: "People both within the church and outside it recognize that movies are also providing primary stories around which we shape our lives. Movies block out the distractions around us and encourage an attentiveness toward life. Presenting to viewers aspects of their daily lives, both intimate and profound, movies exercise our moral and religious imagination" (2006, 13).

Movies, then, provide a cultural genre in which theology is discussed through the stories presented (movies will be discussed further below). Instead of ignoring these stories (which leads to split-level Christianity) or uncritically accepting the stories portrayed in movies (which leads to syncretism), critical contextualization engages Scripture with these stories for discipleship.

Critical Contextualization of Stories

Discipleship is fostered as the biblical stories engage and interpret indigenous stories. At times, indigenous stories also stimulate reflection on biblical stories. While this can be done alone, it is often more powerful when done in community, such as a storytelling event.

One discipleship practice for postmoderns that I have used is a "storytelling night" at a local coffee shop. Prior to the event, disciples meet and discuss indigenous stories that interact with biblical stories. Some of the indigenous stories are funny, others are serious, but all of them are personal. After meeting as a group to discuss the engagement of these stories, we then discuss some storytelling principles. Finally, the participants all practice their stories several times. They are invited to bring their family and friends to this event. Anyone who tells a story that night is treated to free coffee. Ultimately, this event has led to further discussion with the disciples and also with bystanders at the shop who are "sucked into" the stories.

Proverbs

Proverbs are pithy, creative sayings that often summarize the meaning of a story. A proverb is also a mnemonic device to help storytellers and listeners remember the meaning long after the event is over. They also provide a window into the soul of the culture. These insights can then be engaged with Scripture for contextual discipleship.

For example, Stan Nussbaum (1998, 1–4) surveyed 234 American proverbs and found common themes that describe the "Ten Commandments of American Culture," including:

1. You can't argue with success (be a success).
2. Live and let live (be tolerant).
3. Time flies when you're having fun (have lots of fun).
4. Shop till you drop.
5. Just do it.
6. No pain, no gain (get tough; don't whine).
7. Enough is enough (stand up for your rights).

8. Time is money (don't waste time).

9. Rules are made to be broken (think for yourself).

10. God helps those who help themselves (work hard).

Each of these cultural themes can be discussed and critiqued with Scripture so that disciples can critically evaluate their own worldview. This engagement provides hope for transformation.

Other books have been written about biblical proverbs and their use in the workplace. For example, Michael Zigarelli (2004) provides a contemporary business story and then applies a biblical proverb to describe how to manage business decisions.

In addition, short, pithy sayings are such potent memory devices that good communicators often develop their own proverb-like sayings. For example, I can still remember many years ago being challenged by a message of Rev. Johnson Asare in Ghana that included the refrain, "If we move, God moves: If we sit, God sits."

In postmodern contexts, proverbs can be likened to taglines or Twitter posts. These short, catchy phrases communicate with a few words in ways that many words cannot. Disciplers can develop their own proverb-like phrases, such as Mike Breen and Steve Cockram's phrase "If you make disciples, you always get the church. But if you make a church, you rarely get disciples" (2011, Kindle locations 84–85).

Dance

Postmoderns are often not content to learn about spirituality; rather, they want to participate in and experience it. Leonard Sweet notes, "Postmoderns want interactive, immersive, 'in your face' participation in the mysteries of God. Pentecostals talk about 'moving the service.' To 'move the service' is to facilitate intimacy with God through dance, speech, sound, touch, etc." (2000, 72).

Dance is a cultural expression that provides cultural identity. If dancers are forbidden to dance in church, they will not dance there but will likely dance elsewhere. This promotes split-level Christianity. However, if dance is not critiqued, it may lead to syncretism, as some dances may be sexually suggestive.

An example of Christian dance for postmoderns is demonstrated at http://www.youtube.com/watch?v=uUeUiecis10. Adam Sieff and his worship team are shown teaching teenagers a dance to talk it (their faith) like they walk it (in practice). Since these youth are going to dance anyway, they are being taught a Christian approach to dance that engages their faith with their culture. The goal is to promote deeper discipleship through contextualization.

Music

For postmoderns, music is ubiquitous and formative. Craig Detweiler and Barry Taylor note, "If we understand pop music as a key component in the development of identity, a fertile ground for the matrix of meanings that characterize postmodern life, we should not be surprised that pop music has much to say about the shaping of contemporary notions of God and religion" (2003, 130).

Music, then, is not a secondary concern for postmodern discipleship; rather, this genre is a constant presence that shapes identity and spiritual motivations. In describing the ever-present and shaping power of music, Tom Beaudoin (1998) has described pop music as the amniotic fluid of contemporary society. The most influential writers in Dublin are now musicians such as Bono and the Edge of U2 instead of author James Joyce (Detweiler and Taylor 2003, 21).

Nondiscursive Teaching

Music teaches through nondiscursive means. Instead of direct analytical points to be remembered, music creates an atmosphere that touches the heart of a disciple for transformation. Detweiler and Taylor explain,

> In a post-rational, post-literal world, the communication of thoughts and ideas through "atmosphere" might prove to be a more effective means of communicating the gospel. St. Francis told his followers, "Preach the gospel wherever you can, and when all else fails, use words." For today's [postmodern] people, St. Francis may say, "Sing the gospel wherever you can, and when all else fails, use words." (2003, 141)

If the music of the disciple is not identified and engaged in discipleship, this powerful shaper of identity and motivations will be untouched, leading to split-level Christianity. However, a simple survey of pop music recognizes that not all pop music is spiritually uplifting. A simple acceptance of all pop music leads to syncretism.

Critical Contextualization of Music

The same process of critical contextualization needs to be applied to the genre of music. Instead of rejecting all pop music too quickly, though, the discipler may be surprised to find spiritual discussions outside the contemporary Christian music world. For example, "artists such as Nick Cave, Bruce Cockburn, Creed, Moby, and U2 speak about spirituality from a distinctly Christian bias but have little or nothing to do with organized religion" (Detweiler and

Taylor 2003, 151). Different music styles may also be combined. Craig Miller notes that postmoderns thrive on a variety of musical forms:

> Along with the organ and piano, these congregations use guitars, drums, synthesizers, conga drums, string, brass, woodwind instruments, marimbas, and so forth. They are limited only by their imagination. . . . They use rock, classic rock, country, folk, Celtic, alternative, jazz, gospel, classical, and Christian contemporary, plus the various styles of world music such as Jamaican or Mariachi and the like. To communicate the message they add the use of drama, dance. (1996, 174)

Creativity Encouraged

Instead of stifling musical expression, postmodern discipleship should encourage creative expressions that are faithful to Scripture. This includes the music of contemporary artists who express Christian values, as well as the music of Christian contemporary artists. A creative form of hip-hop from a Christian perspective is FOG's worship-hop. See http://www.youtube.com/watch?v=knL-JMzFl9w.

Postmoderns yearn for a creative expression of faith that is articulated poetically in song, metaphor, and symbols. Theology that is stripped down to analytical statements feels like "theology in a body bag" (Detweiler and Taylor 2003, 153). The use of music liberates theology so that it lives and moves among us, as Jesus did on earth.

Drama

Drama can be presented in many contexts. In contemporary Western culture, movies combine the genres of storytelling, music, and drama in a two-hour space of time. Movie lines shape an important part of postmodern thinking; I have observed postmoderns quoting movie lines back and forth to each other. At times, the movie lines and story plots are embedded with theology. Detweiler and Taylor note, "There is a conversation about God going on in popular culture that the church is not engaged in and is often unaware of" (2003, 23). Unless the church engages the drama contained in movies with Scripture, disciples will unconsciously shape their theology by the most powerful movies.

Movies

Christ United Methodist Church in Lexington, Kentucky, exemplifies one approach that a church can take to engage movies with Scripture. A Wednesday-night group meets at the church to discuss "The Gospel according to Pop

Culture." In this format, a small interpretive community was formed that watches thirty minutes of a movie and then spends the next thirty minutes in discussion. Scripture is used to interpret the content of the movie. Recently, when viewing the movie *Harry Potter and the Sorcerer's Stone*, the participants asked questions such as:

- What characteristics does Harry demonstrate that are compatible with characteristics considered virtuous and acceptable in the Christian faith?
- Who are the Voldemorts of our day and age, and what qualities do they have?
- What kind of trolls do we face in our lives?
- How is Harry's solution to the troll problem similar to our solutions?
- How would you use scenes and events from this movie segment to help explain Christian beliefs to a person who is not familiar with the church, the Bible, or Christian theology?

They use such questions to dig down to some of the roots and identify values in American culture. Each person is allowed time to be heard, and everyone is encouraged to consult with others in order to enlarge the interpretive community's awareness and experience. This exercise allows practical discussion of relevant concerns. For example, a discussion developed concerning the enthusiasm of the seekers who were going after the golden snitches. In light of Luke 15 concerning Jesus's parables of the lost sheep, the lost coin, and the lost son, group members discussed how lost people are like golden snitches to God, and we are to be active as seekers in reaching them. When people come to Christ, the heavens erupt in joy, just as the crowd erupted when Harry finally caught the golden snitch. Other discussions focused on the presence of spiritual forces in our world and the need to discuss this with our children. Relevant scriptures, such as Revelation 12 and 1 Peter 5, were then introduced to facilitate this discussion. While this practice could go much deeper, the use of Scripture to examine issues within an interpretive community is a major step toward articulating an informed response to the Harry Potter movie. The critical contextualization of movies provides a discipleship opportunity as the disciple engages movies with Scripture.

Drama in Church

Drama has been used effectively in church services as well. It can come in the form of enacted biblical stories or dramatized life events that address the biblical theme on which the preacher will elaborate. In both cases, I have observed postmoderns absorbed in the drama such that it touched both their heads and their hearts. One creative use of drama in church is the "enacted prayer," first developed by Jeff Barker at Northwestern College. Barker explains how this developed:

> One day while we were praying before rehearsal, we prayed for a man in our church who was desperately ill in the hospital. We prayed that God would go to his room at the hospital and heal him and return him home to his family. Suddenly we realized that we could easily create an image of our prayer by acting it out. We did, and the prayer took on a more vital reality for us. We decided to pray that same prayer, using the same dramatic form, on Sunday morning in worship. Since I am a worship leader at our church, this was easily integrated into the service. . . . The prayer was quite moving, and the man did return from the hospital, both in the prayer and in life. (2017)

This creative prayer form incorporates the creativity and participation that is valued by postmoderns. Other creative uses of drama can foster growth for disciples, including participatory educational theater (PET).

Participatory Educational Theater

PET transforms spectators of drama into actors. A problem is first enacted, then the drama is temporarily halted. Spectators are then asked what they would do to resolve the issue that is dramatized. Whoever has something to contribute is then invited to take the place of one of the actors in order to demonstrate how he or she recommends addressing the issue. As Sweet observes, "Postmoderns . . . perceive, comprehend, and interact with the world as much as participants as observers" (2000, 54). The PET method of problem solving appeals to these postmodern tendencies, as my following personal account illustrates:

> Gradually, the couches fill as the youth gather to discuss their upcoming immersion experience on a Native American reservation. After twenty minutes of discussion, the meeting takes an abrupt turn.
> "I need a volunteer to step in when I call on you. You will observe how Dave acts out a situation, and then you will take Dave's place and do it better," I announce.
> They do not know that Dave and I have met before the meeting to act out how a visitor should not greet a Native American elder. We discussed how Natives may interpret a strong handshake as aggression, how looking into the eyes of the elder may represent disrespect, and how their concept of time is different from that of many Americans.
> I take the role of a Native elder on the reservation who is being approached by a youth on this immersion team.
> Dave bounces into the room with youthful vigor, locks hands in a tight handshake, looks me straight in the eye, and says, "Hi, we have been waiting for thirty minutes for you to show up. Where have you been?"

My eyes express pain and disappointment during the conversation. Eventually, I say, "That was painful for the Native American being visited. How could this be done better?"

One youth takes Dave's place and reenacts the same scene. This time, he does not look directly into my eyes; rather, he diverts his eyes away periodically.

"Very good. Did you see how his eyes were showing respect?" I ask. "The handshake, though, is still expressing an aggressive attitude. This indicates that this person cannot be trusted. Who can reenact this?"

Hesitantly, a girl rises to take his place. She greets me with a soft handshake and avoids direct eye contact. So far, so good. I save the most difficult task for last, though.

With a serious look and stern voice, I protest, "Why are you here on our sacred land? Don't you know that whites have mistreated us in the past?"

Her eyes widen, and she steps back. Not knowing what to say, she shrugs and replies, "I didn't know you felt that way. Can you explain this to me?"

"Natives often look to the past to determine the next steps for today, while Americans often look to the future to set goals for the future. Instead of ignoring the past, your learner's attitude will help resolve tensions that you may encounter on the reservation," I explain.

While other lessons are taught today, the ones that are enacted appear to sink in. This PET experiment is a significant step in demonstrating how disciplers can become good news so that they can share good news. This ability may make the difference for this intercultural immersion to be a positive discipleship experience for these youth.

Through participation, postmoderns do not simply learn about facts and opinions on issues; instead, they experience the issues. This desire for experience emerges in other areas of life, not simply the "spiritual areas."

Holistic Discipleship

Holistic discipleship concerns the whole person, both the spiritual and the secular areas of life. Postmoderns critique the foundations of both the spiritual and the secular world. They question simple notions of progress, metanarratives, and universal knowledge as "no more than claims to social and political domination" (Kirk 2007, 299). Postmodernity seeks to listen to marginalized and alternative voices in order to critique the existing economic, social, political, and even religious power structures. Disciplers need to assist postmoderns in this critique of various foundations of culture by experiences within culture that are then reflected on through words and deeds.

Postmoderns want to learn how to address cultural issues by experiencing them. Sweet explains, "Moderns want to figure out what life's about. Postmoderns want to experience what life is, especially experience life for themselves. Postmoderns are not willing to live at even an arms'-length distance from experience. They want life to explode all around them. . . . They want it laced with experience" (2000, 33).

Instead of ignoring postmodern concerns in the cultural sectors of economics/technology, social organization/relationships, and ideology/beliefs, discipleship must address these areas with a Christian response. Craig Miller notes, "The local church must create a place of integrity, compassion, and authenticity in which postmoderns can find a safe place to seek God" (1996, 167). The areas in which postmoderns are seeking God are not solely spiritual areas; rather, they may start with trying to understand and respond to poverty.

Economics

I have observed that many postmoderns are increasingly concerned with social justice. They want to know why economic poverty still exists in a world that has abundant resources. They are not content with simple answers such as "the poor are simply lazy." They also want to know what they can do about it. A good way to start exploring this issue is through immersion experiences with the poor.

For a seminary course, I have invited students to live on the streets with me for a week. They can bring only a sleeping bag, a Bible, a pen, twenty-five dollars, and an optional toothbrush. Through this experience, students interact with the chronically poor, the working poor, and the situationally poor. In the evenings, the students ask questions and reflect on God's presence with a depth that does not often occur in the classroom. Often there are many startling discoveries. They find many of the poor are open and desirous of spiritual conversations. Students observe how meaningful work dignifies a person, and conversely how a person's sense of worth is diminished when he or she has no meaningful work. Theologically, perhaps the greatest revelation comes from realizing that the mission of Jesus is intimately connected to the poor. The students start to see Scripture differently as they discover the connection between discipleship and interacting with the poor.

The American Bible Society published *The Poverty and Justice Bible*, which highlights verses that discuss poverty and justice. James Catford, former chief executive of the Bible Society, notes that the Scriptures mention poverty over 2,100 times, and he asks, "How can the issues of poverty and justice be left out of the 'basics' if they are so deeply enshrined in the Bible's pages?" (2008, 2). Students living on the streets for a week begin to ask the same question. The discipleship issue is then brought home to them as they consider that their own discipleship is perhaps stunted when they do not spend time with the poor.

Western society is structured such that the middle and upper class can go through their entire routine for a week, month, or even a year with very little intimate contact with the poor. Jesus connected the gospel to the poor, yet we tend to separate the two. Is it possible that we are missing an essential understanding of the gospel when we are not in the midst of the poor?

An important area of discipleship for postmoderns is to interact with the poor. As we do, Jesus's presence is felt, as described when Jesus said to the disciples, "I tell you the truth, whatever you did for one of the least of these brothers and sisters of mine, you did for me" (Matt. 25:40). St. Francis of Assisi noted that the face of Christ is revealed to us in the faces of the poor. Intentional efforts are needed to interact with the poor, either through week-long experiences, weekend encounters, or through regular visits to friends in poverty, soup kitchens, and the like. Instead of regarding this practice as something that disciples do simply to help others, engagement with the poor helps disciples grow in their love of Jesus. This discipleship practice helps postmoderns fulfill the Great Commandment to love God and to love others.

Technology

Another major influence on postmodern culture is technology. The postmodern generation is the first one to be raised in the media-rich environment of computers, cell phones, and the internet. While this rapid and pervasive change in technology has brought untold benefits, it comes not without a price. Neil Postman (1993) has warned that the unquestioned acceptance of technology and the resultant information glut shape postmodern culture in unsuspecting ways. Instead of people simply using technology, technology now shapes postmoderns as it monopolizes other sectors of culture. Postman calls this "technopoly." The functional integration of a culture, described in chapter 10, anticipates that a change in one sector of culture results in a change in the other sectors. As any kid waiting to share a pie with his or her siblings knows, when mother makes one piece inordinately large, the other pieces will correspondingly shrink, as portrayed in figure 11.3.

Figure 11.3
Increasing size of economics/technology sector

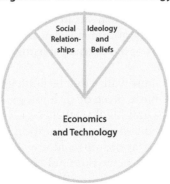

Three Yearnings of Postmoderns

John Stott notes that postmoderns are yearning for three things:

1. Transcendence—a sense or a connection with what is beyond immediate and material things and beings.
2. Significance—a sense that they are meaningful, have purpose, and make a difference.
3. Community—a sense that in a fragmenting world and society they belong to a family (1988).

Reprinted from Pocock, Van Rheenen, and McConnell (2005, 116)

Reflection and Discussion

1. How are these yearnings manifested in the lives of disciples?
2. What excluded middle issues may arise when these longings are not addressed?
3. How can the creative use of the genres described in the preceding chapters address these longings?

Discipleship with postmoderns, then, must take into account the pervasive effects of technology, since social relationships and ideology/beliefs may atrophy as a result of the expanding reach of technology. For example, disciples may not question the effects of listening to music on their favorite device while walking to class, at the gym, on the bus, and so on. Unfortunately, this technology removes them from the social world around them. Their hyperindividual ideology further isolates them from a communal identity.

Consider also the growing connectivity of social networking such as Facebook. While this technology connects postmoderns with many Facebook "friends," when they need to talk with someone at midnight, there is no one they can turn to, since their face-to-face social relationships have withered. Consider also the technological benefits in health care. Increasingly, we turn to technology alone to provide answers to what ails us, neglecting the fact that broken social relationships or a weakened spiritual life may be contributing to depression and fatigue.

Postmodern disciples must realize that technology is not value-free. That is, the adoption of one more piece of technology will create a change in their social relationships and ideology/beliefs. For each piece of technology that postmoderns want to add, the question should be asked, "How will this affect my social relationships and my ideology/belief system?" It may come as a shock that the newest technology is actually weakening their social relationships.

Social Relationships

Postmoderns are often hungry for community, a place where everyone knows their name. Sweet notes, "The paradox is this: the pursuit of individualism has led us to this place of hunger for connectedness, for communities not of blood or nation but communities of choice" (2000, 109–10). In a hyperindividualistic Western culture that encourages privacy and specialization, true community becomes increasingly rare. Yet the hunger is still there.

John Wesley noted a similar problem, that young converts needed a small community for nurturing in their faith. He pulled these disciples together into small groups for "accountable discipleship" (Watson 1986). This discipleship approach encouraged people to share about their obedience to God amid their intimate issues so that they would move toward holiness. These "class meetings" were not formed along divisions of age, sex, or marital status; rather, they were formed based on where the members and leader lived (ibid., 37). The formation of the class meetings in this manner strengthened multiplex relationships instead of adding more simplex relationships (see fig. 11.4).

Figure 11.4
Simplex vs. multiplex relationships

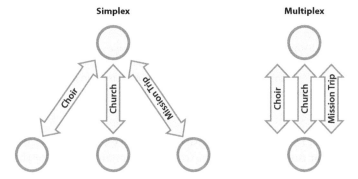

The small group approach is most effective when these groups are based on multiplex relationships instead of solely simplex relationships. Simplex relationships are those in which people are joined by a single bond, such as a pastor-church member relationship (C. Kraft 1996, 317). They relate to one another in just one context. Their relationship is rather weak, since they know about one another only what they observe in that one status/role bond.

Multiplex relationships, however, exist when people relate to one another in more than one social context. As such, they will have various status/role bonds to connect them, thereby forming stronger relationships. For example, a pastor recently told me that his present small group is one of the closest he has ever had. Its members are willing to dig into deep issues and concerns.

How Do We Know What We Know?

Many of the cultural battles that postmodern disciples face deal with the underlying question, "How do we know what we know?" This is the question that epistemology seeks to address. Ian Barbour (1974) has identified three commonly assumed epistemologies (see fig. 11.5). They will be discussed in order to identify the epistemological assumptions that often underlie views of Scripture and culture. These epistemologies can be classified as various degrees of realism:

1. *Instrumentalist epistemology (also called subjective realist epistemology):* Assumes that knowledge is totally subjective, since it is created by culture. This view holds that one cannot know any exact truth, since models "are neither true nor false, but only more or less useful mental devices" (Barbour 1974, 36–37). Religion is considered a "useful fiction" in that it is "a mental construct used instrumentally for particular purposes

but not assumed to be either true or false" (1974, 38). This is the typical postmodern epistemology, reflected in the expression "Whatever!" This view can be likened to the person who says to the optometrist, "Of course I need glasses—everyone has them. Can I try the orange-tinted lenses for a while, please?"

2. *Naive realist epistemology (also called positivist or total realist epistemology):* Assumes that knowledge is totally objective, can be understood by scientific observations, and is an exact "picture of reality" without any distortions (Barbour 1974, 33–35). This position denies that cultural or historical contexts affect the way people view reality, since their view of reality is "the way it is" for all people everywhere. This epistemology was the underlying view for most of modern science and modern mission (the period of modernity),

He realized that this is largely because the members' relationships are mainly multiplex. Not only is there the pastor-church member relationship; they also sing in the choir together. In addition, they made a short-term mission trip together that bonded them tightly. While small groups based on simplex relationships are helpful in spiritual formation, small groups built around multiplex relationships are the most transformative for discipleship. Multiplex relationships actually return to society what the Industrial Revolution (with the resulting specialization) removed.

When small groups are randomly assigned in a church, it often results in people adding one more simplex relationship to a packed list of other simplex relationships. While these relationships can be helpful, they tend to be not as strong as multiplex relationships, which tend to be thicker. The thicker the relationship, the deeper the transfer of values. As a result, multiplex relationships tend to be more transformative; therefore, they are recommended for discipleship efforts. This is particularly important in a hyperindividualistic culture.

which often resulted in arrogance and ethnocentrism. It can be likened to the person who declares to the optometrist, "I don't need glasses; I can see perfectly" (despite the fact that the person's vision is not really perfect).

3. *Critical realist epistemology:* Assumes that knowledge is both objective and subjective. There is an objective reality that can be observed and understood; however, our understanding of it is not complete due to the limitations of cultural and historical contexts. Barbour notes that valid theories are true and useful, but they "are abstract symbol systems which inadequately represent particular aspects of the world for specific purposes" (1974, 37). He concludes, "They are partial and inadequate ways of imagining what is not observable" (48). This approach leads to a confidence in disciples' view of reality that is tempered with humility and a willingness to learn. The critical realist view can be likened to the person who declares to the optometrist, "I can see well most of the time, but I need glasses to see the blurry objects and to know what I am missing!"

These underlying epistemologies shape disciples' view of both Scripture and culture without them even considering the impact.

Adapted from Moon (2009a, 114–15)

Reflection and Discussion

1. Which epistemology do you use to understand Scripture and culture?
2. How does this affect your discipleship approach to excluded middle issues?
3. Hiebert (1999) posits that critical realist epistemology is the most tenable for Christian disciples. What cultural forces exerted on disciples push them away from critical realism and toward instrumentalism (postmoderns) or naive realism (moderns)?

Ideology/Beliefs

In addition to critiquing hyperindividualism, postmoderns question the underlying ideological foundations of consumerism and secularism. If these concerns are not addressed, Christianity becomes simply one more layer added to a worldview largely shaped by individual, consumer, secular assumptions. These assumptions affect important decisions in surprising ways.

Timothy and Kathy Keller note how the consumer mind-set has dominated the marriage relationship in contemporary Western culture:

The marketplace has become so dominant that the consumer model characterizes most relationships that historically were covenantal, including marriage. Today we stay connected to people only as long as they are meeting our particular needs at an acceptable cost to us. When we cease to make a profit—that is, when the relationship appears to require more love and affirmation from us than we are getting back—then we "cut our losses" and drop the relationship. This has also been called "commodification," a process by which social relationships are reduced to economic exchange relationships, and so the very idea of "covenant" is disappearing in our culture. Covenant is therefore a concept that is increasingly foreign to us, and yet the Bible says it is the essence of marriage, so we must take some time to understand it. (2011, 62)

Critique of contemporary Western beliefs/ideology is needed to produce a biblical approach to intimate issues. It is also necessary to critique postmodern assumptions concerning epistemology. The postmodern penchant for pluralism, tolerance, and multiple perspectives can easily lead to an instrumentalist epistemology that rejects the unique revelation of God in Christ. Scripture can be misread as just one more voice among a sea of others. This error can lead disciples into syncretism. Instead of reacting with a naive realist epistemology that regards everything as clearly black and white (which leads to split-level Christianity), a critical realist epistemology balances the objectivity of the Bible with our subjective understanding of it. A critical realist epistemology promotes contextual discipleship.

Figure 11.5
Epistemologies

Instrumentalism   Critical Realism   Naïve Realism

Degree of Realism

Summary

Postmodernity began as a critique in Western culture of the assumptions of modernity. Together with the rise of postmodernity came a change in learning preference to one that relies on oral learning methods for transformation. Discipleship in postmodern culture must adapt to this learning preference. While this preference is considered a recent culture change in the West, intercultural disciplers recognize this learning pattern from premodern cultures around the world. Premodern discipleship approaches can be applied to postmodern disciples to transform their worldview. This chapter discussed a few points to keep in mind when discipling postmoderns:

1. Symbols are important components for postmodern spirituality. They can be incorporated at the workplace, at home, at school, and elsewhere. Labyrinths provide a unique symbolic representation of life. In addition, the tabernacle prayer pattern is a creative symbolic prayer form.

2. Rituals mediate spiritual experience for postmoderns. Rituals are particularly helpful in maintaining continuity amid life transitions. Life-cycle transitions that are particularly pertinent for postmoderns include the stages of adolescence and the odyssey years. Intensification occurs during the calendrical rituals of camps and the Eucharist. Crisis rituals include healing, dedication/cleansing, and intercultural mission experiences.

3. Storytelling is one of the primary means to communicate beliefs to postmoderns. This includes interiorizing biblical stories and learning indigenous stories. Indigenous stories frequently emerge from moments of crisis, courage, conflict, commemoration, comedy, chastisement, charismatic events, and celebration. For postmoderns, stories are also often shaped by the media, particularly movies. Discipleship occurs as indigenous stories are critically contextualized with biblical stories at events such as storytelling at a coffee shop.

4. Proverbs offer a creative genre for uncovering values in postmodern culture. The engagement of cultural proverbs with Scripture promotes contextual discipleship of excluded middle issues in postmodern culture.

5. Dance, music, and drama offer participatory and experiential genres to engage postmoderns. They provide nondiscursive options for critical contextualization that creatively transforms disciples.

6. Holistic discipleship encourages the use of words and deeds to critique the secular and spiritual foundations of culture. Immersion in relationships with those who are economically poor fosters an understanding of and empathy for the poor that helps disciples see the image of Jesus in the face of the poor. Social poverty can be addressed by multiplex relationships in small groups. Underlying ideology and beliefs such as individualism, consumerism, secularism, and epistemology also need to be critiqued for transformation.

Activity for Discipling

1. Look at the symbols in your workplace. Consider placing a symbol in a central location that will remind you that God desires meaningful work to dignify you and be an expression of the kingdom of God. When selecting this symbol, consider the properties of polarization, condensation, and unification discussed in chapter 4.

2. Identify your own excluded middle issues. Consider how a ritual can be constructed to help maintain continuity amid transition. Use the principles discussed in chapter 5 to construct this ritual.

3. Plan a short-term mission trip to another culture for the purpose of discipleship. Take time to prepare for each of the three stages of a ritual structure: separation, transition, and reincorporation, as described in chapter 5.

4. Look for popular pithy sayings or proverbs. Compare these with Scripture. Then summarize your learning in a pithy statement.

5. Look for evidence of the image of God in pop music, movies, and dance. Also, point out the stain of sin in the same genres. Practice differentiating the two.

6. View the enacted prayer and the description of its discovery by Jeff Barker (http://www.youtube.com/watch?v=TUUTnWWl9Ws). Enact a prayer for an excluded middle issue.

7. Develop a relationship with a poor person. You can do this, for example, in an immersion experience or by visiting a soup kitchen. Initiate spiritual discussions and look for the face of Jesus in the people you meet.

8. Form a small group in your church based on multiplex relationships. Observe how the greater familiarity results in deeper conversations leading to greater transformation.

9. Consider the three sectors of culture: economics/technology, social relationships, and ideology/beliefs. Which sector have you focused most of your attention on, and how has this affected the other sectors? What excluded middle issues may arise as you consider your weakest sector? Consider the assumptions of hyperindividualism, consumerism, secularism, and instrumentalism. How do they affect discipleship?

10. In a small group, read a book on postmodernism and discuss the theological challenges and opportunities that postmodernism presents for discipleship (Grenz 1996).

A New Location and Method, but the Same Content

William O'Neal

Church every Sunday, Sunday school, and confirmation—these church activities had little noticeable or meaningful impact on John, a sophomore in college. As he reflected back on how he spent his Sundays sitting on hard wooden benches listening to a man in white garments tell a story of his previous week, he was glad that this Sunday he was still in his bed. John grew up in two worlds that never mingled. He went to church, as the society around him expected, but after Sunday there was no relationship that tied him back to church. His relationship to the church, therefore, was very distant.

He was now under distress, however, from the pluralistic culture of college, which made him doubt every truth he thought he once knew. The whirlwind of opinions and criticism for thinking differently from those who held them made him nauseated. Depression set in like an unwelcome guest as he felt there was no solid ground to save him from the constant roiling thoughts.

While driving one day, John's father called and invited him to participate in a weekend Christian retreat called Outback America. John's hunger for sustenance overrode his hesitation to experience more church, and he agreed to attend with his father. The retreat focused on uniting families by teaching each member to live a Christian life. The father and son were paired with other fathers and sons in a group throughout the weekend.

For the first time in his life, he heard Christians who integrated their faith in every aspect of their life, including work, hobbies, and relationships. The speakers' occupations were diverse: lawyers, doctors, businessmen, pastors, laborers, and more. The faith of these men and women was integral to every facet of their lives and shaped the way they lived out their vocations.

During the week, Outback America presenters used symbols such as "the cord of three strands" to teach biblical messages. Holding a rope in his hand as it dangled to the floor, the presenter explained, "Each strand of the rope symbolizes something. One strand is for God, another is for accountability, and the last strand is for you. In order to have a strong relationship with God that is not easily broken, you have to be entwined with God and your faith community."

John was stunned.

He had never been so intrigued by biblical lessons before in his life, but the presenter's use of symbols, music, rituals, and personal stories drew him into their lessons. He was open to hearing their messages because of the method used to share who God is, as explained in Scripture. Throughout the week he felt deep convictions about the way he was living his life. He also felt freedom, knowing there was a loving God, but he was afraid to discover what life would be like after leaving this safe haven.

In the very last hour of the retreat, John was convicted by the Holy Spirit and confessed Christ as his savior. Once the retreat was over, though, the hardest part was about to begin. Reentering college with no support was difficult.

Even though he was alone in his new journey, he was committed to reading his Bible, fasting, and praying. As God grew John's faith, he yearned for more.

Six months later, John finally was filled with a desire to share his new faith. He had grown up going to church, but he had no idea how to affect his friends. Now he was left with a question: How would he share the joy of Christ he had received in a meaningful way with others, instead of replicating the experience of his youth?

To learn ways to disciple others, John participated in a Bible study his new home church offered. Unfortunately, the method did not click with him. Every member of the group would read a chapter from the assigned book alone, read Scripture relating to it, and then answer analytical questions at the end. Although this is not a bad format, it did not engage John spiritually. It just seemed like a task he had to complete to graduate from another class.

Struggling to live out his new faith, John befriended another college student in his church. As their friendship blossomed, their conversations started to focus on the need to create a group for college students. The purpose of the group would be to build genuine relationships, engage the spiritual struggles of college students, and disciple students to live out their faith in all areas of their lives.

As the two students hashed out ways to form their group, they realized that neither the traditional ways they had grown up with nor the techniques from the study groups at church would be effective in this context. They needed a new method that created multiplex relationships, used symbols and rituals to navigate students through excluded middle issues, and ultimately was dedicated to holistic discipleship. They realized that using culturally relevant ways of learning—such as drama, symbols, and movies—would be the way to reach postmoderns. They decided to construct the group as follows . . .

Reflection and Discussion

1. Explain why the methods of discipleship mattered and why there was a need for change.
2. What examples from Scripture show varying types of discipleship?
3. Given postmoderns' preference for digitoral learning, what are useful discipleship tools to engage them?
4. How, where, and why can symbols, rituals, movies, and so on be implemented in discipleship to address excluded middle issues of postmoderns?
5. How can the location of meetings matter? What settings will create space for discipleship?

Conclusion

Ginggelung ale nyina ale bo le chaab, allege ba kpaling chaab kama. (The tongue and the mouth stay together, but they fight each other.)

—Builsa proverb

Who Can Help Us?

"I can't believe they just asked that question! How ironic," I think. If not for appearing rude, I would have laughed out loud. They are simply being honest and sharing from their hearts.

Jane has been a friend for many years. We had a joyful reunion when she recently came home from her missionary service in sub-Saharan Africa. With excitement in her voice and her hands talking almost as fast as her words, she describes the phenomenal growth of the churches in sub-Sahara Africa. The joy and excitement are hard to contain as she bubbles over with one story after another of God's faithfulness expressed in the growth of the church. Gradually, though, her smile wears away as she leaned closer to confide. "It is great to see the churches growing, but I am concerned about the lack of discipleship. The African church leaders asked me to find a discipleship program that I can take back with me to help. Do you know of a discipleship program that can help us?" This seemingly innocent question floats between us like a hot air balloon as I think back to another conversation I had just the other day.

A few days ago, I was at a restaurant chatting with another church leader who was also working "in the trenches." Amid eating pancakes, he eagerly recounted the incredible growth in his American church over the past five years. I cradled the coffee mug to warm my hands as his stories of God's blessings warmed my heart as well. Putting down the fork, though, he looked me in the eyes and confided, "I have heard about the phenomenal growth of the church in the non-Western world. I am wondering if they can help us with this problem that we have of discipleship. People will come to church, but their lives are not changed and we

Intercultural Competency

What character traits are necessary for intercultural disciplers? Of course, they require some level of intercultural competence. While several models have been proposed to describe intercultural competence, Scott Moreau, Evvy Campbell, and Susan Greener (2014) provide the following list of character traits for intercultural competence. These character traits have applications for intercultural disciplers:

1. Higher emphasis on people, less on task; approachable: establishes contact with others easily; intercultural receptivity: interested in people, especially from other cultures
2. Ability to not criticize the host people; shows respect: treats others in ways that make them feel valued; capacity to communicate respect
3. Tolerance of ambiguity
4. Flexibility: open to culture learning
5. Empathy (demonstrated through culturally appropriate means of listening and accurate perceiving of the other's point of view); cultural perspectivism: the capacity to imaginatively enter into another cultural viewpoint
6. Openness in communication style; nondogmatic; social openness; the inclination to interact with people regardless of their differences
7. High cognitive complexity (not quickly judging in black-and-white terminology; not accepting simplistic stereotypes); capacity to be nonjudgmental
8. Good personal relationship skills in the home culture; ability to trust others; capacity for turn taking
9. Maintains a sense of personal control; positive orientation: expects that one can succeed living and working in another culture
10. Innovativeness; enterprise: tends to approach tasks and activities in new and creative ways; venturesome: inclined toward that which is novel or different
11. Proper self-esteem, including confidence in communication skills; forthrightness: acts and speaks out readily; social confidence: tends to be self-assured
12. Perseverance: tends to remain in a situation and feel positive about it even in the face of some difficulties
13. Capacity to personalize one's knowledge and perceptions

Moreau, Campbell, and
Greener (2014, 229)

Reflection and Discussion

1. Which of the above character traits for intercultural disciplers are the most essential traits to develop prior to entering another culture?
2. Which of the above character traits can be learned on entering another culture?
3. How may these traits be expressed differently in various cultures?

have a hard time getting them to grow deeper. You were a missionary—do you think those churches can help us with our discipleship problem?"

The irony is that both people in my story recognize the need for discipleship, and they are looking to others for help. Unfortunately, we are all in a similar position. Evangelical church leaders from around the world summarized in the Cape Town Commitment: "We lament the scandal of our shallowness and lack of discipleship. . . . To fail in discipleship and disciple-making, is to fail at the most basic level of our mission" (Lausanne Movement 2011, 70–71).

Instead of continuing to use monocultural and monogenerational discipleship patterns, an intercultural approach is needed to move us forward. While existing approaches are easier and more comfortable for those in control, they simply do not gain traction for the long haul. As the African proverb reminds us, "If you want to go fast, go alone; if you want to go far, go together." We have tried to simply go fast for too long. We end up stuck. If we use an intercultural discipleship approach, the way home is much more promising. But it takes work . . . and humility.

God has provided cultural genres that are needed to dislodge disciples from the conforming grip of culture. These genres are locally grown and available for assistance in the form of symbols, rituals, stories, proverbs, music, dance, drama, and deeds with words. It is true that the contextualization of these culturally available genres requires effort and care, but history confirms that it can be done.

We have already discussed historical paradigms of successful intercultural disciplers by surveying selected examples from time periods such as the formation of the nation of Israel, the early church, the Celtic movement, and the Second Great Awakening. In addition to these historical perspectives, we observed patterns from successful intercultural disciplers around the world. These disciplers were not superheroes; they simply recognized God's work in the local culture and were willing to humbly admit that perspectives from various cultures help us overcome the limitations of one culture alone.

Humility Needed

Intercultural discipleship requires some humility to admit that no one society has all of the answers. This may be the most difficult sticking point to overcome. Ethnocentrism lurks inside all cultures, ready to confine us to the strictures of our own culture and time period. I fully expect resistance and even misunderstanding, since intercultural discipleship requires multicultural and multigenerational exchange. This may, at times, create pain similar to that experienced when teeth accidentally bite the tongue. Instead of giving up and remaining stuck in existing ruts, however, a Builsa proverb reminds us, "The tongue and the mouth stay together, but they fight each other."

Intercultural discipleship maintains the tension of cultural differences in order to gain the benefits of staying together. While prepackaged, "assembly-line" discipleship methods from outside the local culture speak to large groups of people, handcrafted discipleship can address the particular excluded middle issues. Disciplers must be willing to learn from local cultures for intercultural discipleship to gain traction. Print-based methods have long been a staple of discipleship, but an integration with oral approaches addresses varying learning preferences.

> A gifted discipler is someone who invites people into a covenantal relationship with him or her, but challenges that person to live into his or her true identity in very direct yet graceful ways. Without both dynamics working together, you will not see people grow into the people God has created them to be.
>
> Mike Breen and Steve Cockram (2011, Kindle locations 178–80)

This may place disciplers on unfamiliar ground. Instead of relying on a cognitive focus alone, we also need an emotive focus for transformation to occur. This may make some disciplers uncomfortable. A material/scientific orientation provides helpful tools for biblical interpretation. A spirit-power orientation also provides insight for biblical application. Balancing these two is not easy. It may appear risky to some. An integration of both a redemption theology and a creation theology provides a balanced discipleship, but it requires a willingness to listen to local theologies. While discipleship often focuses on a personal, individual relationship with Jesus, a collective approach does the same and also transforms people. This process is not necessarily familiar, comfortable, easy, risk free, or quick, but intercultural discipleship provides hope for getting disciples unstuck.

There Is No Quick Fix

I hope that you realize by now that there is no quick and simple way to fix the discipleship problem. Intercultural discipleship requires a deep engagement in the local culture such that local genres can be identified and contextualized. The starting point for discipleship will vary due to the various genres that are prevalent and valued in various cultures. Contextualization takes time in order to engage the local culture with Scripture.

In addition, intercultural discipleship requires intimate relationships to form between the discipler and the people being discipled. Relationships take time to build trust and intimacy, such that excluded middle issues can be identified and addressed. Greg Ogden suggests that one year is required for a triad to form (one discipler meets with two disciples), such that intimacy and transformation begin. In the second year, the disciples then each start another triad of their own (2003, 189).

Stages of Growth

Since discipleship is a long-term process, there should be recognizable stages of growth to anticipate along the way. Ogden notes that Jesus's example provided five stages of growth from what he calls a "pre-disciple" to a mature disciple, as demonstrated in table C.1 (2003, 82).

TABLE C.1				
Five Stages of Growth in Jesus's Discipleship				
	Pre-disciple	Stage 1	Stage 2	Stage 3	Stage 4
Jesus's role	Inviter	Living example	Provocative teacher	Supportive coach	Ultimate delegator
Disciples' role	Seeker	Observer and imitator	Student and questioner	Short-term missionary	Apostle

While the stages of intercultural discipleship may not be as linear as indicated in table C.1, Jesus's example indicates that the discipleship relationship changes over time. Both the discipler and the disciples assume new roles as the relationships progress. Eventually, the goal is for the disciples to be sent out (i.e., like apostles) to make disciples of others.

Ogden also observes that the apostle Paul's discipleship approach involved stages of growth that can be compared to the maturation process of children to adults. In particular, Ogden described Paul's "parental empowerment model" of discipleship (modified slightly) as shown in table C.2 (2003, 105).

TABLE C.2				
Four Stages of Growth in Paul's Discipleship				
	Infancy	Childhood	Adolescence	Adulthood
Life stage need	Modeling, direction	Unconditional love, protection	Identity in Christ	Mutuality, reciprocity
Paul's role	Model	Hero	Coach	Peer
Disciples' role	Imitation	Identification	Experimentation	Participation

There are obvious similarities and differences in Jesus's and Paul's approaches to discipleship. For intercultural disciplers, the important point to consider is that worldview transformation is a process that changes over time. While each disciple will have different excluded middle issues and various culturally available genres to address these issues, disciplers' roles will change as they encourage the growing disciples to center their lives on the kingdom of God and obey Christ's commands in culture. This process takes time and commitment.

Signs of Success

While intercultural discipleship takes time, there are signs to look for that signal success. Here are some markers to signal that discipleship is on the right track:

1. The people whom you discipled are now intentionally discipling others. This is spiritual reproduction. If you are meeting with disciples for an extended period of time, these disciples should eventually be discipling others. If not, spiritual multiplication doesn't occur, and the discipleship process has been misunderstood or misapplied. The goal of a discipleship group is *not* to add more members to the group; rather, the goal is to empower the disciples to form discipleship relationships with other young disciples. This multiplication effect is the genius behind Jesus's method of discipleship (Coleman 1993).

2. The identification and addressing of excluded middle issues is another sign of success. By addressing these issues, disciples are empowered to center their lives on the kingdom of God.

3. Disciples' worldviews are being transformed to reflect the kingdom of God. Look for signs of the kingdom in the decisions that disciples make. Look for the ways that they utilize two "holy documents"—their calendar and their money. There should be a radical change in how these things are viewed and used.

4. Disciples are observing and applying culturally available genres to address discipleship concerns. When this occurs, disciples have recognized the work of the Holy Spirit in their own contexts, such that the discipleship process is infinitely reproducible, even though the particular issues may change over time.

Warning: Ruts!

Since that day of being stuck in the mud and finally freed, I have learned to watch out for ruts ahead of me so that I do not subject my family to further

Realities of Cross-Cultural Friendship

Since discipleship is largely a relational process, intercultural disciplers need to be aware of realities related to forming cross-cultural friendships. Harriet Hill (1993) summarizes the following insights about cross-cultural friendships that have implications for intercultural disciplers:

1. Cross-cultural friendship must be intentional. In monocultural situations, we often gravitate effortlessly toward those who become our friends. But establishing cross-cultural friendships requires more intent.

2. Cross-cultural friendship requires proximity. . . .Those who can live in the middle of the community have a great advantage. Those who cannot must regularly get close to the people.

3. Cross-cultural friendship must appreciate differences and similarities. . . . We must balance the understanding of our differences with a realization of our common humanness.

4. Cross-cultural friendship will cross economic classes. This barrier seems at times more difficult than crossing cultures. . . . The contrast of our income and theirs spews out a host of problems. We feel guilty about having so much, both materially and in terms of opportunity. We are accustomed to a certain lifestyle and function very poorly when all of our props are removed.

5. Cross-cultural friendship involves vulnerability. . . . When cross-cultural workers experience the death of a child, they often report suddenly being taken into a new level of intimacy with the people. In the depths of their grief, all modeling and role playing is set aside, bonding with the people occurs to an extent never thought possible.

6. Cross-cultural friendship must be selective. . . . Without selecting a few people as close friends, our attention will be too diffused to be significant. But with a few friends, you will gain a window on the culture.

7. Cross-cultural friendship must be flexible. The goal is friendship, but the strategies must remain flexible. Each situation is different, and each missionary is different. Your lifestyle might look significantly different than someone else's, but if you both have good relationships with the people, you've both succeeded.

Cited in Moreau, Campbell, and Greener (2014, 249–50)

Reflection and Discussion

1. For each of the points above, replace the words "cross-cultural friendship" with the words "intercultural discipleship." Compare/contrast these statements with the previous chapters.

2. Which of these statements have you noticed to be true of friendship within your own culture? Which are the most pronounced when you enter a new culture?

3. How do these points help you select and nurture relationships for intercultural discipleship?

mishaps. It is much better to recognize ruts beforehand than to struggle for freedom afterward. There are two common ruts awaiting the well-intended traveler on the discipleship path.

The first rut is syncretism, the blending of elements of one faith system with another. This is to be avoided in order to maintain biblical faithfulness. Dodging this rut, though, may unwittingly steer the disciple toward the other common rut of split-level Christianity. When intimate issues in culture are avoided, Christians go to church for certain answers, but they revert to other sources to address other life issues. Both syncretism and split-level Christianity steer the disciple away from a kingdom-centered life.

Goal for the Journey

The end goal is not simply more information. Discipleship should result in transformation. This transformation occurs as Jesus followers center their lives on the kingdom of God and obey Christ's commands in culture, utilizing culturally available genres. Instead of leaving us to spin our wheels, intercultural discipleship frees us from the deep ruts we find ourselves in and enables disciples to make it home . . . with the help of others.

Ceremony for the Installation of a Teacher

Prior to class, the teacher selects a "ritual specialist" to help the students meet and decide who will represent them in the areas of wisdom, scholarship, and godliness. They can choose the criteria for the representatives they want, and they can alter the categories of representation, if they see the need. For example, the representatives chosen could be based on the oldest (represents wisdom), the closest to graduation (representing scholarship), and the closest to ordination (representing godliness). The students then select symbols that they will give as gifts to the new teacher.

The ritual specialist meets with the students to make a list of characteristics of bad teachers. All students are urged to frankly and openly participate in this task. Once the long list is made, students then choose the top five characteristics. The same is done in terms of making a list of characteristics of good teachers.

Once the lists are completed, the ritual specialist describes the ceremony briefly to the students. When they are ready, they call the teacher back into the room.

Ritual Specialist: *[Name], the students have met and discussed some of the bad experiences they have had with teachers in the past. We are describing*

This ritual is adapted from an African chief installation ritual. I was initially exposed to this adapted ritual by Mathias Zahniser in his Cross-Cultural Discipling class at Asbury Theological Seminary. This ritual draws from Turner (1995, 170–71).

these experiences to alert you to the complaints that will arise if you exhibit these characteristics. Some characteristics of bad teachers that we want you to avoid are:

_____

_____

_____

_____

_____

Ritual Specialist: *We have chosen three representatives to assist you in your new role. The first represents the wisdom of our community. Please come forward.*

Wisdom Representative (bringing symbol of wisdom the students have chosen): This person explains the symbol's significance to the teacher and the class. The representative then offers a prayer (or asks another class member to do so) for God the Father to fill the teacher with wisdom to help guide the class.

Ritual Specialist: *Our second representative stands for scholarship in our community. Please come forward.*

Scholarship Representative (bringing symbol of scholarship the students have chosen): This person explains the symbol's significance to the teacher and the class. The representative then offers a prayer (or asks another class member to do so) for Jesus to empower the teacher with scholarship to bring the class to a deeper and broader understanding.

Ritual Specialist: *[Name], the students have also met and discussed some of the good experiences they have had with teachers in the past. We are describing these experiences in order to encourage you to live up to the good example others have set before you. We exhort you to exhibit these characteristics as you guide our class. Some characteristics of good teachers that we want you to exhibit are:*

_____

_____

_____

_____

_____

Ritual Specialist: *Our third representative stands for godliness. Please come forward.*

Godliness Representative (bringing symbol of godliness the students have chosen): This person explains the significance to the teacher and the class. The representative then offers a prayer (or asks another group member to do so) for God to fill the teacher with the Holy Spirit to empower him or her to live a godly example for the class to follow.

Ritual Specialist: *Have you heard and understood the characteristics of good and bad teachers?*

Teacher: *Yes, I have* (the teacher may ask for additional explanation if a particular characteristic is not clear).

Ritual Specialist: *Will you strive to fulfill the good qualities and avoid the bad qualities of teachers?*

Teacher: *By God's grace, I will.*

Ritual Specialist (as he or she puts the academic robe on the teacher): *Our class then recognizes you as our teacher. We are eager to obey the wisdom that our Father God has given you, to heed the scholarship that comes from the mind of Christ, and to follow the example of godliness that the Holy Spirit empowers you to lead.*
The ritual specialist offers a prayer.
Do you have any words for us to hear?

Teacher: *Yes, I also have thought about my experiences with students. I have come up with a list of the qualities that make a good student and those that make a bad student. These characteristics are:*

The teacher then gives carefully selected and symbolic gifts to the students.

Teacher: *Do you, as students, strive to exhibit the qualities of good students and avoid the qualities of bad students? If so, respond, "By God's grace, we will."*

Students (in unison): *By God's grace, we will.*

Teacher (as he or she brings a symbol of studenthood and explains its significance): *I accept the responsibility to be your teacher.*
Final prayer by teacher.

273

Appendix B

Activities for Teaching

Chapter 1: How Did We Get in This Spiritual Rut?

1. Go to http://www.hunter.cuny.edu/socwork/nrcfcpp/pass/learning-circles
/five/Brokensquares.pdf (or Google "cooperative squares") and cut paper
into the shapes denoted. Put the shapes in envelopes in groups of five (I
suggest different color paper for every group of five).

2. Arrange the class in groups of five. Extra people will be observers and
enforcers of the rules. Discuss the rules briefly and explain that the
objective is for each person to complete a square of the same size.

3. As the game progresses, observe those who find a quick solution to their
square and then do not participate any longer (which unknowingly prevents the rest of the group from succeeding). Look for people who try
to gather all the pieces and solve the problem themselves. Identify those
who get frustrated or lose hope and then observe how they respond.

4. Once all the groups complete the task, discuss the following questions:
What feelings or reactions did you have during the game? Did you have
something unique to give or receive? Was there a turning point in the
game? Suppose you were constructing a discipleship program for your
church instead of squares. What can we learn from critical pieces that
other cultures may have? How can those pieces help your own discipleship? What limits you from recognizing these needed pieces? How can
we give and receive these pieces? Which of the cultural assumptions in
table 1.1 limit your discipleship approach?

Chapter 2: Issues That Get Us Stuck

1. With the class, view "Sacred Rites and Rituals" from the *Ancient Mysteries* television show ("Sacred Rites and Rituals" 1996). Look for important elements that religions around the world use in the discipleship process. If possible, view this episode with people from another culture and ask about their experiences with discipleship. These people may be Christian or not-yet Christian.

2. Discuss the following questions:
   a. What excluded middle issues can you identify that are addressed in the episode?
   b. How does the ritual affect the individuals and the community?
   c. If someone from this culture were to become a Christian, could some of these rituals be useful for discipleship? How would they need to be contextualized?

Chapter 3: What Is Intercultural Discipleship?

1. Download the "Orality Assessment Tool" (http://wmausa.org/wp-content/uploads/2016/12/Orality-Assessment-Tool-Worksheet.pdf).

2. Complete the Learning Preference Assessment for yourself. Determine whether you have a preference for oral or for print learning. A total score of eighty or below indicates that you prefer to learn and be transformed when learning comes in oral forms.

3. Ask your students to complete the assessment. Remind them that this tool simply assesses their learning preference without any correlation to intelligence or IQ. The assessment provides forty learning preference pairs in areas such as learning via dialogue with others/traditions/stories, engaging real-life experiences, learning in context, and the importance of sound and drama. Determine the learning preference of your disciples.

4. Ask the class to contrast/compare their learning experiences based on their preference for oral versus print learning. How may this affect the discipleship approach that will be most effective for them?

Chapter 4: Symbols Speak When Words Can't

1. View with class *The Tabernacle* (https://www.visionvideo.com/dvd/4791D/tabernacle), which depicts the tabernacle that God instructed the Israelites to construct in the wilderness. Carefully observe the symbols used and discuss the following points:

    a. Which symbols are used?

    b. How do they stir your emotions to help you want to do what you should do?

    c. In addition to the polarization property, look for evidence of the condensation and unification properties of symbols.

2. What excluded middle issues do you think the symbols address?

3. What biblical stories are also being drawn on for the tabernacle ritual?

4. How would these symbols inside the ritual transform the Israelites' worldview?

5. Pastor David Yonggi Cho from South Korea uses the symbols in the tabernacle to develop a prayer pattern for disciples (http://tabernacle -prayer.com/tabernacle-prayer-basics). In this prayer pattern, disciples close their eyes and imagine that they are walking through the tabernacle, stopping to pause at each symbol along the way. Each symbol has New Testament significance that allows the disciple to encounter God's presence. I regularly use this pattern and have also done this exercise with small groups. After reading about the use of each symbol for a prayer journey, ask the students to form a circle as you lead them through this prayer pattern as a group. Following the prayer, discuss which symbols connected with you and why.

Chapter 5: Rituals Drive Meaning Deep into the Bone

1. Watch the following videos and look for the rite-of-passage structure. Consider the use of symbols, how liminality is created, and the resulting effects of the ritual on the individual and the community:

    a. "Rite of Passage," from *Dr. Quinn, Medicine Woman* (Sullivan and Davidson 1993).

    b. "The Hajj: One American's Pilgrimage to Mecca" (Koppel 1997). This is an ABC News *Nightline* show that aired on April 18, 1997.

2. Research some of the history behind the symbols and rituals used for Christian holidays such as Christmas and Easter. Consider which symbols/rituals the early church introduced and how the church modified other existing symbols/rituals. Discuss how symbols/rituals are appropriated and renegotiated for each generation. An entertaining and informative source for Christian symbols/rituals is the "Advent Calendar on DVD" (Vision Video 2006).

Chapter 6: Contextualization Process—Tailored Pants Fit Just Right

1. Enact the ritual described in appendix A for the installation of a new teacher. It is adapted from an African chieftaincy ritual (Turner 1995, 170–72), and can be used for your Sunday school, small group, seminary class, and so on. After enacting the ritual, discuss how participants selected the symbols, what they communicated, how the three phases of the ritual structure worked, and what effects the ritual had on the teacher and the class. I first participated in this ritual in a class by Mathias Zahniser, "Cross-Cultural Discipling," in January 2003. Since then, I have conducted it each year in the seminary classroom, which has resulted in a marked increase in commitment to the class work and other class members.

2. Watch the DVD "Contextualization in Action" (http://createinternational.com/store/#action) to view various contextualization practices from around the world. How are the principles of critical contextualization demonstrated in the rituals shown? What is the role of the *satsang* ritual, and what important symbols are used to communicate Christian meaning that shapes a Christian worldview?

3. Watch the video "This Is the Night" (http://www.commonword.ca/ResourceView/18/12675), which portrays the catechesis process in a Roman Catholic church in Texas. Look for the rich use of symbols and myths in the ritual process. How does this affect the participants? How does this affect the observers? Consider how the "dignity of effort" is communicated in the ritual. Could aspects of this ritual be applied in your own church?

Chapter 7: Stories Portray It, Not Just Say It

1. To view an entertaining portrayal of the statement "We become the stories that we tell," watch the movie *Big Fish* (http://www.sonypictures.com/movies/bigfish). Consider the stories that you are telling to yourself and others. How are they shaping you?

2. A metanarrative is an overarching story that makes sense of individual underlying stories. To see the role that a metanarrative plays in our lives, watch the movie *Lady in the Water* (http://www.imdb.com/title/tt0452637). Consider how people get lost when their own individual story becomes too large and they miss the metanarrative. What does the manager mean when he tells the character named Story, "You saved me!"? What is the overarching metanarrative of Scripture, and how does this save us from ourselves, others, and evil?

3. The card game "Nano-fictionary" (http://www.looneylabs.com/games /nanofictionary) teaches people to construct good stories. Play the game in groups of five and watch how students collect various cards (setting, character, conflict, and resolution) to construct humorous stories. The enthusiasm and fun generated from this exercise can be used to introduce the process of telling biblical or cultural stories.

4. Ask each student to bring a short story (two to three minutes long). Follow the steps in sidebar 7.3 to guide them through the art of storytelling.

Chapter 8: Proverbs Are Worth a Thousand Words

1. Review the list of top ten values that Stan Nussbaum (2005) identifies in American proverbs (see sidebar 8.4). Break into groups and ask each group to pick one or two proverbs. If possible, make sure that at least one American is in each group.

2. As a group, try the critical contextualization process for each of these values. Which aspects does Scripture affirm, modify, or reject?

3. How do these values compare to the host culture for your intercultural ministry?

4. How will these value differences affect your discipleship in this host culture?

Chapter 9: Music, Dance, and Drama—We Become What We Hum

1. Visit http://www.wiconi.com and observe the Native American liturgy, including dance and music. Consider the emic perspective and what discipleship looks like without these important genres. Discuss what effect this would have on Native people trying to integrate their identity in Christ with their Native identity.

2. Wiconi International invites Christians to visit the Rosebud Native Lakota Sioux reservation in Mission, South Dakota, for one week each July. Some take this for a seminary class with Sioux Falls Seminary, while others attend for personal growth. They usually participate in Native American rituals, dance, and music in order to discuss the topic of intercultural discipleship and contextualization.

3. Julisa Rowe provided a list of thirty-five types and eleven usages of drama in cross-cultural contexts (see http://www.ethnodrama.com). Review the list and identify one biblical story or theme that can be enacted in class.

Chapter 10: Holistic Discipleship Connects Word and Deed

1. Watch the video "Transformations" (The Sentinel Group 2002; https://www.youtube.com/watch?v=Dyrho_hoz5s). Consider the poverty that existed in the ideology/beliefs sector. How was this addressed? What was the result? What was the role of the church body for transformation?

2. Watch the video "Poverty Cure Project" and join the discussion on http://www.povertycure.org. How does holistic discipleship change when the focus moves from observing the causes of poverty to identifying what makes people flourish?

Chapter 11: Discipleship for Postmoderns

1. Watch the video *The Tabernacle* (https://www.visionvideo.com/dvd/4791D/tabernacle) and imagine that you are in the wilderness. Then close your eyes and picture yourself moving through the tabernacle, stopping at each station, as described by Dr. Cho.

2. Visit a prayer labyrinth nearby. Encourage disciples to experience God in their own journeys. The discipler can place objects/symbols along the labyrinth ahead of time to stimulate reflection for disciples.

3. Contact local coffee-shop owners and ask them whether you can host a storytelling night. Gather people and prepare them to interiorize biblical stories, and then engage them with indigenous stories for contextualization. Enjoy the storytelling night, particularly the discussions that arise at the coffee shop.

4. Watch the Tony Campolo video from the series *Serving Like Christ Together: Six Sessions on Ministry* (Rathbun 2005). Discuss how engaging the poor is necessary for discipleship.

Reference List

Achebe, Chinua. 1959. *Things Fall Apart.* New York: Anchor Books.

Allitt, Patrick N. 2001. *American Religious History: Course Guidebook.* Chantilly, VA: Great Courses.

Anderson, Matthew Lee. 2012. "A Black and White Issue?" *Relevant*, no. 56 (April): 74–77.

Ankele, John. 2011. *Rise Up and Walk.* http://www.olddogdocumentaries.com/vid _ruaw.html.

Arnett, Jeffrey Jensen. 2004. *Emerging Adulthood: The Winding Road from the Late Teens through the Twenties.* New York: Oxford University Press.

Asogwa, Maazi Chijioke. 2002. "Re-kindling an Interest in an Endangered Language: A Way Forward for Igbo." In *Endangered Languages and Their Literatures: Proceedings of the Sixth FEL Conference*, edited by R. McKenna Brown, 47–50. Bath, UK: Foundation for Endangered Languages.

Atemboa, George. 1998. "The Impact of the Slave Trade on the Builsa." In *The Slave Trade and Reconciliation: A Northern Ghanaian Perspective*, edited by Allison Howell, 23–30. Accra, Ghana: Assemblies of God Literature Centre.

Atkins, Wendy. 2012. "Transforming Worldview through Song." *Evangelical Missions Quarterly* 48 (1): 36–43.

Bailey, David M. 2013. "Honoring Diverse Heart Languages in a Christian Community." In Krabill 2013, 443–46.

Barbour, Ian G. 1974. *Myths, Models, and Paradigms: A Comparative Study in Science and Religion.* San Francisco: HarperCollins.

Barker, Jeff. 2011. *The Storytelling Church: Adventures in Reclaiming the Role of Story in Worship.* Webber Institute Books. Cleveland, TN: Parson's Porch Books.

———. 2017. "Enacted Prayer." *Rich Drama*. Accessed March 6, 2017. http://rich drama.com/BookStore/EnactedPrayer.htm.

Barnes, Elizabeth. 1995. *The Story of Discipleship: Christ, Humanity, and Church in Narrative Perspective*. Nashville: Abingdon.

Beaudoin, Tom. 1998. *Virtual Faith: The Irreverent Spiritual Quest of Generation X*. San Francisco: Jossey-Bass.

Bediako, Kwame. 1995. *Christianity in Africa: The Renewal of a Non-Western Religion*. Maryknoll, NY: Orbis Books.

———. 1999. "Gospel and Culture: Guest Editorial." *Journal of African Christian Thought* 2 (2): 1.

———. 2001. "Scripture as the Hermeneutic of Culture and Tradition." *Journal of African Christian Thought* 4 (1): 2–11.

Boa, Kenneth. 2001. *Conformed to His Image*. Grand Rapids: Zondervan.

Boogaart, Thomas A. 2008. "Drama and the Sacred: Recovering the Dramatic Tradition in Scripture and Worship." In *Touching the Altar: The Old Testament for Christian Worship*, edited by Carol Bechtel, 35–61. Calvin Institute of Christian Worship Liturgical Studies. Grand Rapids: Eerdmans.

Boomershine, Thomas E. 1988. *Story Journey: An Invitation to the Gospel as Storytelling*. Nashville: Abingdon.

Bowie, Fiona. 2005. "Ritual and Performance." In *Introduction to World Religions*, edited by Christopher Partridge, 32–33. Minneapolis: Fortress.

Bowman, Jim, and Carla Bowman. 2013. "Story and Song in Kpele-Dafo: An Innovative Church Planting Model among an Oral Culture of Togo." In Krabill 2013, 229–31.

———. 2014. "Story and Song: An Innovative Church Planting Model." *Mission Frontiers* 36 (5): 33.

Breen, Mike, and Steve Cockram. 2011. *Building a Discipling Culture*. 2nd ed. Kindle ed. Pawleys Island, SC: 3DM.

Brooks, David. 2011. *The Social Animal: Hidden Sources of Love, Character, and Achievement*. New York: Random House.

Brown, Joseph E. 1989. *The Sacred Pipe: Black Elk's Account of the Seven Rites of the Oglala Sioux*. Civilization of the American Indians. Norman: University of Oklahoma Press.

Brown, Rick. 2004. "Communicating God's Message in Oral Cultures." *International Journal of Frontier Missions* 21 (3): 122–28.

Bucko, Raymond A. 1998. *The Lakota Ritual of the Sweat Lodge: History and Contemporary Practice*. Lincoln: University of Nebraska Press.

Bulatao, Jaime C. 1992. *Phenomena and Their Interpretation: Landmark Essays, 1957–1989*. Manila: Ateneo de Manila.

Burkholder, Galen. 2011. "Case Study: A Locally Sustainable and Multiplying Approach for Majority World Churches." *Evangelical Missions Quarterly* 47 (4): 482–85.

Caldwell, Larry. 2005. "Towards an Ethnohermeneutical Model for a Lowland Filipino Context." *Journal of Asian Mission* 7 (2): 169–93.

Catford, James. 2008. "The Core." In *The Poverty and Justice Bible*, 1–32. Swindon, UK: British and Foreign Bible Society.

Chadiha, Jeffri. 2016. "Marching Forward: Michael Johnson's Fight for Selma." *Analysis*. February 24. http://www.nfl.com/news/story/0ap3000000638034/article/marching -forward-michael-johnsons-fight-for-selma.

Charles, Mark. 2013. "A Laughing Party and Contextualized Worship." In Krabill 2013, 267–69.

Chiang, Samuel, ed. 2010. *Orality Breakouts: Using Heart Language to Transform Hearts*. Hong Kong: International Orality Network.

Clarke, Jim. 2011. *Creating Rituals: A New Way of Healing for Everyday Life*. Mahwah, NJ: Paulist Press.

Claydon, David. 2004a. "Lausanne Occasional Paper 42: Prayer in Evangelism." In *Lausanne 2004 Forum on World Evangelization*. 2004 Forum Occasional Papers. Pattaya, Thailand: Lausanne Committee for World Evangelization. http://www .lausanne.org/en/documents/lops/857-lop-42.html.

———. 2004b. "Lausanne Occasional Paper 46: Redeeming the Arts: The Restoration of the Arts to God's Creational Intention." In *Lausanne 2004 Forum on World Evangelization*. 2004 Forum Occasional Papers. Pattaya, Thailand: Lausanne Committee for World Evangelization. http://www.lausanne.org/en/documents/lops/861 -lop-46.html.

Coleman, Robert E. 1993. *The Master Plan of Evangelism*. Grand Rapids: Revell.

Colijn, Brenda. 2010. *Images of Salvation in the New Testament*. Downers Grove, IL: IVP Academic.

Corbett, Steve, and Brian Fikkert. 2009. *When Helping Hurts: Alleviating Poverty without Hurting the Poor . . . and Ourselves*. Chicago: Moody.

Cosgrove, Francis M., Jr. 1988. *Essentials of Discipleship: What It Takes to Follow Christ*. Dallas: Roper Press.

Cotter, George. 1989. "Words of Wisdom." *Maryknoll* 83 (2): 17.

Courson, Jim. 1998. "Deepening the Bonds of Christian Community: Applying Rite of Passage Structure to the Discipling Process in Taiwan." *Missiology: An International Review* 26 (3): 301–13.

Crabtree, Charles T. 2008. "The Crisis of Discipleship in the American Church." *Enrichment Journal* (Winter). http://enrichmentjournal.ag.org/200801/200801_022 _Discipleship.cfm.

Craddock, Fred. 2001. *Craddock Stories*. Edited by Michael Graves and Richard Ward. St. Louis: Chalice.

Curtis, Brent, and John Eldredge. 1997. *The Sacred Romance: Drawing Closer to the Heart of God*. Nashville: Thomas Nelson.

Davis, Charles A. 2015. *Making Disciples across Cultures: Missional Principles for a Diverse World*. Downers Grove, IL: InterVarsity.

"Decade of Discipleship." 2017. *C. S. Lewis Institute*. Accessed April 4, 2017. http://www.cslewisinstitute.org/Decade_of_Discipleship.

De Neui, Paul Henry. 2005. "String-Tying Ritual as Christian Communication in Northeast Thailand." PhD diss., Fuller Theological Seminary.

Detweiler, Craig, and Barry Taylor. 2003. *Matrix of Meanings: Finding God in Pop Culture*. Engaging Culture. Grand Rapids: Baker Academic.

Dobson, Dr. James. 1999. *Preparing for Adolescence: How to Survive the Coming Years of Change*. CD. Ventura, CA: Regal.

Driver, Tom F. 1991. *The Magic of Ritual: Our Need for Liberating Rites That Transform Our Lives and Our Communities*. New York: HarperCollins.

Durand, Pascal, and Joseph Nkumbulwa. 2012. "African Proverb of the Month: January 2012." *African Proverbs, Sayings, and Stories*. http://www.afriprov.org/index.php/african-proverb-of-the-month/51-2012proverbofthemonth/598-apothmjan2012.html.

Eims, LeRoy. 1976. *What Every Christian Should Know about Growing: Basic Steps to Discipleship*. Wheaton: Victor Books.

———. 1978. *The Lost Art of Disciple Making*. Grand Rapids: Zondervan.

Ela, Jean-Marc. 2009. *My Faith as an African*. Eugene, OR: Wipf & Stock.

Eliade, Mircea. 1959. *The Sacred and the Profane: The Nature of Religion*. New York: Harcourt, Brace.

———. 1998. *Myth and Reality*. Prospect Heights, IL: Waveland Press.

Ellis, Catherine J. 1985. *Aboriginal Music: Education for Living: Cross-Cultural Experiences from South Australia*. St. Lucia: University of Queensland Press.

Ellwood, Robert S. 1983. *Introducing Religion: From Inside and Outside*. Englewood Cliffs, NJ: Prentice-Hall.

Farley, Edward. 1996. *Deep Symbols: Their Postmodern Effacement and Reclamation*. Valley Forge, PA: Trinity Press International.

Farrel, Pam, and Doreen Hanna. 2009. *Raising a Modern-Day Princess*. Carol Stream, IL: Tyndale House.

The Feast. 2011. Part 3 of *A History of Christian Worship: Ancient Ways, Future Paths*. DVD. Directed by Tom Dallis. Dayton, OH: Ensign Media.

Feinstein, David, and Peg E. Mayo. 1990. *How We Can Turn Loss and the Fear of Death into an Affirmation of Life*. San Francisco: Harper.

Finn, Thomas M. 1989. "Ritual Process and the Survival of Early Christianity: A Study of the Apostolic Tradition of Hippolytus." *Journal of Ritual Studies* 3 (1): 69–85.

Flory, Richard, and Donald Miller. 2000. *GenX Religion*. New York: Routledge.

Forster, Greg. 2013a. "Theology That Works: Making Disciples Who Practice Fruitful Work and Economic Wisdom in Modern America." *Oikonomia Network*. http://oikonomianetwork.org/wp-content/uploads/2014/02/Theology-that-Works-v2-FINAL.pdf.

———. 2013b. "Twelve Elements of Economic Wisdom." *Economic Wisdom Project*. http://oikonomianetwork.org/wp-content/uploads/2015/03/TwelveElements EconomicWisdom8.pdf.

Friedman, Matthew, and Jonathon Toon. 2008. "The Liminality of Ramazan in the Context of the 'Isai Jamat." Unpublished paper in author's possession.

Gasque, Laurel. 2007. "Art." In *Dictionary of Mission Theology: Evangelical Foundations*, edited by John Corrie, 26–29. Downers Grove, IL: InterVarsity.

Geertz, Clifford. 1973. *The Interpretation of Cultures*. New York: Basic Books.

Gilliland, Dean. 2000. "Contextualization." In Moreau, Netland, and Van Engen 2000, 225–27.

Grenz, Stanley J. 1996. *A Primer on Postmodernism*. Grand Rapids: Eerdmans.

Grimes, R. L. 2000. *Deeply into the Bone: Re-inventing Rites of Passage*. Berkeley: University of California Press.

Hall, Edward T. 1959. *The Silent Language*. New York: Doubleday.

Harries, Jim. 2012. "Witchcraft, Envy, Development, and Christian Mission in Africa." *Missiology: An International Review* 40 (2): 129–39.

Harris, Robin P. 2013. "The Great Misconception: Why Music Is Not a Universal Language." In Krabill 2013, 82–89.

Hascall, John S. 1996. "The Sacred Circle: Native American Liturgy." In *Native and Christian: Indigenous Voices on Religious Identity in the United States and Canada*, edited by James Treat, 179–83. New York: Routledge.

Hassrick, Royal B. 1964. *The Sioux: Life and Customs of a Warrior Society*. Civilization of the American Indian 72. Norman: University of Oklahoma Press.

Haynes, Brian. 2009. *Shift: What It Takes to Finally Reach Families Today*. Loveland, CO: Group.

Healey, Joseph, and Donald Sybertz. 2000. *Towards an African Narrative Theology*. Maryknoll, NY: Orbis Books.

Hiebert, Paul G. 1982. "The Flaw of the Excluded Middle." *Missiology: An International Review* 10 (1): 35–47.

———. 1985. *Anthropological Insights for Missionaries*. Grand Rapids: Baker.

———. 1987. "Critical Contextualization." *International Bulletin of Missionary Research* 11 (3): 104–11.

———. 1993. "Popular Religions." In *Toward the 21st Century in Christian Mission*, edited by J. M. Phillips and R. T. Coote, 253–66. Grand Rapids: Eerdmans.

———. 1994a. *Anthropological Reflections on Missiological Issues*. Grand Rapids: Baker.

———. 1994b. "The Category Christian in the Mission Task." In Hiebert 1994a, 107–36.

———. 1999. *Missiological Implications of Epistemological Shifts: Affirming Truth in a Modern/Postmodern World*. Christian Mission and Modern Culture. Harrisburg, PA: Trinity Press International.

———. 2008. *Transforming Worldviews: An Anthropological Understanding of How People Change*. Grand Rapids: Baker Academic.

Hiebert, Paul G., R. D. Shaw, and T. Tiénou. 1999a. "Split Level Christianity." In Hiebert, Shaw, and Tiénou 1999b, 15–29.

———. 1999b. *Understanding Folk Religion: A Christian Response to Popular Beliefs and Practices*. Grand Rapids: Baker.

Hill, Harriet. 1993. "Lifting the Fog on Incarnational Ministry." *Evangelical Quarterly* 29 (July): 262–69.

———. 2013. "The Arts and Trauma Healing in Situations of Violence and Conflict." In Krabill 2013, 177–78. Pasadena, CA: William Carey.

Holstein, James A., and Jaber F. Gubrium. 2000. *The Self We Live By: Narrative Identity in a Postmodern World*. Oxford: Oxford University Press.

Hughes, Dewi. 2008. *Power and Poverty: Divine and Human Rule in a World of Need*. Downers Grove, IL: InterVarsity.

Hull, Bill. 2006. *The Complete Book of Discipleship: On Being and Making Followers of Christ*. Navigators Reference Library. Colorado Springs: NavPress.

Hull, John K. 2004. "Faith Development through Crosscultural Interaction and Liminality: Bonding to the Meaning of Scripture through the Short-Term Mission Experience." DMiss diss. Asbury Theological Seminary, Wilmore, KY.

Hunter, George G., III. 2000. *The Celtic Way of Evangelism: How Christianity Can Reach the West . . . Again*. Nashville: Abingdon.

Jenkins, Philip. 2011. *The Next Christendom: The Coming of Global Christianity*. 3rd ed. New York: Oxford University Press.

Job, Rueben P., et al., eds. 1989. *The United Methodist Hymnal: Book of United Methodist Worship*. Nashville: United Methodist Publishing House.

Johnson, Todd E., and Dale Savidge. 2009. *Performing the Sacred: Theology and Theatre in Dialogue*. Grand Rapids: Baker Academic.

Johnston, Robert K. 2006. *Reel Spirituality: Theology and Film in Dialogue*. 2nd ed. Engaging Culture Series. Grand Rapids: Baker Academic.

Johnston, Susan. 2009. *Religion, Myth, and Magic: The Anthropology of Religion*. Modern Scholar Course Guide. Prince Frederick, MD: Recorded Books.

Jones, Scott J. 2003. *The Evangelistic Love of God and Neighbor: A Theology of Witness and Discipleship*. Kindle ed. Nashville: Abingdon.

Jones, Tommy. 2001. *Postmodern Youth Ministry*. Grand Rapids: Zondervan.

Kalilombe, Patrick A. 1969. "Preface." In *Bantu Wisdom: A Collection of Proverbs*, 3. Kachebere, Malawi: n.p.

Keller, Timothy, with Kathy Keller. 2011. *The Meaning of Marriage: Facing the Complexities of Commitment with the Wisdom of God*. New York: Dutton.

Kimball, Charles. 2008. *Comparative Religion: Course Guidebook*. Great Courses. Chantilly, VA: Teaching Company.

King, Roberta. 2006. "Singing the Lord's Song in a Global World: The Dynamics of Doing Critical Contextualization through Music." *Evangelical Missions Quarterly* 42 (1): 68–74.

———. 2009. *Pathways in Christian Music Communication.* American Society of Missiology Monograph 3. Eugene, OR: Pickwick.

———. 2013. "Do They Have Sin?" In Krabill 2013, 184. Pasadena, CA: William Carey.

Kirk, J. Andrew. 2007. "Postmodernity." In *Dictionary of Mission Theology: Evangelical Foundations,* 298–303. Downers Grove, IL: InterVarsity.

Koppel, Ted. 1997. "The Hajj: One American's Pilgrimage to Mecca." *Nightline.* Originally aired April 18, 1997. ABC News.

Krabill, James. 1995. *The Hymnody of the Harrist Church among the Dida of South-Central Ivory Coast (1913–1949): A Historico-Religious Study.* Frankfurt am Main: Peter Lang.

———, ed. 2013. *Worship and Mission for the Global Church: An Ethnodoxology Handbook.* Pasadena, CA: William Carey.

———. 2014. "Culturally Appropriate Music." *Mission Frontiers* 36 (5): 13–15.

Krabill, James R., and Jeanette Krabill. 2016. "Scriptural Impact through a Dramatic Reenactment." *Orality Journal* 5 (1): 83–86.

Kraft, Charles H. 1996. *Anthropology for Christian Witness.* Maryknoll, NY: Orbis.

Kraft, Marguerite G. 1995. *Understanding Spiritual Power: A Forgotten Dimension of Cross-Cultural Mission and Ministry.* Edited by J. A. Scherer. American Society of Missiology 22. Eugene, OR: Wipf & Stock.

Lausanne Movement. 2011. *The Cape Town Commitment: A Confession of Faith and a Call to Action.* Didasko Files. Peabody, MA: Hendrickson.

Lawrence, Gordon, and Charles Martin. 2001. "How Frequent Is My Type?" *The Myers & Briggs Foundation.* http://www.myersbriggs.org/my-mbti-personality -type/my-mbti-results/how-frequent-is-my-type.htm.

Leeds-Hurwitz, Wendy. 1993. *Semiotics and Communication: Signs, Codes, Cultures.* Edited by J. Bryant. Hillsdale, NJ: Lawrence Erlbaum Associates.

Lewis, Robert. 2007. *Raising a Modern-Day Knight: A Father's Role in Guiding His Son to Authentic Manhood.* Carol Stream, IL: Tyndale House.

Lienhard, Ruth. 2001. "A Good Conscience: Differences between Honor and Justice Orientation." *Missiology: An International Review* 29 (2): 131–41.

Lindfors, B. 1973. "Wole Soyinka and the Horses of Speech." In *Essays on African Literature,* edited by W. L. Ballard, 79–97. Atlanta: Georgia State University.

Lindsey, Ursula. 2015. "The Ties That Bind Jihadists: Scholars Explore the Culture of Radical Islam." *Chronicle of Higher Education,* The Chronicle Review, November 30, 2015. http://chronicle.com/article/The-Ties-That-Bind-Jihadists/234161/?utm _source=nextdraft&utm_medium=email.

Little, Don. 2015. *Effective Discipling in Muslim Communities: Scripture, History, and Seasoned Practices.* Kindle ed. Downers Grove, IL: IVP Academic.

Little, Juanita. 1996. "The Story and Faith Journey of a Native Catechist." In *Native and Christian: Indigenous Voices on Religious Identity in the United States and Canada*, edited by James Treat, 209–18. New York: Routledge.

Lopez, Barry. 1998. *Crow and Weasel*. New York: Square Fish.

Lovejoy, Grant. 2007. "The Extent of Orality." *Dharma Deepika: A South Asian Journal of Missiological Research* 11 (25): 24–34.

Lovejoy, Grant, and David Claydon. 2005. "Making Disciples of Oral Learners: Lausanne Occasional Paper 54." *2004 Lausanne Forum Occasional Papers*. http://www.lausanne.org/documents/2004forum/LOP54_IG25.pdf.

Luke, P. Y., and J. B. Carman. 1968. *Village Christians and Hindu Culture*. London: Lutterworth.

Lupton, Robert. 2011. *Toxic Charity: How Churches and Charities Hurt Those They Help (and How to Reverse It)*. New York: HarperOne.

Maguire, Jack. 1998. *The Power of Personal Storytelling: Spinning Tales to Connect with Others*. New York: Tarcher/Putnam.

McIntyre, Alasdair. 1981. *After Virtue: A Study in Moral Theory*. Notre Dame, IN: University of Notre Dame Press.

Meineck, Peter. 2005. *Classical Mythology: The Greeks*. Modern Scholar Course Guide. Prince Frederick, MD: Recorded Books.

Micah Network. 2001. "Micah Network Declaration on Integral Mission." http://www.micahnetwork.org/sites/default/files/doc/page/mn_integral_mission_declaration_en.pdf.

Miller, Craig Kennet. 1996. *Postmoderns: The Beliefs, Hopes, and Fears of Young Americans (1965–1981)*. Nashville: Discipleship Resources.

Minuchin, Patricia, Jorge Colapinto, and Salvador Minuchin. 2007. *Working with Families of the Poor*. 2nd ed. Guilford Family Therapy Series. New York: Guilford.

Mitchell, Kateri. 1996. "Program Development and Native American Catechesis." In *Native and Christian: Indigenous Voices on Religious Identity in the United States and Canada*, edited by James Treat, 170–78. New York: Routledge.

Moon, W. Jay. 2004. "Sweet Talk in Africa: Using Proverbs in Ministry." *Evangelical Missions Quarterly* 40 (2): 162–69.

———. 2009a. *African Proverbs Reveal Christianity in Culture: A Narrative Portrayal of Builsa Proverbs Contextualizing Christianity in Culture*. American Society of Missiology Monograph 5. Eugene, OR: Pickwick.

———. 2009b. "Indigenous Proverbs, Rituals, and Stories: Evidence of God's Prevenient Grace in Oral Cultures." In *World Mission in the Wesleyan Spirit*, edited by D. Whiteman and G. Anderson, 260–69. Maryknoll, NY: Orbis.

———. 2010. "Discipling through the Eyes of Oral Learners." *Missiology: An International Review* 38 (2): 127–40.

———. 2012a. "Guest Editor's Notes." *Missiology: An International Review* 40 (2): 123–25.

————. 2012b. "Holistic Discipleship: Integrating Community Development in the Discipleship Process." *Evangelical Missions Quarterly* 48 (1): 16–22.

————. 2012c. *Ordinary Missionary: A Narrative Approach to Introducing World Missions*. Eugene, OR: Resource Publications.

————. 2012d. "Rituals and Symbols in Community Development." *Missiology: An International Review* 40 (2): 141–52.

————. 2012e. "Understanding Oral Learners." *Teaching Theology and Religion* 15 (1): 29–39.

————. 2015. "Re-wiring the Brain: Theological Education among Oral Learners." In *Reflecting on and Equipping for Christian Mission*, edited by Stephen B. Bevans, Teresa Chai, J. Nelson Jennings, Knud Jørgensen, and Dietrich Werner, 166–77. Regnum Edinburgh Centenary Series 27. Eugene, OR: Wipf & Stock.

————. 2016. "Fad or Renaissance: Misconceptions of the Orality Movement." *International Bulletin of Missionary Research* 40 (1): 6–21.

Moon, W. Jay, and Bob Armstrong. 2016. "Case Study: Blue Jean Selma." Unpublished paper in author's possession.

Moore, Waylon B. 1981. *Multiplying Disciples: The New Testament Method for Church Growth*. Colorado Springs: NavPress.

Moreau, A. Scott. 2000. "Syncretism." In Moreau, Netland, and Van Engen 2000, 924–25.

Moreau, A. Scott, Evvy Campbell, and Susan Greener. 2014. *Effective Intercultural Communication: A Christian Perspective*. Encountering Mission 7. Grand Rapids: Baker Academic.

Moreau, A. Scott, Harold Netland, and Charles Van Engen. 2000. *Evangelical Dictionary of World Missions*. Baker Reference Library. Grand Rapids: Baker.

Morgan, Janine Paden. 2011. "Emerging Eucharist: 'This Is His Story, This Is My Song.'" *Missiology: An International Review* 39 (4): 445–57.

Morgan, Richard L. 2002. *Remembering Your Story: Creating Your Own Spiritual Autobiography*. Nashville: Upper Room Books.

Morley, Patrick, David Delk, and Brett Clemmer. 2006. *No Man Left Behind: How to Build and Sustain a Thriving Disciple-Making Ministry for Every Man in Your Church*. Chicago: Moody.

Motty, Bauta D. 2013. *Indigenous Christian Disciple-Making*. Jos, Nigeria: ECWA Productions.

Mulholland, M. Robert, Jr. 1993. *Invitation to a Journey: A Road Map for Spiritual Formation*. Downers Grove, IL: InterVarsity.

The Music. 2011. Part 4 of *A History of Christian Worship: Ancient Ways, Future Paths*. DVD. Directed by Tom Dallis. Dayton, OH: Ensign Media.

Myers, Bryant. 1990. "The Sacrament of Well Digging." *MARC Newsletter* 90, no. 3 (June): 3–4.

————. 1999. *Walking with the Poor: Principles and Practices of Transformational Development*. Maryknoll, NY: Orbis.

National Native American Cooperative. 2011. "Thunder in the Desert Events Schedule." December 30. http://www.usaindianinfo.org/scheduleofevents.html.

Neeley, Paul. 2013. "Creating a Farm Blessing Church Service." In Krabill 2013, 254–55.

Nerburn, Kent. 1999. *The Wisdom of the Native Americans*. Novato, CA: New World Library.

Nida, Eugene A. 1975. *Customs and Cultures: Anthropology for Christian Missions*. Eugene, OR: Wipf & Stock.

NMC. 2005. "A Global Imperative: The Report of the 21st Century Literacy Summit." http://www.adobe.com/education/pdf/globalimperative.pdf.

Novelli, Michael. 2008. *Shaped by the Story: Helping Students Encounter God in a New Way*. Grand Rapids: Zondervan.

Nussbaum, Stan. 1996. *The Wisdom of African Proverbs*. CD, Version 1.03. Colorado Springs: Global Mapping International.

———. 1998. *The ABC's of American Culture: Understanding the American People through Their Common Sayings*. Colorado Springs: Global Mapping International.

———. 2005. *Why Are Americans like That?: A Visitor's Guide to American Cultural Values and Expectations*. Colorado Springs: Enculturation Books.

Ogden, Greg. 2003. *Transforming Discipleship: Making Disciples a Few at a Time*. Downers Grove, IL: InterVarsity.

Okpewho, Isidore. 1992. *African Oral Literature*. Bloomington: Indiana University Press.

Olson, Harriett J. 2004. *The Book of Discipline of the United Methodist Church*. Nashville: United Methodist Publishing House.

Ong, Walter J. 1982. *Orality and Literacy*. London: Routledge.

Ott, Craig. 2014. "The Power of Biblical Metaphors for the Contextualized Communication of the Gospel." *Missiology: An International Review* 42 (4): 357–74.

Parris, Matthew. 2008. "As an Atheist, I Truly Believe Africa Needs God." http://www.thetimes.co.uk/tto/opinion/columnists/matthewparris/article2044345.ece.

Pass, D. B. 2007. "Music." In *Dictionary of Mission Theology: Evangelical Foundations*, edited by John Corrie, 250–51. Downers Grove, IL: InterVarsity.

Peirce, Charles S. (1940) 1955. *Philosophical Writings of Peirce*. Edited by J. Buchler. New York: Dover.

Peterson, Eugene. 2000. *A Long Obedience in the Same Direction: Discipleship in an Instant Society*. 2nd ed. Downers Grove, IL: InterVarsity.

———. 2004. *THE MESSAGE: The Bible in Contemporary Language*. Colorado Springs: NavPress.

Pike, Kenneth L. 1954. *Language in Relation to a Unified Theory of the Structure of Human Behavior*. The Hague: Mouton.

Piper, John. 1993. *Let the Nations Be Glad! The Supremacy of God in Missions*. Grand Rapids: Baker.

Pobee, John. 1989. "Oral Theology and Christian Oral Tradition: Challenge to Traditional Archival Concept." *Communicatio Socialis Yearbook* 8:83–86.

———. 1996. "Statement on the Working Consultation on 'African Proverbs and Christian Missions.'" In Nussbaum 1996.

Pocock, Michael, Gailyn Van Rheenen, and Douglas McConnell. 2005. *The Changing Face of World Missions: Engaging Contemporary Issues and Trends*. Encountering Mission 2. Grand Rapids: Baker Academic.

Postman, Neil. 1993. *Technopoly: The Surrender of Culture to Technology*. New York: Vintage Books.

Rathbun, T. J. 2005. *Serving Christ in Others: Tony Campolo*. DVD. Vol. Serving Like Christ Together. Experiencing Christ Together. Grand Rapids: Zondervan.

Raymond, Janice. 2012. "Proverbs as a Window into Mongolian Culture and a Resource for Developing a Contextualized Approach for Evangelism." PhD diss., Fuller Theological Seminary, Pasadena, CA.

Richardson, Don. 1981. *Eternity in Their Hearts*. Ventura, CA: Regal.

Roach, Elizabeth M. 1988. "Transformation of Christian Ritual in the Pacific: Samoan White Sunday." *Missiology: An International Review* 16 (2): 173–82.

Rowe, Julisa. 2006. "Ethnodramatology 101." http://ethnodrama.com/resources.html.

———. 2013. "Ethnodramatology for Community Engagement." In Krabill 2013, 61–63.

Sachs, Jonah. 2012. *Winning the Story Wars: Why Those Who Tell (and Live) the Best Stories Will Rule the Future*. Boston: Harvard Business Review Press.

"Sacred Rites and Rituals." 1996. *Ancient Mysteries*, season 4, episode 7. A&E.

Saussure, Ferdinand de. 1983. *Course in General Linguistics*. Chicago: Open Court Classics.

Schaper, Donna, and Carole Ann Camp. 2012. *Labyrinths from the Outside In: Walking to Spiritual Insight, A Beginners Guide*. Woodstock, VT: SkyLight Paths.

Schipper, Mineke. 1985. *Unheard Words: Women and Literature in Africa, the Arab World, Asia, the Caribbean and Latin America*. London: Allison & Busby.

Schrag, Brian. 2014. "Ethnodoxology: Facilitating Local Arts Expressions for Kingdom Purposes." *Mission Frontiers* 36 (5): 6–8.

Schreiter, Robert J. 1985. *Constructing Local Theologies*. Maryknoll, NY: Orbis Books.

Senkbeil, Peter L. 2007. "Drama/Theatre." In *Dictionary of Mission Theology: Evangelical Foundations*, edited by John Corrie, 102–4. Downers Grove, IL: InterVarsity.

The Sentinel Group. 2002. *Transformations*. http://www.TransformNations.com.

Steffen, T. A. 1996. *Reconnecting God's Story to Ministry: Crosscultural Storytelling at Home and Abroad*. La Habra, CA: Center for Organizational & Ministry Development.

Storti, Craig. 2007. *The Art of Crossing Cultures*. 2nd ed. Yarmouth, MA: Intercultural Press.

Stott, John. 1988. "The World's Challenge to the Church. Part 1. Griffith Thomas Lectureship at Dallas Theological Seminary, on Christian Missiology in the Twenty-First Century." *Bibliotheca Sacra* 145 (578): 123–32.

Sullivan, Beth, and Sara Davidson. 1993. "Rite of Passage." *Dr. Quinn, Medicine Woman*, season 1, episode 13. Directed by Chuck Bowman. CBS.

Swanson, Allen J. 1989. "Decisions or Disciples? A Study in Evangelism Effectiveness in Taiwan." *Missiology: An International Review* 17 (1): 53–68.

Sweet, Leonard. 2000. *Post-Modern Pilgrims: First Century Passion for the 21st Century World*. Nashville: Broadman & Holman.

Tarr, Delbert. 1994. *Double Image: Biblical Insights from African Parables*. Mahwah, NJ: Paulist Press.

Taylor, Julie. 2012. "Beyond Song: Transforming the Reality of God's Kingdom through All the Arts." *Evangelical Missions Quarterly* 48 (1): 38–39.

Terry, John Mark. 2000. "Indigenous Churches." In Moreau, Netland, and Van Engen 2000, 483–85.

Tillich, Paul. 1955. "Theology and Symbolism." In *Religious Symbolism*, edited by F. E. Johnson, 107–16. New York: Institute for Religious and Social Studies. Distributed by Harper.

Tippett, Alan R. 1987. *Introduction to Missiology*. Pasadena, CA: William Carey Library.

Turner, Victor. 1967. *The Forest of Symbols: Aspects of Ndembu Ritual*. Ithaca, NY: Cornell University Press.

———. 1995. *The Ritual Process: Structure and Anti-structure*. New York: Aldine De Gruyter.

Twiss, Richard. 2000. *One Church, Many Tribes*. Ventura, CA: Regal Books.

———. 2002. *Dancing Our Prayers: Perspectives on Syncretism, Critical Contextualization, and Cultural Practices in First Nations Ministry*. Vancouver, WA: Wiconi.

Vahakangas, Auli. 2009. *Christian Couples Coping with Childlessness: Narratives from Machame, Kilimanjaro*. American Society of Missiology Monograph 4. Eugene, OR: Pickwick.

Van der Hart, Onno. 1983. *Rituals in Psychotherapy: Transition and Continuity*. New York: Irvington.

Van Gennep, Arnold. 1960. *Rites of Passage*. Chicago: University of Chicago Press.

Vine, W. E., Merrill F. Unger, and William White Jr. 1985. *Vine's Expository Dictionary of Biblical Words*. Nashville: Thomas Nelson.

Vision Video. 2006. *Advent Calendar on DVD*. https://www.visionvideo.com/dvd/501053D /advent-calendar-ON-DVD?.

Wagner, C. Peter. 1987. *Strategies for Church Growth*. Ventura, CA: Regal Books.

Walsh, John. 2003. *The Art of Storytelling: Easy Steps to Presenting an Unforgettable Story*. Chicago: Moody.

Watson, David Lowes. 1986. *Accountable Discipleship: Handbook for Covenant Discipleship Groups in the Congregation*. Nashville: Discipleship Resources.

Weber, Robert E., ed. 2003. *Ancient-Future Evangelism: Making Your Church a Faith-Forming Community*. Grand Rapids: Baker.

Wesley, John. 1984. *The Works of John Wesley*. Vol. 14. Peabody, MA: Hendrickson.

Whiteman, Darrell L. 1997. "Contextualization: The Theory, the Gap, the Challenge." *International Bulletin of Missionary Research* 21 (1): 2–7.

———. 2001. "Definitions of Culture—Unpublished Class notes, 'MB 700 Anthropology for Christian Mission.'" In author's possession.

Willard, Dallas. 1998. *The Divine Conspiracy: Rediscovering Our Hidden Life in God*. San Francisco: HarperCollins.

Willard, Dallas, and Gary Black Jr. 2014. *The Divine Conspiracy Continued: Fulfilling God's Kingdom on Earth*. New York: HarperOne.

Wright, N. T. 1992. *The New Testament People of God*. Minneapolis: Fortress.

Yamamori, Tetsunao. 1993. *Penetrating Missions' Final Frontier : A New Strategy for Unreached Peoples*. Downers Grove, IL: InterVarsity.

Zahniser, A. H. Mathias. 1997. *Symbol and Ceremony: Making Disciples across Cultures*. Monrovia, CA: MARC.

Zigarelli, Michael A. 2004. *Management by Proverbs: Applying Timeless Wisdom in the Workplace*. Singapore: Moody Imprint.

Index

Printed and bound by CPI Group (UK) Ltd, Croydon, CR0 4YY

13/04/2025
14656459-0004